SCHOOL ZONE

PAMELA WILCOX, GRAHAM C. OUSEY,
AND MARIE SKUBAK TILLYER

SCHOOL ZONE

A Problem Analysis of Student

Offending and Victimization

TEMPLE UNIVERSITY PRESS
Philadelphia • *Rome* • *Tokyo*

TEMPLE UNIVERSITY PRESS
Philadelphia, Pennsylvania 19122
tupress.temple.edu

Library of Congress Cataloging-in-Publication Data

Names: Wilcox, Pamela, 1968– author. | Ousey, Graham C., 1968– author. |
Tillyer, Marie Skubak, 1981– author.
Title: School zone : a problem analysis of student offending and
victimization / Pamela Wilcox, Graham C. Ousey, and Marie Skubak
Tillyer.
Description: Philadelphia : Temple University Press, 2022. | Includes
bibliographical references and index. | Summary: "This book combines
offender, victim, and environmental perspectives to show how leading
theories of crime are correctly and incorrectly applied to the school
environment. It also evaluates data on a range of crimes at school
ranging from theft to violence to verbal and physical assault and
evaluates prevention strategies"— Provided by publisher.
Identifiers: LCCN 2021040399 (print) | LCCN 2021040400 (ebook) | ISBN
9781439920367 (cloth) | ISBN 9781439920374 (paperback) | ISBN
9781439920381 (pdf)
Subjects: LCSH: Students—Crimes against—United States. | School
violence—United States. | Juvenile delinquency—United States. |
Victims of juvenile crime—United States.
Classification: LCC HV6250.4.S78 W55 2022 (print) | LCC HV6250.4.S78
(ebook) | DDC 362.88088/37—dc23/eng/20211227
LC record available at https://lccn.loc.gov/2021040399
LC ebook record available at https://lccn.loc.gov/2021040400

♾The paper used in this publication meets the requirements of the
American National Standard for Information Sciences—Permanence
of Paper for Printed Library Materials, ANSI Z39.48-1992

Printed in the United States of America

9 8 7 6 5 4 3 2 1

We dedicate this book to

Michael Rosenberg;

Sherri, Danielle, and Grayson Ousey;

and Rob, Caleb, and Jack Tillyer.

Contents

Acknowledgments

We wish to thank Hyunjung Shim and Kelsey Leibelsperger for valuable assistance at various points in this project. We are especially indebted to Dr. Richard R. Clayton for his collaboration on the Rural Substance abuse and Violence Project (RSVP). He served as Principal Investigator on the NIH grant that funded the data collection effort (DA11317). In that role, he fostered our examination of topics of great interest to us, including student offending, victimization, and perceptions of school safety. Without his mentorship and support in this regard, many of the analyses that serve as the backbone to this book would not have been possible.

SCHOOL ZONE

1

The School-Crime Connection

Variation across People,
Places, and Time

Schools are safe and nurturing places where caring nonfamily adults protect students and guide their intellectual and social development. That is the ideal, anyway. In many cases, reality is close to the ideal, but not always or everywhere. Although schools are generally safe places, students' school experiences differ, both in terms of exposure to crime and in the strategies implemented to prevent it. These differences occur between individuals located in the same schools and between students attending separate schools. Moreover, experiences vary widely for individuals who attend schools in different time periods.

Evidence of variation in school experiences across individuals, places, and time exists in many forms. Empirical evidence from social research is a primary form of evidence and is the focus of much of this book. However, the simplest form is anecdotal evidence derived from each of our own "lived experiences" or personal stories. Consider the experiences of the three authors of this book. In many ways, these experiences are homogeneous, reflecting positions of relative privilege within our society's racial and social class stratification system. However, our lived experiences also illustrate personal, contextual, and temporal variations in school crime or safety concerns. Pamela Wilcox's story hints at the importance of place, highlighting vastly different experiences of students across school settings—even settings that are quite close geographically. At the same time, it highlights variation in experiences with school crime across students within the same setting, especially variation in offending behavior. The personal story of Graham

Ousey involves a contrast between his own school experiences and those of his children, providing anecdotal examples of how similar student behaviors are defined and reacted to differently over time. Moreover, it illustrates noted differences in experiences with school crime across individual students in any one place-time setting, especially differences in victimization experiences. Finally, Marie Skubak Tillyer's story also contrasts her own experience and that of her children, highlighting how incidents of school shootings, while still rare, have altered school safety policies in a single generation.

School Crime and Spatial Divides

Pamela Wilcox attended public schools in a middle-class, inner-ring suburb of a midsize midwestern city. She graduated from high school in the mid-1980s. During the decade spanning 1980 to 1990, the population of her suburban community was approximately 60,000 and overwhelmingly racially and ethnically homogeneous—census data indicate that over 97% of community residents were White, with persons of Asian descent constituting the largest racial/ethnic minority group at just over 1% of the suburb's population. Educational attainment was strongly encouraged in the community during this time, and over 90% of the adult population held a high-school degree (U.S. Census Bureau, 1992). Additionally, there was discernable community pride in the local schools, as residents consistently backed the schools through volunteerism and financial support in the form of tax levies (Gower et al., 2005). Such local support produced results: the school district was consistently considered high performing based on state standards and was even named a "Top 100" school district in 1995 by *Money* magazine. Commensurate with the community's strong emphasis on education and local schools, fewer than 5% of households were impoverished during the 1980s (U.S. Census Bureau, 1992).

Over 2,000 students were enrolled in the community's high school while Wilcox attended. There were no locked doors, buzzers for entry, or metal detectors to pass through. Police, school resource officers, private security, and drug-sniffing dogs were not present in the school. She recalls no security cameras. The truth is, nobody thought or talked much about strategies to ensure school safety because problematic incidents were uncommon and relatively minor. "Bad behavior" tended to consist of the sporadic fight breaking out in hallways during class changes or the occasional incident of someone getting "busted" for bringing alcohol to a football game. Perusal of archived clippings from the local newspapers revealed few headlines associated with crime at her school in the 1980s—an exception being a story written about a burglary of the high school's physical education building, during which time "at least eight bags of sports clothing and equipment [were] taken" ("Stolen Uniforms Sought," 1984).

Just a few miles away, inner-city school students in that same midwestern metropolitan area experienced different, and more traumatic, events. Wilcox's community was geographically contiguous to the central city, yet the two environments seemed worlds apart in terms of social structure. The central city, consisting of a total population of 182,000 in 1990, was in decline. Built on a manufacturing base, deindustrialization hit the city hard, leading to significant population loss throughout the 1980s.

In addition to its population instability, the city was much more racially and economically diverse than Wilcox's suburban community during the 1980s (and still is today). Census data indicate that the population was 58% White and 40% African American around the time she was in high school, and the overall poverty rate in the central city was around 25% (over five times greater than in Wilcox's residential suburb). Moreover, there were alarming pockets of concentrated disadvantage, with rates of poverty above 40% in 14 of its census tracts in 1990 (Gower et al., 2005). Indicative of segregation, there were obvious racial disparities in experiences with such disadvantage. Fully 54.3% of the African American children in the central city were living in poverty according to the 1990 census (Gower et al., 2005). Undoubtedly related to the city's socioeconomic struggles, educational achievement and pride in local schools were lower in the central city than what Wilcox had experienced in her nearby suburb. Approximately a quarter of the adults were without high-school degrees. Additionally, there was consistent local media attention devoted to the struggling school district, and public opinion polls suggested that fewer than 25% of residents rated the local schools as either "good" or "excellent" (Gower et al., 2005).

Around the same time Wilcox attended her suburban school just a few miles away, students attending the schools within the central-city context faced classroom disturbances (e.g., pulled fire alarms, disrespect toward teachers), substance abuse, weapon-involved fights, gang violence, and suspensions numbering in the thousands (e.g., see Ancona, 1985; Madison, 1986). In one telling example occurring in the year prior to Wilcox's high-school graduation, a 17-year-old male central-city student was assaulted at school by local gang members. Members of a rival gang, in turn, showed up on the school campus a few days later with a firearm, allegedly seeking retaliation (Sullivan, 1985). One year after Wilcox's graduation, a 17-year-old central-city female student was stabbed in the chest by another female student during a scuffle on the school bus ("Stabbing occurs on school bus," 1987). Violence continued, perhaps even escalated, in the early 1990s, as inner-city-youth crime climbed nationally. In the course of mere weeks in 1992, a track star at one of the public city high schools was shot in the back by other teens who robbed him of his jacket and shoes, a female high-school student was "knocked cold" at a bus stop, and a nine-year-old boy was forced to have oral sex in an elementary school locker room (Lamb, 1992). Earlier that same year, the city's superintendent ordered walk-through metal detectors for all middle- and high-school students after the stabbing of a middle-school student. At the time of the metal detector installation, the district indicated they had confiscated 59 weapons from students during the preceding six months of the school year (Scruggs, 1992). Along with metal detectors, the inner-city school district employed 18 unarmed security officers to patrol the grounds around the middle- and high-school campuses (Scruggs, 1992). City police also patrolled each weekday afternoon at the downtown spot where students switched buses after school—the spot of several large fights among teens that involved shootings (Bray, 1991).

School Crime and Historical Divides

Like Wilcox, Graham Ousey attended high school in the 1980s, graduating in 1986. His school was the only public high school in a small city (~20,000 population) located in central Virginia. It was, and is today, a blue-collar community with many adults working in manufacturing plants and others serving in the military or working as contractors for the Department of Defense. In the 1980s, the population was somewhat racially diverse but highly segregated. Whites made up roughly 72% of the population, and African Americans made up about 26% of the residents. About 14% of the population had income below the poverty line, placing it close to the national average at the time (Manson, Schroeder, Van Riper, and Ruggles, 2018).

Crime occurred in the city, but Ousey recalls moving freely throughout the city on foot, by bike, and, when older, by car. The general lack of concern about crime was evident in school as well. School doors were unlocked during the day; there were no buzzers required for entry; and security personnel, surveillance cameras, and metal detectors were nonexistent. While there were occasionally incidents that were classifiable as criminal—hallway fistfights, drug possession, drug use, thefts of money or clothing—they were generally handled "in-house" by school personnel handing out school-related discipline, usually in consultation with parents. Ousey recalls infrequent but routine instances (maybe one per year) when the police would visit the school with canine teams to search hall and gym lockers for illegal drugs. Mostly these events added a little excitement to the school day as students speculated whether anyone would be arrested. Contraband rarely turned up in these searches. On the other hand, bullying was a regular occurrence, and

Ousey recalls that an unlucky few bore the brunt of mistreatment. The behavior was not condoned, but neither was it highly condemned. It was perceived as an unfortunate, but mostly harmless, aspect of the transition through adolescent life.

"Shelter in place" or "active shooter" drills, or general concerns about armed intruders, were unheard of in the school experiences of Wilcox and Ousey. The idea of someone literally attacking the school was so far beyond the imagination, it was perceived comically by many students. Indeed, Ousey recalls that as his high-school graduation drew close, a rumor began circulating that one frequently bullied student had created a "hit list" containing all of those who had teased or mistreated him during school. These rumors seemed inspired by movies like the 1982 film *National Lampoon's Class Reunion*, which depicted a former student returning to a 10-year class reunion to exact revenge for mistreatment that occurred during his senior year. Ousey recalls few students taking the rumors seriously, with many actively joking about the absurdity of such an attack during regular school-day banter.

Times have certainly changed. Although violent crime rates dropped substantially in the United States after the early 1990s, awareness and concern about violence has become a much more prominent part of the school experiences of students today. This is true not only in disadvantaged communities with higher levels of crime but also in higher-wealth, lower-crime communities. For example, Ousey's children have grown up in a context of significantly greater privilege than he did. They are recent graduates of a public high school that *U.S. News & World Report* ranks among the top 20 schools in the state of Virginia. It is located in a well-educated and financially secure county where 95% of the population aged 25-plus has a high-school diploma, 50% have graduated from college, the median household income is $81,000, and the poverty rate is only 7% (U.S. Census Bureau, 2018). It is also a safe place to live. Its 2019 violent crime rate was less than one-third of the U.S. violent crime rate, and gun violence and murder are rare (Virginia State Police, 2020; U.S. Department of Justice, Federal Bureau of Investigation, 2020). Despite these facts, Ousey's kids experienced at least one "lockdown/shooter" drill per year going back as far as middle school. Prior to these events, students were informed the drills were a precautionary preparation for an armed intruder attacking the school. Students learned they should close and lock classroom doors, turn off lights, hide behind desks, or otherwise locate themselves in areas not visible to someone peering through the small window embedded in the classroom door. In addition, bullying prevention programming was also a regular presence in the educational experience of Ousey's kids. Antibullying educational programs were presented each year. Moreover, despite its location in a peaceful community, the school maintained an on-campus school safety officer, all entrances were monitored by surveillance cameras, visitors were required to enter through a single front door location, and entry required communication with school staff prior to being "buzzed" in to the vestibule by the main office.

Marie Skubak Tillyer is younger than Pamela Wilcox and Graham Ousey and attended a Catholic high school in the Midwest in the late 1990s. The school, which served approximately 1,000 students at the time, was located in a middle-class residential neighborhood north of the central city with 98% White residents. Students, however, were drawn from a much larger geographic area because of the school's religious tradition. While many aspects of Tillyer's experiences are similar to Wilcox's and Ousey's, one noteworthy difference is that the shooting at Columbine High School occurred just six weeks prior to Tillyer's high-school graduation. On April 20, 1999, two high-school seniors killed 12 fellow students and one teacher before taking their own lives at Columbine High School in Littleton, Colorado. Tillyer remembers the shock and sadness in the aftermath but notes that, at the time, a mass shooting in school seemed like such a unique, once-in-a-generation event. Unfortunately, we know now it was simply the first of several horrifying events that shape how we view school safety today. Over a decade later—on December 14, 2012—a 20-year-old man walked into Sandy Hook Elementary School in Newtown, Connecticut, and killed 22 children and six adults. And on February 14, 2018, a 19-year-old former student at Marjory Stoneman Douglas High School in Parkland, Florida, returned to the school grounds and killed 17 people (including students and teachers) and wounded 17 others. Each of these events received national media attention for weeks and changed the discourse on school crime from a problem of the inner city to a problem that could happen anywhere, with unfathomable consequences. Indeed, 20 years after Tillyer's high-school graduation in 1999, her young children practice active shooter drills in their suburban Texas elementary school. Thus, crime awareness and preparation that was far from the imagination of earlier generations of students has become central to the experiences of present-day students in U.S. schools.

School Crime and Individual Differences

While school crime experiences—whether in the form of offending behavior, victimization, or security efforts—vary among students in different communities or across historical periods, there are also stark individual-level differences in school crime experiences within any particular place-time setting. The stories of Wilcox and Ousey, in particular, illustrate how the risks of offending and victimization, respectively, vary greatly across individual students. For example, the crimes described above that occurred among students in the inner city adjacent to Wilcox's suburban community were relatively alarming, but only a small fraction of students was responsible for such acts. Archived news stories from the local community in the 1980s suggest that students, teachers, and administrators in the inner-city schools expressed frustration about how incidents involving a few students tended to harm the image of the entire school or school district, where the overwhelming majority of students were not involved in criminal misconduct. For example, while inner-city student violence tended to grab the headlines, officials at one school pointed out that "11 percent of students are involved in honors programs and 51 percent of students apply to 4-year colleges" (Madison, 1987). In fact, students in the same school blamed the media for exaggerating violent incidents involving a few individuals while largely overlooking the involvement of many more students in prosocial activities such as the annual blood drive or their vibrant performing arts program (Madison, 1987). Thus, even in a "high-crime" school district (relative to neighboring districts), offending behavior appeared concentrated among a small number of individual students. These patterns of concentration of offending behavior mirror those seen for decades in criminological research. Indeed, they reflect Marvin Wolfgang and colleagues' famous study finding that a "chronic 6 percent" of boys from a Philadelphia birth cohort accounted for more than half of the crimes committed by the entire cohort through age 18 (Wolfgang, Figlio, and Sellin, 1972).

Similarly, Ousey's recollection that relatively few unfortunate kids experienced the vast majority of mistreatment and harassment by fellow students is consistent with a pattern evinced over decades of large-scale research studies. For example, in one of the more famous studies of victimization concentration, Graham Farrell and Ken Pease's analysis of data from the British Crime Survey found that just 4.3% of sampled respondents experienced 43.5% of the entire sample's reported victimization incidents (Farrell and Pease, 1993). More recently, and more directly relevant to school-based crime incidents, Tillyer and colleagues reported that just 6.2% of a sample of middle- and high-school students across Kentucky experienced 40.6% of the total reported assaults (Tillyer, Wilcox, and Fissel, 2018).

Looking beyond variations in patterns of offending and victimization, there are also differences in how students experience "school safety" within a given place-time context. First, students have unique perceptions of their overall safety at school, and they express varying levels of fear of school crime (Wilcox, Campbell Augustine, Bryan, and Roberts, 2005). Second, while the use of measures aimed at making schools less vulnerable to attack (e.g., armed police, metal detectors, active-shooter preparedness training) is now widespread, students are often differentially exposed to particular types of discipline in response to offending. For some, the experience of harsh, exclusionary school discipline practices is more common, whereas for others, therapeutic or restorative disciplinary practices predominate (Hirschfield, 2018; Hughes, Bailey, Warren, and Stewart, 2022; Jonson, 2017; Kupchik, 2010, 2016, 2020; Morris and Perry, 2017; Payne and Welch, 2010; Ramey, 2015; Rocque and Paternoster, 2011). Thus, while variations in school crime across unique places and times are important considerations, so, too, are cross-individual differences in school-based offending, victimization, fear, and punishment within any single place-time context.

Purpose of the Book: Understanding School Crime through Problem Analysis

Although limited, the preceding anecdotes help illustrate that experiences with school crime and safety vary across places, time, and individuals in the United States. Understanding and explaining those variations is a major focus of this book. For most students, schools are institutions that provide a caring, safe environment for learning and growth. Yet, they also are places where diverse individuals converge in settings with distinct social, cultural, and physical features (Gottfredson and Gottfredson, 1985; Gottfredson, 2001). These convergences sometimes result in disapproved behaviors, including some that are violations of criminal codes or that threaten student well-being. Unfortunately, "school crime safety" is a term that has increasingly been intertwined with concerns about mass shootings in suburban schools since the late 1990s, such as those mentioned earlier (for reviews, see Butler, Kulig, Fisher, and Wilcox, 2019; Jonson, 2017). While these events are devastating and justify prevention efforts, they are as unusual as they are extreme (Addington, 2009; Chouhy, Madero-Hernandez, and Turanovic, 2017; Fox and Fridel, 2019; Musu-Gillette et al., 2018; Rocque, 2012). A negative consequence of the focus on school shootings is that it tends to obscure student-involved delinquency and victimization that is less extreme but more common: theft; weapon carrying; drug possession; and the verbal, physical, and sexual harassment of classmates. These phenomena also warrant focused attention on description, explanation, and prevention. This book is an effort in that direction.

The book is a culmination of our effort over the past 15 years to study crime among students located across diverse middle- and high-school settings. It seeks answers to several core questions: Why are some students more likely to engage in delinquency than others? Why are some students more prone to experience victimization? Why do some schools exhibit higher rates of crime than other schools? How do individual students and schools respond to crime or threats thereof? It integrates knowledge gained from our own research, as well as lessons learned from studies by other

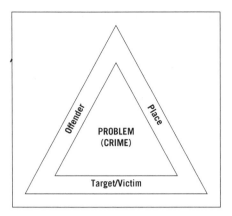

Figure 1.1 The problem analysis triangle
(Adapted from https://popcenter.asu.edu/content/problem-analysis-triangle-0. Redrawn with permission from the ASU Center for Problem-Oriented Policing. Downloaded on October 3, 2019.)

scholars, to provide deeper understanding of the patterns and causes of variation in individual-level and aggregate-level school-based offending and victimization experiences, while also addressing the adequacy of wide-ranging criminological explanations and crime prevention policies.

Our investigation of student offending and victimization—focused on adolescents in middle- and high-school settings in the United States—is anchored by the problem analysis framework. This framework emerged from scholars such as Ronald Clarke, John Eck, and Marcus Felson, and it is often portrayed by a simple triangle as shown in Figure 1.1. The "problem analysis triangle" views crime (or a crime-related problem) as an outcome emerging from the convergence between a motivated offender, a suitable target/victim, and a conducive environmental setting (e.g., Brantingham and Brantingham, 1981, 1993; Clarke 2010).

Problem analysis focuses on relatively small-scale settings or contexts in which motivated offenders access targets or victims, including street intersections, street segments, and street addresses. Indeed, several decades of research show that crime events cluster at such small-scale places, now commonly referred to as "hot spots" for crime (Sherman, Gartin, and Buerger, 1989; Weisburd, Groff, and Yang, 2012; Braga, Hureau, and Papachristos, 2011). However, the problem analysis perspective on crime also identifies both large- and small-scale public facilities as places where crime emerges. Marcus Felson (1987) first noted the important role of facilities as hosts of the convergence of motivated offenders and suitable targets in contemporary society. He claimed that many routine daily activities take place at facilities in modern-day life, thus making them susceptible to becoming hot spots. Additionally, a focus on crime at facilities, as opposed to street segments, offers potential benefits for crime prevention: formal organizations can take responsibility for discouraging crime through facility design and management, rather than relying on public policing. A good deal of research over the past several decades has supported the idea that offender-target convergence is high in facilities—places such as parking lots, railway stations, shopping centers, taverns, convenience stores, and *schools* (Crowe, 1990; Eck, Clarke, and Guerette, 2007; Felson et al., 1996; Smith, 1996).

Schools are especially salient facilities for investigating crime among young people. As Garofalo, Siegel, and Laub (1987, p. 321) noted some three decades ago, students are pools of potential crime offenders and victims who are typically in contact for eight hours a day, five days a week. Often their convergence occurs in situations where capable guardians (e.g., responsible adults, security) are absent.[1] This book endorses the idea that schools are important facilities hosting crime. It considers schools as key places where a better understanding of youth crime can develop through consideration of all sides of the problem analysis triangle.

Criminologists utilizing the problem analysis framework often treat offender motivation as an assumed "constant" and prioritize the analysis of variation in the other sides of the problem analysis triangle: targets/victims and places. They contend that focusing on the immediate situational circumstances associated with a crime event, not background factors that supply individual motivation, is the best means to understand and prevent crime. We depart somewhat from this approach, arguing that offender motivation is an important dimension of explanation that warrants examination, along with targets and places, within the problem analysis framework. Our position accords with eminent criminologist Francis Cullen. In his Sutherland Address to the American Society of Criminology, Cullen urged a more holistic approach: "The mistake . . . is to assume that 'motivated offenders' can be taken for granted and, in turn, to give only marginal attention to the way in which criminal decision making is bounded by factors that offenders import into the crime situation . . . the future of criminology will be advanced by exploring the nexus between propensity and opportunity—between offender and situation" (Cullen, 2011, p. 315; see also Cullen and Kulig, 2018; Wilcox, Gialopsos, and Land, 2013; Wilcox and Cullen, 2018). Hence, in *School Zone*, we consider all three sides of the crime problem analysis triangle: (1) factors that motivate some students to engage in delin-

---

1. We thought it worth mentioning that the completion of this book occurred during the COVID-19 pandemic, which, at least temporarily, dramatically changed patterns of convergence of offenders and victims in facilities such as schools due to lockdowns forcing remote learning.

quency; (2) factors that make some students suitable targets, susceptible to victimization; and (3) characteristics of schools that facilitate or, conversely, constrain the convergence of the motivated offender and the suitable target.

A Look Ahead

We organize the remaining chapters according to the three sides of the problem analysis triangle sketched above. However, before diving headlong into research on offending, victimization, and criminogenic school settings, we provide in Chapter 2 a broad overview of key concepts that aid in understanding each of these dimensions of school crime. The concepts draw from a diverse array of criminological theories. Included are theories aimed at explaining why some students have a greater proclivity to engage in offending, theories building insights on why some students are more likely targets for victimization, and theories addressing factors that make certain school environments more likely to host crime incidents. Theories of offender motivation, theories of crime victims, and theories of crime places have traditionally been considered and examined somewhat separately, with the first thought to represent the domain of "traditional criminology," while the latter two types of theory are often associated with what has been termed "environmental criminology." As indicated above, most criminologists using a problem analysis approach to understanding crime do so with a heavy (if not exclusive) emphasis on environmental criminology, while setting aside the issue of offender motivation. In contrast, our problem analysis will blend both traditional criminology and environmental criminology, and, in the process, will address theoretical explanations for student offending, student victimization, and schools as crime places.

After providing an overview of theoretical concepts relevant to understanding school crime, Chapter 3 discusses data sources that are used to study school-based crime. The focus of that discussion is intentionally broad, covering an array of datasets. It also highlights the Rural Substance abuse and Violence Project (RSVP). RSVP was a multiyear data-collection effort conducted in the early 2000s, led by Richard Clayton and funded by the National Institute on Drug Abuse (R01 DA11317). Two authors of this book, Pamela Wilcox and Graham Ousey, served as coinvestigators on RSVP, which collected longitudinal data on students as well as contextual information about schools from teachers, administrators, and field observations made by the researchers. To date, nearly three dozen peer-reviewed journal articles using RSVP data have been published, many coauthored by the current authors: Wilcox, Ousey, or Tillyer. *School Zone* synthesizes many of the findings from the RSVP-based studies with research on other data sources to provide a cohesive, comprehensive volume on individual and contextual factors associated with school crime.

Chapters 4 through 7 represent the heart of the book, addressing what we know about school crime from empirical studies, with all sides of the problem analysis triangle (offender, victim, place) serving as our organizational guide. In Chapter 4, we review the empirical evidence regarding various types of delinquent offending occurring in schools, including violence, weapon carrying, property crime, and substance use. Discussion includes prevalence and patterns of behaviors as well as the key motivational factors observed in available research. In particular, the focus is on the offending motivation factors identified and discussed more generally in Chapter 2.

In Chapter 5, our attention turns to empirical studies addressing risk of victimization among students. This review takes stock of research on general victimization as well as categories or specific types of victimization—violent victimization, theft victimization, and sexual victimization as examples.[2] It also considers research on short- and long-term repeat victimization among students. As with our review of research on offending, the research discussed in Chapter 5 provides information on prevalence and trends in victimization as well as key risk factors for experiencing victimization, with the latter discussion framed around the key theoretical concepts introduced in Chapter 2. Finally, Chapter 5 also considers research on students' worries about crime at school, assessments of victimization risk at school, and behaviors employed to reduce victimization risk at school.

Chapter 6 addresses the potential comorbidity of student offending and victimization since a victim-offender overlap has been observed in general population samples. It reviews research examining the evidence of the victim-offender overlap among students. Drawing again from some theoretical perspectives outlined in Chapter 2, it considers whether overlap is due to similar underlying forces causing both offending and victimization (a population heterogeneity perspective), or, alternatively, whether there is a causal linkage between student offending and student victimization (i.e., offending causes subsequent victimization, or vice versa).

In Chapter 7, we consider empirical research addressing variations in rates of crime across school contexts, with special focus on characteristics of the school environment that make schools more or less susceptible to student offending and/or victimization. Here, we consider two major mechanisms: (1) whether characteristics of school environments are directly

---

2. In Chapters 3 and 5, we report on trends in bullying victimization in addition to criminal victimization experienced by students at school. However, given our reliance on theories and perspectives developed to explain and understand *crime*, the focus of the book is on violent, property, sexual, and drug crimes, rather than on other forms of bullying.

related to offending and victimization, independent of student differences, and (2) whether school characteristics interact with student characteristics, potentially mitigating or enhancing the effects of individual-level correlates of student offending and/or victimization. The discussion centers on the key concepts from "crime and place" theories described in Chapter 2.

Finally, in Chapter 8, we discuss common school crime prevention efforts and their relationships to the theories and empirical research reviewed in the previous chapters. In doing so, we assess the extent to which currently popular strategies of school crime prevention align with the problem analysis framework and scientific understandings of student offending and victimization.

2

Making Sense of School Crime

Key Perspectives

Recall from Chapter 1 that our examination of student offending and victimization is organized around the problem analysis framework—a perspective that views crime as an outcome that occurs when a motivated offender and a suitable target/victim converge in a place or setting characterized by weak guardianship. Therefore, we attempt to understand why some students offend more often than other students do, why some students are more prone to victimization than others are, and why some schools are more dangerous environments than other schools. In this chapter, we review concepts and criminological theories that appear most useful for those purposes. In later chapters, we review findings from research on school crime to illuminate the value of these concepts and theories.

We divide the current chapter into three major sections. First, we discuss theoretical perspectives addressing between-student differences in offending propensity, or *delinquency*. Understanding why some students are more predisposed to offend is fundamentally important, but crime events require more than just a motivated offender. They also require that motivated offenders encounter and overcome or procure from victims/targets. Thus, theories of student victimization risk are also key. The second major section of the chapter discusses these victimization theories. Finally, the motivated student offender must encounter students suitable for victimization within a school environment permissive enough that it does not prevent the crime. As such, perspectives describing how differences in the school environment affect the likelihood of crime are important as well.

We should stress that the theoretical concepts and perspectives discussed in the chapter's three major sections do not constitute an exhaustive set of potential explanations of offending, victimization, and crime places. Rather, we focus on perspectives receiving the most attention in the school-based crime research literature discussed in Chapters 4 through 7.

Understanding Offending

Students typically follow school rules during time spent in classes or when engaged in other school-related activities. Moreover, they abide by codes of right and wrong, and of politeness and courtesy learned from parents and guardians. Of course, there are exceptions. Most often, those exceptions are minor acts of misbehavior, such as showing up late or skipping a class, or smoking tobacco on campus where not permitted. Less often, the misbehavior is more serious—a criminal act that breaks a legal statute defined by the state. Some examples of these crimes are larceny-theft, assault, illicit drug possession, or robbery.

Why do students, particularly middle- and high-school students, engage in criminal acts? This intriguing question is simple to state but complex to answer. For much of the last century, criminologists have proposed explanations for why individuals offend. Some of these explanations emphasize *sources of motivation* that compel us to crime, while others identify *sources of constraint* that hold us back in the face of criminal temptations. In the following pages, we discuss several important explanations of crime that invoke either motivation or constraint mechanisms to help answer why students in school may engage in criminal offending.

Strain

Strain explanations of crime argue that individuals are motivated to commit crimes by acute and/or chronic aversive social experiences. These aversive experiences yield negative emotions, especially frustration and anger, which motivate a criminal-behavior response. Persistent blockages in opportunity, unfair treatment within social institutions, criminal victimization, adverse childhood experiences (often referred to as ACEs), and abusive interpersonal interactions are all commonly identified sources of strain. Early strain explanations of crime emerged from the work of American sociologist Robert Merton (1938). Merton argued that individuals develop criminal motivations when they are unable to achieve the major success goal defined by American culture—monetary wealth—through approved methods of achievement, such as getting a strong formal education and a well-paying career. Anyone can be susceptible to this kind of strain, but it may be especially acute for the lower class because obstacles beyond their control often block their routes for achieving success via approved means, like education. For example, even when motivated to get a good education, low-income individuals may have access to poor-quality schools, and their home environments may not be conducive for studying, completing academic projects, and the like. The resulting disconnect between their goals for success and their means of attainment creates a growing sense of frustration and disillusionment. In response, Merton suggested that they often turn to "innovation," using criminal behavior to achieve the desired goal of monetary wealth.

Robert Agnew (2006) expanded Merton's singular focus on goal blockages as the main sources of strains that motivate crime. He argues that strains also emerge when individuals lose things that they value, including friendships, romantic relationships, or valued property. Likewise, we experience strains when people we interact with treat us poorly. Discrimination, unwarranted hostility, or physical and emotional abuse are all examples. Each of these kinds of strain generate negative emotions such as sadness, frustration, or anger. Those emotions, in turn, motivate a corrective action, or "coping" response. Crime is one possible corrective action because it allows individuals to escape strains, to get revenge against others who harmed them, and to alleviate their experience of negative emotions (Agnew, 2006). Thus, the general strain explanation of crime suggests that several types of strain create negative emotions, which can motivate criminal behavior. Yet only some individuals will cope with strains through criminal behavior. Many individuals cope with strains in legal ways, such as talking to a friend, consulting a therapist, or hiring a lawyer. However, others lack the resources or ability to cope with strains through legal means for several reasons. First, some individuals have personality traits such as negative emotionality that make it more challenging for them to cope with strains in prosocial ways (Agnew, Brezina, Wright, and Cullen, 2002). Second, a lack of financial resources may prevent some individuals from hiring professionals to help them address problems or grievances. Third, those with few social supports may not have the family and friend connections needed to help neutralize negative feelings and prevent destructive behavioral responses. Finally, because some individuals operate within permissive social environments, there is no real disincentive for coping with strains through crime. For these individuals, strains are likely to produce criminality rather than the utilization of a legal coping strategy.

Interpersonal conflicts are a common part of social life, including in schools. Strain explanations of crime suggest that such conflict is an impetus leading some students to crime at school. This is because students who experience the dissolution of a friendship, or who are victims of bullying, are likely to feel anger or experience depression. They will want to do something to eradicate these bad feelings or the sources from which they originate. Some students cope with their bad feelings in acceptable ways, seeking support from their other friends, from school staff (teachers, guidance counselors), or from their families. Some will channel their negative emotions into conventional activities like sports, exercise, or artistic expressions. For others, however, coping strategies are highly counterproductive. They physically lash out against those who have harmed them (retaliatory violence) or against innocent proxies who happen to be in the wrong place at the wrong time (non-retaliatory violence). Or, they turn their aggressive feelings toward property, engaging in acts of vandalism or theft as a means of cathartic expression. Finally, some neutralize negative emotions by using illegal drugs on school grounds or during school-sponsored activities (e.g., sports).

Besides interpersonal conflicts among students, strains arise in school when students are frustrated in attempts to attain desired goals. Failure to achieve good grades or to qualify for a school club, social group, or sports team creates strains that engender negative emotions. Using crime to cope with these or the previously mentioned strains is most probable when students lack strong networks of social support (e.g., social bonds), have insufficient means to acquire help from third parties (e.g., professional counselors), or have personality characteristics (e.g., short tempers) that make them particularly reactive to the experience of anger or other negative emotions (Agnew, 2006).

Social Learning

Social learning explanations argue that crime is a normal, learned behavior. Many, if not most, people engage in acts of crime—even if just minor infractions—sometime during their lives. The important question is why does crime become a regular, repeated behavior for the few but only an isolated episode for the many? The social learning explanation of crime points to socialization processes for the answer. For criminologist Edwin Sutherland, *differential association* was the key (Sutherland, 1947). This idea suggests that the characteristics of a person's intimate social networks and their interactions within those networks shape their likelihood of criminal behavior. Through face-to-face interactions with intimate personal groups (e.g., family, close friends) some individuals learn techniques, motives, and rationalizations for crime. More specifically, they learn attitudes or beliefs that support criminal behavior, called "definitions favorable to crime." Individuals whose intimate peer-group associations include greater exposure to others who engage in and positively evaluate crime are more likely to acquire these definitions favorable to crime. When definitions favorable to crime exceed definitions unfavorable to crime, criminal behavior becomes likely.

Ronald Akers (1973) added two pieces to Sutherland's ideas about how crime is learned. First, he argued that in addition to face-to-face interactions with intimate peer groups, individuals learn definitions favorable to crime from the media and from role models with whom they have little or no direct interaction (e.g., celebrities). Second, Akers proposed additional mechanisms for learning crime-supportive attitudes and rationalizations. One is *imitation*, which involves repeating a behavior after directly observing it modeled by others. Another is learning by *differential reinforcement*. By the latter, Akers refers to the balance of rewards and/or punishments that an individual receives for engaging in particular behaviors. Those who associate with others who praise or assign status to law-violating behaviors are more likely to continue such behaviors. In contrast, those associating with others who shame and punish such actions are likely to avoid repeating them. Akers also argued that differential reinforcement may occur vicariously, as when we observe someone else receiving rewarding or punishing consequences for their criminal behavior.

Social learning suggests the characteristics of the peers with whom a student associates is key to their involvement in criminal offending. Because schools bring diverse students together in classes and extracurricular activities, they create opportunities for students to influence each other. Indeed, it is an awareness of these opportunities that leads some parents to advise their children to "choose friends wisely" or "don't give in to peer pressure." As the concept of differential association suggests, individuals who become friends with others holding definitions favorable to crime are at higher risk of committing violations of school rules or societal laws. The influence of these associations is especially great if the time friends spend together is large and their emotional connection is close. Beyond the spreading of crime-supporting attitudes through intimate friendships, social learning offers that some students learn deviant behavior by observing and mimicking the behavior of others. To the extent that adolescent culture assigns status to kids who are mavericks that thumb their noses at the rules, some may see "walking on the wild side" as worthwhile and advantageous. Indeed, rule breaking is sometimes seen as adultlike behavior among adolescents, thereby conferring greater social status to those who engage in it and motivating others to follow suit (Moffitt, 1993).

Biological and Psychological Traits

Trait explanations of crime assert there is a fundamental person-based difference between criminals and noncriminals. This difference is usually a biological or psychological "trait." It may have roots in genetics or biology, or it may have origins in early-life social environments. Regardless of origin, these explanations argue that once developed, some traits predispose individuals to a high propensity for crime throughout their life course. In other words, traits are persistent and stable risk factors that individuals carry.

The earliest trait explanations assumed criminals were biologically inferior, evolutionary throwbacks who were impulsive, aggressive, and lacking in empathetic emotions (Lombroso and Horton, 1911). Those early trait explanations lost credibility due to ignorant and racist assumptions (DeLisi, 2013). Moving beyond troublesome assumptions, a new class of trait-based explanations have made useful contributions to contemporary research on criminal offending. Rooted in more rigorous scientific thinking than early trait theories, modern trait arguments contend that biological factors and social factors interact, mutually reinforcing each other in their effects on criminal offending. One trait explanation focuses on genetic differences and the heritability of gene variations that are associated with some criminal behaviors. Evidence of heritability and genetic influences on crime come from studies of twins raised together, twins reared apart, and adoption studies. These studies estimate that between 40 and 60% of variation in antisocial behavior and criminality is inherited (Peskin et al., 2013; Raine, 2014). No specific "crime gene" is identifiable in these studies, but a combination of genes paired with difficult social environments may give individuals greater propensity to engage in antisocial or criminal behavior (Peskin et al., 2013). A second trait explanation focuses on dysfunction in the brain and the ways it influences behavior. Brain imaging studies show that criminal psychopaths have unusually low volume of gray matter in the frontotemporal regions of the brain (Yang et al., 2005; Yang, Raine, Colletti, Toga, and Narr, 2010), while murderers and other criminals have impaired functioning in the prefrontal cortex and other parts of the brain (Peskin et al., 2013; Raine, 2014; Raine, Buchsbaum, and LaCasse, 1997). Finally, a third trait-based explanation argues that a particular configuration of personality traits is associated with higher-than-normal crime propensity. Avshalom Caspi and his colleagues (1994), for example, contend that higher levels of criminal propensity are associated with two personality "supertraits" identified by personality psychologists: (1) constraint and (2) negative emotionality. Individuals with a configuration of low scores on the constraint trait and high scores on the negative emotionality trait are more likely to be involved in both minor and severe criminal behavior. Why? One argument is that these individuals are more likely to perceive threats in others' actions and are unable to contain their impulses for aggressive responses to those threats.

Trait explanations are relevant to understanding the offending behavior of students in schools. Elementary-school experiences may have some hand in shaping an individual's personality characteristics, but most trait explanations of crime suggest the origins of an individual's propensity for crime is based in genetics or reflects environmental exposures and experiences that happen very early in life (e.g., ages 0–5 years). This means that much of the crucial period of individual trait development occurs before individuals enter school settings. However, neither genes nor traits developed early in life are fully determinative of the behavioral outcomes that students will experience. While the school may not be where individual propensities for crime are forged, the nature of the school environment may be crucial in shaping how that propensity plays out in behavior. For example, students who rank high on the personality trait of "negative emotionality" may be more likely to interpret hostile intent in others' actions or to react aggressively to irritating or stressful situations. Thus, they are more likely to interpret light-hearted banter among peers as an ill-intended personal affront and to respond with an aggressive and criminal act of retaliation. Designing educational settings that attend to individual trait differences such as this offers a means to minimizing chances that trait-linked behavioral impulses produce acts of criminal offending.

Social Control and Social Bonds

All explanations discussed above emphasize concepts aimed at understanding why individuals are motivated to commit crimes. Social control explanations, in contrast, seek to understand what demotivates us. These explanations view humans as naturally self-interested, pleasure-seeking beings. They also recognize that crime often is a self-rewarding behavior. Therefore, the motivation for crime is inherent, and the trick is to explain what keeps us from pursuing its rewards.

Major societal institutions play an important role in the development of constraints on our behavior. The family and the education system, for example, serve to socialize individuals so that they "buy in" to the norms of right and wrong defined by, and shared among, members of society. When socialization is successful, individuals invest in the activities, relationships, and belief systems that conventional society prescribes. In general, these investments yield constraints on our behaviors and prevent criminal offending. However, the processes involved in conventional socialization sometimes break down or fail. When this happens, crime becomes more likely.

Travis Hirschi (1969) argues that the probability of criminal behavior depends on the strength of *social bonds* that exist between individuals and society's major social institutions. This social bond consists of four elements: attachment, commitment, involvement, and belief. Hirschi (1969) suggests these elements are interrelated, with weakness in one implying weakness in others as well. Attachment exists when individuals are sensitive to the opinions of others—when they care about upholding the behavioral expectations set by their family, friends, teachers, and other respected members of society. Commitment exists when individuals invest in the activities that society finds wholesome, worthwhile, and productive. These investments include getting a good formal education, working in an honest occupation, and pursuing achieved positions and social statuses that society regards as prestigious or worthy of distinction. Individuals who place value on these activities and make efforts to participate in them are constrained by a fear that they will lose their investments in conventional life if caught engaging in criminal behavior. Individuals without such commitments are unconstrained by such fears. Involvement reflects the amount of time in a 24-hour day that performing conventional social roles occupies. For the person committed to the activities of conventional life (e.g., school, work, religion), each day is packed with a busy cycle of appointments, meetings, deadlines, and obligations. This cycle limits the opportunity for deviance and crime. In contrast, life for individuals lacking in such conventional activities is unstructured. Freedom and opportunity to engage in crime is thus much greater. Finally, belief exists when individuals perceive that the rules and laws of society are legitimate and worthy of adherence. Those with such beliefs are constrained and unlikely to break the law. When bonds weaken, however, one's belief in the legitimacy of societal laws may be shaken, making crime a more likely outcome.

The social control/social bond explanation tells us that school-based student misbehavior occurs primarily when students lack connections to conventional society. For some students, this lack of connection results from a disorganized home life in which supervision is scarce and conflict is common. These individuals enter schools without the socialization groundwork needed to follow basic institutional rules of the structured school environment. Hence, they are ripe for school-based misbehavior and, in time, for crime. Yet the school presents a new set of structures that may potentially fill in deficits in family bonding. Teachers welcome students into their classrooms and provide a structured and caring environment. They supervise and guide student learning and maturation, and they mediate conflicts with others. More generally, they teach self-discipline and orient students to conventional academic and life goals. Because of these efforts, some students will inevitably develop key attachments to their teachers and the school as an institution. These school-related social bonds increase sensitivity to others' behavioral expectations, making them work harder to avoid transgressions. In short, attachments to teachers and school are important social bonds that should lessen the probability of school-based misbehavior or criminality.

In addition, students in schools often develop close friendship connections to one another. Social control theory regards these friendships as additional important sources of bonding to conventional society. Friendships provide meaning, belonging, and support in the school setting. Kids with friends at school are likely to develop positive feelings about school itself. Friends encourage success in each other and serve as reminders of rules when temptations for misbehavior arise. True, caring friendships act as constraining forces, binding individuals to the rules and laws shared by the members of mainstream society. Individuals with more friendships in school are more committed to society's goals and will accept laws as legitimate and worthy of adherence. As a result, those with close connections to teachers or other students are less likely to engage in criminal offending behavior at school (or elsewhere). Individuals lacking such relationships, on the other hand, are more likely to perform poorly, to dislike school, and to exhibit behavior that violates rules and/or criminal codes.

Self-Control

In 1990, Michael Gottfredson and Travis Hirschi developed another control-based explanation of crime. They argued that offenders are individuals with *low self-control*. Self-control is "the tendency to forego acts that provide immediate or near-term pleasures, but that also have negative consequences for the actor" (Gottfredson and Hirschi, 2020, p. 4). Individuals lacking in this tendency are at a heightened risk of crime because they have difficulty resisting short-term pleasures and are unable to attend to the longer-term consequences of their behavior. Self-control develops early in life, perhaps during the first eight years, in response to effective parenting/caregiving. Parents and caregivers who monitor a child's behavior recognize wrongdoing when it occurs, and sanction it appropriately, are providing the tools necessary for the development of self-control (Gottfredson and Hirschi, 1990). In contrast, parenting that neglects those steps will not instill sufficient self-control. This is quite damaging for life prospects because, according to Gottfredson and Hirschi (1990), levels of self-control remain relatively stable beyond age eight. Hence, their arguments suggest that individuals with low self-control are more likely to break rules and engage in delinquency and crimes of nearly all types at all stages of the life span. Moreover, individuals with low self-control are more prone to accidents, criminal victimization, school failure, employment problems, difficult interpersonal relations, substance use, and preventable health problems (Gottfredson and Hirschi, 2020). In sum, individuals without early connection to attentive parents are not likely to develop strong internal constraints needed to limit their natural pleasure-seeking impulses. Consequently, criminal behavior and a range of negative life outcomes become probable for individuals with low self-control.

School-based criminal offending may be a result of insufficient self-control in some students. While all early-elementary-school students are works in progress when it comes to impulse control, teachers will attest that some students lag far behind the majority. Thinking optimistically, schools can help remedy these deficits. They provide a structured environment where a student's behavior is observed and monitored and can be appropriately sanctioned, if necessary. Indeed, targeted early-education interventions have shown some success in strengthening self-control and producing beneficial behavioral results later in life (Hay and Meldrum, 2016). However, early intervention may be crucial. Gottfredson and Hirschi argue that the window for successful modification of self-control largely closes around age eight. Other research offers that self-control can strengthen in adolescence (Hay and Meldrum, 2016; Na and Paternoster, 2012). Regardless, the self-control explanation of student criminality reflects a multistep institutional failure. In preschool years, neglectful or ineffective parenting fails to instill a foundation of impulse control for some students. Therefore, they enter schools lacking in the ability to forego their desires for immediate gratification. As a result, these kids present a challenge for teachers and schools. They have greater difficulty staying on task, remaining in their seats, following along in a line, staying quiet while traversing a hallway, keeping their hands to themselves, and so on. If the school is able to devote focused attention to the needs of these challenging students, sufficient self-control may occur by the time they enter the middle-school setting and temper their criminality risks. However, as Gottfredson and Hirschi (1990) argued, this scenario of the school making up for deficiencies in family socialization is unlikely in practice. This is because a lack of consistent supervision in home life often works against efforts by teachers. Moreover, teachers typically must juggle the demands of many students, which limits their ability to focus specifically on the remediation of self-control deficits in a few students. Thus, the more likely outcome is that by the time the students with low self-control enter middle or high school, they have amassed records of academic struggle (e.g., poor grades) and disciplinary difficulty rather than marked increases in self-control. They are poorly equipped for the highly structured school environment, and this ultimately puts them at high risk of engaging in proscribed behaviors that offend other students, teachers, or school officials. Some of these actions will be serious, rising to the level of criminality.

Summary

The preceding sections of this chapter have pointed to several distinct explanations of student delinquency in schools. These explanations highlight the role of concepts including strains, social learning, individual traits, so-

Concept	Student offending
Strain	Students are motivated to commit crime at school when they have aversive social experiences. These experiences include the inability to achieve desired goals; the loss of valued relationships or possessions; or unfair, unjust, or hostile treatment by others with whom they interact. These aversive experiences lead to negative emotions, which often motivate a crime-based coping response at school.
Social learning	Students are motivated to commit crime at school when they learn criminal behaviors and beliefs, and motives and rationalizations that support them. Learning occurs through face-to-face interactions with peers or significant others. It may also occur by observing the behaviors or expressed beliefs of "distal" others with whom they do not personally interact. The probability of learning school-based crime and beliefs supportive of school-based crime is shaped by whether those behaviors and beliefs are differentially reinforced (rewarded or punished).
Biological/ psychological traits	Student propensity for involvement in school offending is linked to personal traits that are either biological or formed early in life. The source of these traits may be genetic, it may result from brain defect or injury, or it may be a reflection of personality trait development shaped by early-life socialization. Students with "high-risk" traits tend to have difficulty with impulse control during the school day, and they have higher levels of anger, hostility, and related emotions. They also may have difficulty correctly interpreting the intentions of others in social interactions at school.
Social control	Students, like all individuals, are naturally motivated to commit crime. Society constrains their motivations through the social control processes engendered by bonds to family, friends, schools, and other social institutions. For students with strong bonds, crime is inhibited. For students with weak bonds, natural motivations are freed, and school-based crime is likely.
Self-control	Crimes are acts of force and fraud committed in pursuit of self-interest. Students like all individuals, learn to constrain such actions through an early-life socialization process. If parents or caregivers observe the behavior of their children, recognize unacceptable actions, and sanction wrongdoing in appropriate ways, self-control will be instilled. If caregivers neglect these steps, sufficient levels of self-control are not likely. Students with low self-control will be prone to crime at school because they are not able to effectively govern their self-interested desires.

TABLE 2.1 OVERVIEW OF KEY THEORETICAL CONSTRUCTS AND THEIR APPLICATION TO STUDENT OFFENDING

cial bonds, and self-control. Table 2.1 provides a brief summary of how each of these concepts relates to school-based criminal offending of students. In Chapter 4, we review research examining whether theoretical claims about the impact of these concepts on offending are supported by empirical evidence.

Understanding Victimization

The preceding section indicates that while most students follow rules in classes or school-related activities, criminal offending occurs nonetheless. Student offending is sometimes "victimless" behavior, meaning there is no clearly aggrieved crime victim. Common examples of such victimless offenses committed by students include truancy and the possession and use of illegal drugs or alcohol on school grounds. However, other forms of student offending produce direct physical, financial, or emotional harms to one or more students who are *victims* of the misconduct. Examples of student victims under focus in this book include those experiencing physical assault, sexual harassment, sexual assault, robbery, threats, and larceny-theft. All but the last of these examples constitute *violent* or *personal victimization* because aggressive or violent actions by the offender in a direct interpersonal confrontation or interaction produce harm to the victim. In contrast, larceny-theft victimization, or having property stolen without force, is an example of *nonviolent victimization*, or *property victimization*. It involves a financial grievance, and likely an emotional impact, but it does not involve direct interpersonal contact between the victim and offender.

Victims of student offending, both violent and nonviolent alike, can be teachers, other members of school staff, or fellow students. Our focus in the ensuing discussion is students as victims at the hands of their student peers. Fortunately, most students will not experience victimization at school. In fact, recent data suggest that a small percentage (just 2%) of students ages 12–18 report experiencing criminal victimization at school in the six months prior to being queried (Musu, Zhang, Wang, Zhang, and Oudekerk, 2019). Does that relatively small group of students experience victimization due to random misfortune, or is victimization systematically patterned and explainable? Criminological theory and research suggest the latter. Below, we summarize three key concepts criminologists have developed in their efforts to explain victimization. Most pertinent to our focus, these are concepts the research literature commonly uses to understand student victimization in school contexts.

Lifestyle-Routine Activities

A good deal of research in criminology emphasizes lifestyles and routine daily activities as important determinants of victimization risk. Explaining why and how lifestyles and routine activities affect victimization risk initially emerged from the work of two groups of criminologists with somewhat overlapping ideas. First, in the late 1970s, Michael Hindelang and colleagues trumpeted the importance of *lifestyle-exposure* based on analyses of national victimization survey data (Hindelang, Gottfredson, and Garofalo, 1978). In particular, they observed stark differences in victimization rates across demographic groups in the United States based on age, sex, race, marital status, and income. Rates of victimization were elevated among individuals who were young, male, nonwhite, single, and poor. Hindelang and colleagues posited that lifestyle differences created greater exposure to higher-risk places and people for some individuals relative to others. For example, they suggested that young, single males tended to be at relatively high risk of victimization because they were more likely to engage in activity in risky public spaces and times (i.e., in entertainment districts at night) and to have greater contact with high-offending demographic groups (i.e., also young, single males). In short, lifestyles involving nonfamilial, nighttime, public activity, and lifestyles with greater exposure to high-offending groups are presumed associated with heightened risks for victimization.

Around the time that Hindelang and colleagues proposed the lifestyle-exposure concept, another group of scholars—led by Lawrence Cohen, Marcus Felson, and Kenneth Land—published articles that, collectively, articulated the importance of *routine activity* for understanding victimization (e.g., Cohen and Felson, 1979; Cohen, Felson, and Land, 1980; Cohen, Kluegel, and Land, 1981). Noting that robbery and burglary rates increased dramatically starting around 1960 into the mid-1970s (see Table 2.2), they rejected prevailing explanations of crime pointing to poor socioeconomic conditions. This is because the rising crime rates from 1960 to the mid-1970s coincided with improving socioeconomic conditions, such as increasing levels of education and income.

Why then did crime rates increase during this time of apparent socioeconomic prosperity, when motivations for offending should wane? Cohen, Felson, Land, and colleagues took the bold position that crime patterns were less a function of offender motivations and more a function of *criminal opportunity*—the accessibility of *suitable targets* lacking adequate *guardianship*. Treating crime motivations as a "given," they instead focused attention on understanding criminal opportunity in terms of the supply of suitable, inadequately guarded targets—the persons or property overtaken or procured in a predatory crime.

Importantly, Cohen and colleagues' perspective claims that levels of criminal opportunity vary as a function of the routine activities that constitute everyday life (Cohen and Felson, 1979; Cohen et al. 1980). To illustrate, they pointed to sweeping changes in Americans' activity patterns from the late 1940s to the mid-1970s as a culprit in increased criminal opportunity. Specifically, there were substantial increases in college enrollment and labor-force participation among women during this period. There also was a mass proliferation in outside-of-home entertainment options (e.g., eating/drinking at restaurants and bars, shopping at malls, attending sporting events)

TABLE 2.2 UNITED STATES CRIME RATES PER 100,000 POPULATION, 1960–1980		
Year	Violent crime rate	Property crime rate
1960	160.9	1726.3
1961	158.1	1747.9
1962	162.3	1857.5
1963	168.2	2012.1
1964	190.6	2197.5
1965	200.2	2248.8
1966	220.0	2450.9
1967	253.2	2736.5
1968	298.4	3071.8
1969	328.7	3351.3
1970	363.5	3621.0
1971	396.0	3768.8
1972	401.0	3560.4
1973	417.4	3737.0
1974	461.1	4389.3
1975	487.8	4810.7
1976	467.8	4819.5
1977	475.9	4601.7
1978	497.8	4642.5
1979	548.9	5016.6
1980	596.6	5353.3

Source: Uniform Crime Report Data Tool. https://www.ucrdatatool.gov/Search/Crime/State/RunCrimeStatebyState.cfm. Data downloaded on July 14, 2020.

and growth in the purchasing of expensive and/or portable goods for both household and non-household leisure activity (e.g., automobiles, bicycles, TVs, stereos). While such changes were progressive, the routine activity theorists claimed they had the unintended consequence of increasing opportunity for predatory crime. The growth in malls, restaurants, and sporting events drew people into crowded public settings, increasing the supply of suitable targets in places and situations where effective controls were lacking. At the same time, increased participation in higher education and the labor force among women meant that homes stocked with newly available and portable consumer goods were often unattended during the workday. In short, Cohen and colleagues claimed that increases in predatory crimes against people and property resulted from alterations in routine activities, opening up new avenues of opportunity for crime.

The lifestyle-exposure and routine activity perspectives are compatible, both arguing that the patterned activities or lifestyles of individuals create opportunities for offenders. Because of this compatibility, researchers fused them together into *lifestyle-routine activities theory*, or L-RAT. The L-RAT perspective suggests that risks of experiencing victimization varies, most directly, according to four key characteristics of lifestyle and activities (Cohen et al., 1981):

1. *Exposure*—the extent to which potential targets are visible and accessible to motivated offenders
2. *Proximity*—the geographic distance between potential targets and areas with large supplies of motivated offenders
3. *Target suitability*—the desirability of a potential target in combination with its perceived vulnerability
4. *Guardianship*—the extent to which potential targets are protected by persons or objects through mere presence or through some specific action (i.e., surveillance, intervention)

Additionally, social roles and statuses—as indicated by demographic characteristics such as age, gender, race, income, and marital status—affect a potential target's victimization risk more indirectly, as they partly determine lifestyles and activities and, by extension, levels of exposure, proximity, target suitability, and guardianship (see Figure 2.1). In fact, L-RAT suggests that differences in victimization risk across demographic groups is explained by differences in levels of exposure, proximity, target suitability, and guardianship (Cohen et al., 1981).

There is debate about whether L-RAT's four key concepts related to lifestyles and activities are distinctively measurable, but research on community and college samples over the past four decades generally supports the theoretical ideas underlying L-RAT (see Madero-Hernandez and Fisher, 2013; McNeeley, 2015; Wilcox and Cullen, 2018 for reviews). For example, studies indicate that violent victimization—where a person is targeted for robbery or assault, as examples—is higher among those who engage in more frequent "risky" public activity, like going out to bars or parties or using public transportation (e.g., Fisher, Sloan, Cullen, and Lu, 1998; Messner, Lu, Zhang, and Liu, 2007; Miethe and McDowall, 1993). Other work stresses that violent victimization risk is enhanced among those involved in criminal behavior and/or gangs as part of their lifestyle (Lauritsen, Sampson, and Laub, 1991; Wright and Decker, 1997; Wu and Pyrooz, 2016) and/or who live in proximity to inner-city areas (Tseloni, Wittebrood, Farrell, and Pease, 2004). Studies also reveal that nonviolent property victimization—where a person's household or belongings are targeted for burglary or theft, as examples—is higher among individuals leaving their homes unoccupied more frequently, owning a larger number of valuable goods, and engaging in rela-

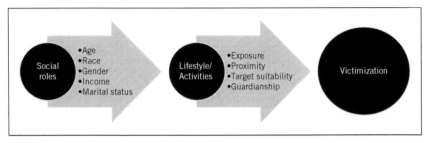

Figure 2.1 Lifestyle-routine activities theory

tively few household safety precautions (i.e., locks, alarms) (Mustaine and Tewksbury, 1998; Wilcox, Madensen, and Tillyer, 2007).

Importantly, lifestyles and activities also are relevant for understanding why some adolescent students are more prone to becoming victims of crime at school. Schools are specific domains of routine daily activity, structuring when, where, and how youths spend much of their time. Nonetheless, even within a school's regimented confines, there is variation in lifestyle and activity patterns across students, with some lifestyles and activities providing more exposure to those motivated to offend (i.e., other students, particularly males) in places and at times where guardianship is lacking. For example, students participate to varying degrees in antisocial activities at school, including bullying, acting out in class, skipping class, or using drugs. Somewhat relatedly, student lifestyles differ in terms of peer associations, with some students hanging around a "rough crowd" of peers known for deviant behavior. On the other hand, some students keep to themselves much of the day or hang around a tight circle of a few close friends, while other students belong to large, popular cliques including numerous opposite-sex friendships. Students also engage to different degrees with their school and its teachers, and they differentially participate in extracurricular activities, such as sports teams or clubs, that occur primarily in after-school hours.

Target Congruence

Several decades after the development of L-RAT, David Finkelhor and Nancy Asdigian (1996) touted *target congruence* as a concept to extend and address limitations of the L-RAT perspective. In particular, they noted that differences in lifestyles and routine activity could not adequately explain some forms of victimization, especially victimization of children at the hands of family members. Moreover, they argued that demographic characteristics might directly affect victimization, net of lifestyles and routine activities. In other words, victimization risk may vary by age, gender, and race for reasons other than lifestyles and activities. To account for this, Finkelhor and Asdigian (1996) elaborated on L-RAT's concept of target suitability by proposing target congruence theory. It offers the idea that the risk of victimization increases for individuals with characteristics that align (i.e., are congruent) with the unique needs, motives, or reactions of offenders. There are three dimensions to target congruence: vulnerability, gratifiability, and antagonism. These concepts help categorize an array of personal characteristics beyond lifestyle and activity that could serve an offender's desires. While quite useful for understanding child-abuse victimization, the concepts are applicable to other types of victimization.

First, *target vulnerability* refers to individual characteristics that make it difficult to combat the predatory actions of an offender. Vulnerability is congruent with an offender's need for minimal resistance from victims. Small size/stature, limited strength/poor fitness, shyness, and physical or mental impairment are all examples of individual traits and states suggesting vulnerability, thus increasing risk of victimization (Elvey and McNeeley, 2019; Felson, 1996). For example, many victims of child sexual abuse are vulnerable not because of their lifestyle or activities but because their nascent stage of human development (1) renders them physically weaker than their perpetrators, and (2) cognitively limits their ability to understand the wrongness of their perpetrator's behavior.

Second, *target gratifiability* refers to characteristics of targets (their possessions, qualities, attributes) that appeal to the desires of an offender—desires that depend on the nature and motive of the crime. In other words, target gratifiability is the extent to which a potential target provides something an offender wants. Pedophiles are, by definition, sexually desirous of prepubescent children. Thus, prepubertal children present target gratifiability to pedophiles not because of their lifestyle but because of their life stage. Beyond child sexual abuse, female gender is a prototypical risk factor for sexual assault victimization in early adulthood, particularly that perpetrated by heterosexual men. As Finkelhor and Asdigian (1996) point out, it is *femaleness*, not lifestyle, that puts women at greater risk than men for experiencing sexual assault victimization. Accounting for lifestyle and activity might explain why some women are at greater risk than other women for sexual assault victimization, but it does not clearly account for why women are at greater risk than men. Femaleness, as representing target gratifiability for a substantial number of perpetrators, helps us understand that gender gap.

Third, *target antagonism* refers to characteristics of targets (their possessions, qualities, and attributes) that arouse destructive reactionary impulses in offenders. For example, temperamental children can wear on parents, sometimes to the point of evoking violent reactions (i.e., shaking a baby to stop their crying). Similarly, individuals with difficult personalities or unpopular behavioral tendencies (e.g., arrogance, impulsivity, eccentricity, mental illness) might provoke others to the point of attack (Silver, 2002). The notion of target antagonism is particularly useful in understanding bias-motivated victimization (i.e., "hate crimes"). Ascribed statuses, such as racial/ethnic or sexual minority status can arouse hatred and anger among those with particular prejudices that sometimes lead to destructive, criminal action (e.g., vandalizing the property belonging to a neighbor who is a racial minority; assaulting a gay peer) (Waldner and Berg, 2008).

The target congruence perspective holds great potential for understanding victimization of students in school contexts. Students vary in the extent to which they possess characteristics, beyond lifestyle or activity, that are congruent with the needs, desires, or reactions of fellow students (who can offend against them). For example, students vary significantly in terms of size and strength, with smaller students likely perceived as vulnerable targets unable to resist aggressions against them. On the other hand, large size (specifically, being overweight) might offer target gratifiability to bullies, as the social undesirability of excess body weight means bullies are likely to generate laughs and other forms of peer approval through their harassment. Beyond size and strength differences, students' variation in gender identity may offer target gratifiability in the school context. In most heteronormative school contexts, female students are likely at greater risk for experiencing harassment, unwanted touching, and more extreme forms of sexual violence, as their gender alone provides sexual gratifiability to the (mostly male) perpetrators of such acts. On the other hand, gender-nonconforming students, or students that carry any number of minority-status characteristics (i.e., race, religion) could be at heightened risk for victimization, likely due to target antagonism—they are prone to victimization because of attributes that evoke aggressive responses from prejudiced peers.

Criminal Propensity

A third perspective explaining victimization emphasizes overlap between criminal offenders and crime victims. Offenders and victims are not mutually exclusive pools of individuals. Moreover, research indicates there is a moderate correlation between criminal offending and victimization. Taken together, this means that a significant number of offenders experience victimization, and a substantial percentage of victims commit offenses. One interpretation of this "victim-offender overlap" is that a similar set of dispositional characteristics put certain individuals at greater risk for both offending and victimization. Therefore, it is worthwhile to consider whether theories of criminal propensity also contribute to our understanding of victimization risk.

Low self-control is an important criminal propensity trait in this regard. Christopher Schreck's (1999) work first drew attention to the idea that individuals with low self-control not only offend at greater rates, as posited by Gottfredson and Hirschi's (1990) general theory of crime (see discussion earlier in this chapter); they also suffer higher rates of victimization. He argued that low self-control tends to enhance both risky lifestyles/activities and target congruence, thereby increasing victimization risk. As such, his perspective shares some similarities to L-RAT and target congruence theory. Importantly, however, Schreck uniquely implied that low self-control was an important underlying root cause of routine activities and perceived target congruence, and, in turn, criminal victimization (see also Pratt, Turanovic, Fox, and Wright, 2014; Schreck, Stewart, and Fisher, 2006; Stewart, Elifson, and Sterk, 2004; Turanovic, Reisig, and Pratt, 2015). For example, individuals with low self-control tend to seek thrills and throw caution to the wind. Moreover, their attraction to risky activities pairs with a low likelihood of taking protective steps that help to control or mitigate negative consequences. According to this logic, the effects of routine activities and lifestyles on victimization risk are the result of a process whereby individuals with low self-control select into lifestyles that increase their vulnerability to crime. Additionally, individuals with low self-control can be antagonistic, making them congruent targets in reactionary crimes. For instance, low self-control can trigger disruptive, obnoxious behavior that provokes aggressive reactions from others.

Beyond the trait of low self-control, other biological, psychological, and social factors underlying criminal behavior may put a person at risk for victimization. For instance, research focused on the psychological origins of criminal propensity shows that individuals low on the trait of agreeableness are at heightened risk of victimization (e.g., Milam, Spitzmueller, and Penney, 2009). Other research suggests that individual adherence to antisocial norms and values—such as norms condoning violence as a way to gain respect—is associated with an increased involvement in criminal offending and increased victimization experiences (McNeeley and Wilcox, 2015a, 2015b; Stewart, Schreck, and Simons, 2006). This research suggests that those who believe in and act according to antisocial norms are antagonistic targets, at risk for retaliatory violence.

The assertion that variation in individual propensity, measured by levels of self-control, is relevant for understanding victimization of students in school contexts overlaps with the argument linking low self-control to student offending articulated earlier in this chapter. Students are expected to sit attentively in classes for many hours each day; they are assessed on mentally complex tasks as opposed to physically complex ones; they are surrounded by peers with whom they are expected to cooperate; and they are expected

TABLE 2.3 OVERVIEW OF KEY THEORETICAL CONSTRUCTS AND THEIR APPLICATION TO STUDENT VICTIMIZATION

Concept	Student victimization
Lifestyle-routine activity	Students most at risk for victimization are those with greater levels of exposure and/or proximity to likely offenders at school, greater levels of target suitability as perceived by peers at school, and lower levels of guardianship at school.
Target congruence	Students most at risk of victimization are those who are vulnerable, gratifiable (depending on needs of the offender), and/or antagonistic.
Criminal propensity	Students most at risk of victimization are those who have characteristics associated with criminal propensity, including low self-control, low agreeableness, and belief in antisocial norms.

to follow rather than bend rules. Given the incongruity between low self-control and these school-based educational expectations, youths with low self-control tend to "act out" in school settings. In turn, acting out may annoy and antagonize other students, sometimes provoking negative (victimizing) responses. Moreover, students with low self-control find risky situations and behaviors attractive, and they eschew precautionary behavior that could reduce victimization risk. Other markers of criminal propensity—such as low scores on the personality trait of agreeableness, or strong beliefs in antisocial values—also vary across students and thus could be key in explaining differential risks of school-based victimization.

Summary

In the preceding discussion, we offered three major concepts to help build understanding of variations in criminal victimization: (1) lifestyle-routine activity, (2) target congruence, and (3) criminal propensity. For review purposes, Table 2.3 briefly summarizes how each of the theoretical concepts relates to students' school-based victimization. A comprehensive review of research examining these concepts and their theorized relationships with student victimization is the focus of Chapter 5.

Understanding Crime Places

Although the explanation of individual-level variation in offending and victimization occupies a significant portion of criminologists' attention, there is also great interest in understanding why crime varies across places. In American criminology, the place-based focus began in the early part of the twentieth century, when research by sociologists in Chicago aimed to understand behavior in its social and physical environmental context. Clifford Shaw and Henry McKay famously mapped homes of juvenile delinquents in Chicago over multiple decades in the early 1900s (e.g., Shaw, 1929; Shaw and McKay, 1942). They observed that the impoverished areas immediately surrounding the central business district consistently had the highest rates of juvenile delinquency. These areas were initial settlements for immigrant groups looking to work in the industrializing city. Across decades, the ethnic composition of these communities shifted as new immigrant ethnic groups replaced previous ones who assimilated and moved to better housing elsewhere in the city. These transitional areas just outside the central business district consistently experienced high rates of crime despite an ever-changing racial/ethnic composition. From their observations of these facts, Shaw and McKay concluded that the consistently high rates of crime could not be due to racial/ethnic characteristics of the individuals because the latter constantly changed. Instead, they posited that crime occurred because of features of these transitional areas, not the features of the people. In sum, Shaw and McKay developed an explanation of crime focused on the *social disorganization* of places as the cause of high rates of crime.

Other scholars followed in the Shaw and McKay tradition, focusing on place-based rather than people-based explanations of crime. However, they offered alternative theories of crime and place, emphasizing concepts beyond social disorganization, including cultural influence and situational opportunity. The concepts theorized as keys to understanding variation in crime are the focus of the subsections that follow. As before, we do not exhaustively review crime and place theories but instead highlight perspectives most relevant for understanding school crime.

Social (Dis)Organization

As just suggested, early American criminologists studying high-crime neighborhoods in industrializing Chicago touted the idea that socially disorganized places fostered high rates of crime. Social disorganization refers to a breakdown in the controlling effect that conventional social rules have on behavior within particular places. This occurs because a weakening in social institutions (families, schools, civic organizations) and networks impedes their ability to clearly articulate and uphold social norms (see, e.g., Shaw, 1929; Shaw and McKay, 1942; Thomas and Znaniecki, 1920). In contrast, organized places clearly convey and enforce conventional norms through strong networks and institutions (Bursik and Grasmick, 1993; Kornhauser, 1978; Sampson and Groves, 1989). When residents in neighborhoods are strongly connected or committed to local institutions, it is easier for everyone to recognize shared values and cooperate in their enforcement.

Recent theoretical statements within the social disorganization tradition challenge the idea that effective control of crime requires strong interpersonal connections. They argue, instead, that residents of a place must share mutual trust and a willingness to intervene for the common good—a characteristic referred to as *collective efficacy* (Sampson, 2012; Sampson, Raudenbush, and Earls, 1997). For example, even in the absence of strong interpersonal ties (i.e., communities where few people get together socially), residents can trust that their neighbors share common values and would come together to address threats to those values. Several decades of research studies support the idea that lower rates of crime are observed in places in which the people within, as a group, exhibit strong collective efficacy (for a recent review, see Wilcox, Cullen, and Feldmeyer, 2018).

The social disorganization/collective efficacy perspective on crime places is also applicable to crime in school contexts. There is good reason to think that crime prevention efforts improve with collective cohesion and coordination among actors in school contexts. Indeed, scholars studying school crime have used similar concepts. Akin to collective efficacy in communities is "school efficacy" (Kirk, 2009; Tillyer et al., 2018) and the related concept of "*communally organized schools*," where "members know, care about, and support one another, have common goals and sense of shared purpose, and to which they actively contribute and feel personally committed" (Solomon, Battistich, Kim, and Watson, 1997, p. 236). Scholars routinely posit that schools effectively stating clear, fair rules and stressing student, parent, and administrator cooperation in defining priorities and addressing problems are the safest (Gottfredson and Gottfredson, 1985; Kirk, 2009; Payne, Gottfredson, and Gottfredson, 2003; Welsh, 2001).

Culture

The cultural (or subcultural) tradition is another criminological perspective aimed at explaining crime across places (Cloward and Ohlin, 1960; Cohen, 1955; Kornhauser, 1978; Merton, 1938; Miller, 1958; Sellin, 1938; Shaw and McKay, 1942; Cohen, Lindesmith, and Schuessler, 1956; Wolfgang and Ferracuti, 1967). Arguments within this theoretical tradition propose that levels of crime differ across places due to distinctive cultural systems. The most prominent is the *deviant subculture* theory. It argues that a coherent set of values and beliefs contradicting with society's mainstream characterize high-crime places (Harding and Hepburn, 2014). Individuals in these places share internalized values defining illegal acts as acceptable and effective means for achieving desired end goals (e.g., social status, power, or money). In short, individuals internalize group norms espousing deviance, and they engage in behavior consistent with those values. Hence, the deviant subculture theory also is called the *culture as individual values* perspective. Crime explanations emphasizing cultural conflict, cultural transmission, and race-, class-, or neighborhood-specific subcultures are oft-cited examples of the deviant subculture perspective (e.g., Kornhauser, 1978; Kubrin, 2015). Moreover, a recent body of studies linking the likelihood of criminal offending with the existence of "oppositional values," "street codes," or "violent subcultures" is also reflective of this theoretical tradition (Brezina, Agnew, Cullen, and Wright, 2004; Felson, Liska, South, and McNulty, 1994; Ousey and Wilcox, 2005; Stewart and Simons, 2010; Swartz, Wilcox, and Ousey, 2017).

A second, emerging cultural perspective in criminology is the *culture in action* perspective (Sampson and Bean, 2006). This perspective proposes that cultural influence is not simply a coherent set of values that prescribe desired ends and the means of achieving them. It is fragmented pieces of information—such as frames, narratives, or scripts—that individuals choose to guide their behavioral responses to contexts or situations (Swidler, 1986; Sampson and Bean, 2006). Culture is viewed as a set of tools allowing individuals "to do different kinds of things in different circumstances" (Swidler, 1986, p. 276). Thus, while individuals hold certain internalized values, their behaviors may not adhere to them. This is because behaving in a situationally appropriate manner (i.e., in ways acceptable to others around us) sometimes requires individuals to apply cultural resources (e.g., context-specific frames or scripts) that contradict their internalized values or beliefs.

Although framed primarily as explanations of neighborhood variations in crime, cultural perspectives are also useful for understanding variations in crime rates across schools. An argument in the deviant subculture tradition (*culture as individual values*) is that in some schools, students maintain deviant sets of norms and values endorsing of rule breaking, mischief, or crime. Sustained exposure to this school-based deviant subculture elevates prospects that individuals internalize, widely share, and act according to the "deviant cultural code" of their school. An argument aligned with a *culture in action* perspective suggests that student offending is high in some schools because the school culture provides tools—scripts, rationalizations, narratives—that encourage delinquent behavior in particular situations. These behaviors may contradict students' personal values, but in the day-to-day situations encountered in the school context, they also may allow students to gain respect, save face, or provide protection from peer victimization.

Situational Opportunity

Another approach to understanding cross-place variation in crime suggests some places have higher rates of crime because they offer plentiful *situation-*

al opportunity—or, opportunity for motivated offenders to encounter suitable, unguarded targets within the immediate environment. Places offering better situational opportunity are those in which (Smith and Clarke, 2012):

- Offending requires minimal *effort* (i.e., the offender faces few, if any, challenges in carrying out the mechanics involved in the crime).
- Offending is *low-risk* (i.e., there is little chance that the offender will be detected).
- Offending is *rewarding* (i.e., the offender can perceive clear gains to be had).
- Offending is *provoked* (i.e., there are stimuli that motivate criminal action).
- Offending is *excusable* (i.e., there are few explanations or reminders about behavioral responsibilities).

To provide a few examples of the indicators of situational opportunity, crime presumably requires minimal *effort* at places that offer few restrictions on movements or actions. Conversely, it is much more difficult to commit a crime at a location where movements into and out of the space are limited, or blocked altogether. It is also more difficult to commit a crime if specific crime-facilitating actions are restricted. For example, acts of firearm violence are more difficult within places that use strategies such as screening with metal detectors, or restricting sales of guns and ammunition.

Crime is, theoretically, *lower risk* to offenders at places using physical designs that limit naturally occurring surveillance (i.e., designs that offer obstructed/blocked sight lines) or at places not using formal or mechanical surveillance aids (i.e., police/security personnel and cameras, respectively). Similarly, locations with ineffective *place management* are also lower-risk environments for perpetrators of crime. In other words, risk is low at places where "managers" of the space are not actively engaged in strategies that deter crime (Madensen and Eck, 2013). Places that ineffectively leverage the guardianship capabilities of unofficial actors within the space, including bystanders, also present relatively few risks to offenders. By offering low risk to offenders, these various situational conditions by extension, provide substantial opportunity for crime.

Crime opportunity is apparent, too, when situational conditions offer obvious rewards, provocations, and excuses for crime. Places offering clear *rewards* are those where beneficial targets are visible, removable, transferable, and non-traceable. Places offering crime *provocations* promote emotional stress, disputes between rivals, peer pressure, or copycat behaviors (i.e., imitation of prior criminal behavior). Finally, *excuses* for crime are more readily available in places that fail to, for example, set clear rules about behavioral expectations, post detailed instructions on how to meet those expectations, or provide prompts to remind people about unacceptable behavior.

Altogether, the indicators of situational opportunity mentioned here are the subject of much research. Numerous studies examine their effectiveness for preventing crime at a variety of place types, including residential complexes, public streets, retail outlets, transportation centers, and recreational spaces. Systematic reviews typically reveal that such places see less crime when they employ strategies to reduce situational opportunity—via increasing effort or risk, or reducing rewards, provocations, or excuses (e.g., see Eck and Guerette, 2012). Most relevant for the focus of this book, schools are another place type for which the concept of situational opportunity is applicable. In fact, opportunity-reduction approaches to combat crime are now commonplace in schools across the United States. Examples include:

- Employing access control in order to make crime more difficult— such as requiring doors be locked and visitors "buzzed in" through a controlled entryway
- Using metal detectors to limit students' access to weaponry necessary for some forms of violence while in school
- Using architectural designs that enhance natural surveillance, thereby increasing the chances that offending is detectable (e.g., in modern schools the walls of the main office are often glass, allowing unobstructed views from the office to other areas of the school building)
- Using cameras as mechanical surveillance and employing school resource officers to increase formal guardianship (Jonson, 2017)
- Using teachers as informal guardians of school space who can effectively curb crime by taking ownership of areas beyond the classroom (Astor, Meyer, and Behre, 1999)
- Banning particular personal items that are hot commodities for theft (i.e., certain types/brands of clothing, cell phones, headphones)
- Taking steps to limit stimuli and situations that provoke offending behaviors, such as staggering times that students are released for recess or lunch to create calmer settings, or creating more efficient serving procedures during lunchtime so that lines are shorter and there is less competition for space
- Engaging in practices aligned with removing excuses for criminal behavior, such as formulating explicit codes of conduct, or posting of rules of behavior throughout school buildings

Of course, just because measures aimed at reducing situational opportunity can be and often are applied in school settings does not mean they are effec-

TABLE 2.4 OVERVIEW OF KEY THEORETICAL CONSTRUCTS AND THEIR APPLICATION TO SCHOOL-LEVEL CRIME INCIDENTS	
Concept	School-level crime incidents
Social (dis)organization	Schools are at risk for higher crime when there is inadequate cooperation among students, parents, and administrators in defining priorities and addressing problems.
Culture	Schools are at risk for higher crime when they have distinctive cultures—cultures that espouse norms contradicting those of mainstream society. Schools can also provide scripts dictating the appropriateness of criminal actions in certain situations.
Situational opportunity	Schools are at risk for higher crime when the environment is structured such that offending requires little effort, is low risk, is rewarding, is provoked, and/or is excusable.

tive. An examination of this question of effectiveness is the subject of the research and policy reviewed in Chapters 7 and 8.

Summary

The sections above highlight the potential importance of social organization or collective efficacy, culture, and situational opportunity for understanding variation in crime across school settings. In Table 2.4 we present an overview of the theoretical linkages between these three concepts and school-based crime incidents. Despite their potential importance, school contexts exhibit a great deal of variation in their social organization/collective efficacy, culture, and situational opportunity. We review the research examining whether cross-school variation in these key factors affects school crime in Chapter 7.

Conclusion

Consider the following scenario, which could happen at virtually any secondary school in the United States: *Right before the bell rings for the start of Monday morning Homeroom, an 11th-grade student receives a video, taken at a weekend party and disseminated via social media. The video shows that the person the 11th grader has been dating is "making out" with someone else—a 10th-grade student at the same school. As soon as students are dismissed from homeroom, the furious 11th-grade student tracks down the 10th grader, throws them up against a locker, and punches them multiple times in the face. Several teachers intervene, but not before the 10th-grade victim is bloody and bruised.*

How do we explain this assault? How do we prevent future occurrences? Those questions underlie the purpose of this book. We suggest that comprehensively explaining and preventing school crime requires thinking about all three elements of the problem analysis triangle: offenders, target/victims, and places. In this chapter, we described criminological perspectives that lay out (1) common reasons for offending, (2) key risk factors for victimization, and (3) characteristics of places that make them susceptible to hosting crime events. Applying these perspectives to the scenario described above, one could infer that the 11th-grade assailant was motivated by strain—a negative stimulus in the form of a video showing their romantic partner cheating with another student. One might also infer that the 11th grader lacked the self-control necessary to handle the situation in a nonviolent manner. Though the scenario lacks details about the 11th-grade assailant's friends, one could infer that they learned from their adolescent peers that violent payback is an expected reaction in the face of humiliation or disrespect. All of these arguments are plausible, and they highlight various common explanations for criminal offending discussed in this chapter.

Understanding what motivated the offending behavior is only part of the story, however, since criminal offenders need targets to victimize and settings in which to carry out their actions. Hence, we must go beyond understanding why the 11th-grade student referenced above was motivated to assault another student. We should attempt to understand what actions and/or characteristics of the 10th-grade victim made them at-risk for attack, and what characteristics of the school played a role in the 11th grader's ability to act on their fury in a violent manner immediately after Homeroom. Theoretical perspectives on criminal victimization and crime places, also discussed in this chapter, offer numerous logical possibilities.

In sum, the theories discussed in this chapter coincide with all three sides of the problem analysis triangle and ultimately offer clear implications for prevention. Theories of offending provide a host of risk factors that schools can target to reduce offending behavior. At the same time, theories of victimization and theories of crime places imply that hardening and better guarding potential targets and/or strengthening the school environment can reduce the opportunities for motivated offenders to carry out their infractions in the school. As stated at the outset of the chapter, our theoretical overview is not intended to cover all possible theoretical explanations for school crime. Rather, our focus is on criminological perspectives commonly tested in research studies of offending and victimization among students in school contexts—research we focus on in much of the remainder of the book. Thus, while the preceding vignette initiates thinking about how the theoretical concepts discussed in this chapter might apply to a hypothetical

ulation of high-school students and is administered biennially, the YRBSS data can track aggregate trends in students' experiences over time. For example, according to the YRBSS data, weapon carrying on school property significantly declined from 11.8% of students in 1993 to 3.8% of students in 2017. In 1993, 7.3% of students reported being threatened or injured with a weapon on school property. This increased to a peak of 9.2% in 2003, and then declined to a low of 6.0% of students in 2017. The percentage of students who reported being in a physical fight on school property has also declined significantly over time from 16.2% of students in 1993 to 8.5% of students in 2017. Despite these noted improvements in student safety at school in recent years, there has been a slight increase in the percentage of students who reported not going to school due to safety concerns, from 4.4% in 1993 to 6.7% in 2017 (Centers for Disease Control and Prevention, n.d.).

Notwithstanding its strengths, the YRBSS data are limited in terms of the ability to *explain* causes of school-based offending and victimization for several reasons. First, due to confidentiality concerns, data are not available by school. Therefore, individual student experiences are not linked to specific school-level characteristics. Second, while the data are collected every two years, the same students are not surveyed over time, so the data do not measure changes over time in an individual's offending or victimization. Third, as the CDC notes, the YRBSS addresses behaviors that contribute to the leading causes of morbidity and mortality among youths and adults, but not the determinants of those behaviors (Brener et al., 2013). In other words, with a few exceptions, the data lack key possible correlates of student offending and victimization. Finally, similar to the NCVS, the data do not explicitly ask about in-school delinquency, with the exception of weapon carrying.

National Study of Delinquency Prevention in Schools

The NSDPS, conducted during 1997 and 1998, was designed to provide a comprehensive description of school-based problem behavior in the United States and schools' efforts to prevent problem behavior and promote a safe and orderly environment (Gottfredson et al., 2000). The 1980s and 1990s saw a rapid growth in prevention programs implemented in schools, and the NSDPS aimed to understand the quality of program implementation (Gottfredson and Gottfredson, 2002). Funded by the NIJ, the Office of Juvenile Justice Delinquency Prevention (OJJDP), and the Department of Education, the NSDPS targeted representative public, private, and Catholic schools in the United States (Gottfredson and Gottfredson, 2002). Schools were stratified by location (urban, suburban, and rural) and level (elementary, middle, and high school) and a total of 1,279 schools were selected. Of the 1,279 sampled schools, 848 participated in Phase I, which surveyed school principals in

1997. During Phase II in the spring of 1998, the originally sampled schools were again targeted for participation, with 635 participating. Principals in all participating schools (elementary, middle, and high schools) were surveyed again. Additionally, in middle and high schools, teachers and students were also surveyed. In total, 13,103 teachers from 403 schools completed the teacher survey and 16,014 students from 310 schools completed the student survey (Gottfredson et al., 2000).

During Phase I, data collection asked principals to identify school activities currently implemented to prevent or reduce delinquency, drug use, or other problem behavior, as well as previous experiences with program implementation and various other school characteristics, including morale, organizational capacity, and staff stability versus turnover (Gottfredson et al., 2000). Principals also identified "activity coordinators," who provided more details about each of the implemented activities. During Phase II, the activity coordinators provide detailed descriptions of prevention activities, as well as information about themselves, available school support, and supervision of the prevention activities. Teacher and student surveys during Phase II included questions about demographics, prevention activities, victimization, delinquent behaviors, school orderliness, and general school climate. Principal surveys during Phase II asked about school disciplinary policies and practices, crimes that occurred at the school, school climate, and principal leadership style and personality.

The NSDPS asked students about specific forms of victimization *in school* occurring during the current school year. This included dichotomous (i.e., "yes and no") questions about theft, physical attacks, forcibly being made to hand over money or things, and being threatened with or without a weapon (Gottfredson et al., 2000). Students were also asked about their delinquent activities in the past 12 months. Five of these questions asked specifically about school-based behaviors: purposely damaging or destroying school property, hitting or threatening to hit a teacher or other adult in school, hitting or threatening to hit other students, stealing or trying to steal something at school, and attending school drunk or high on drugs. Additional questions asked about damaging or destroying property; theft; carrying a weapon; involvement in gang fights; joyriding; using force to take money or things from someone; breaking into a building or car; sniffing glue, paint, or other sprays; and belonging to a gang. These questions did not specify whether the behavior occurred at school, but follow-up questions asked, "If you were in a fight, stole something, damaged property, or used drugs, what time of day did you do these things?" with one option being "during school hours on weekdays (Monday through Friday)." There are also a series of yes/no questions asking about specific forms of substance use in the past 12 months, though the NSDPS does not specify if the behaviors are school-based.

A main strength of the NSDPS is its rich description of the full range of prevention activities schools implement to address problem behaviors in school, with a focus on implementation quality. Specifically, the NSDPS examined the implementation of 14 types of prevention activities:

1. Prevention curriculum, instruction, or training
2. Behavioral programming or behavior modification
3. Counseling, social work, psychological, or therapeutic activity
4. Mentoring, tutoring, coaching, and job apprenticeship/placement
5. Recreation, enrichment, and leisure activity
6. Services or programs for family members
7. Improvements to instructional practices or methods
8. Classroom organization and management practices
9. Activity to change or maintain culture, climate, or expectations for behavior
10. Intergroup relations and school-community interaction
11. Interventions involving a school planning structure or process to manage change
12. Security and surveillance
13. Use of external personnel resources for classroom management and instruction
14. Youth participation in school discipline

For these prevention activities, the NSDPS includes data on organizational capacity, organizational support, program structure, and integration into normal school operations. It also includes various indicators of intensity, including the level of use by school personnel, the frequency of operation, the number of lessons or sessions, duration, frequency of student participation, ratio of providers to students in the school, and the proportion of students exposed or participating (Gottfredson and Gottfredson, 2002). In addition to these prevention activities, the teacher survey also provides data on elements of school climate, such as teachers' perceptions of relationships between students, teachers, administrators; levels of collaboration between and among faculty and administrators; degree of support for teachers; and the extent to which the school has common goals and norms (Payne et al., 2003; Payne, 2008). Finally, the NSDPS sampling methodology, which yields a sample representative of all schools serving students in grades K through 12 in the 50 states and the District of Columbia, is a strength of the dataset (Gottfredson and Gottfredson, 2002).

While the NSDPS is valuable for understanding school prevention activities and climate, it is not well suited for addressing some research questions related to school crime and safety. First, the cross-sectional nature of the Phase II data prohibits the analysis of temporal changes in student victimization and/or delinquency risk over time. Moreover, the victimization and delinquency items are framed as "yes" or "no" responses, precluding any investigation into the frequency of students' involvement in school crime (e.g., repeat victimization).

School Survey on Crime and Safety (SSOCS)

The U.S. Department of Education's NCES manages the SSOCS, which aims to provide national-level estimates of school crime, disorder, disciplinary practices, programs, and policies in U.S. public schools (Diliberti, Jackson, Correa, Padgett, and Hansen, 2019). SSOCS data come from random samples of K through 12 U.S. public schools. For example, during the 2017–2018 school year, a nationally representative, stratified, random sample of 4,803 U.S. public schools was selected, and questionnaires were received from 2,762 schools. Weighting of the data produces a sample representative of the population of public schools in the U.S. (Diliberti et al., 2019).

Public school administrators and principals provide the data included in the survey. The SSOCS occurs during the spring and, to date, has been conducted for each of following academic years: 1999–2000, 2003–2004, 2005–2006, 2007–2008, 2009–2010, 2015–2016, 2017–2018, and 2019–2020. The U.S. Census Bureau administered recent SSOCS data collection, with support from the NIJ's Comprehensive School Safety Initiative.

In the SSOCS, principals and other school administrators report on a variety of school practices and programs. Questions address usage of access control policy, metal detectors, classroom locks, drug-sniffing dogs, drug testing, uniforms and dress codes, book bag policies, security cameras, classroom telephones, access limits on school computers and social networks, and prohibitions of cell phones (U.S. Department of Education, 2016). They also ask if the school has written plans to address a range of scenarios, including active shooters, national disasters, and bomb threats, and if students drill on emergency procedures including evacuation, lockdown, and shelter in place. The survey also includes questions about specific formal programs intended to prevent or reduce violence, including prevention curriculum, behavioral modification interventions, counseling, and so on. Finally, the SSOCS measures additional school-level characteristics, including parent and community involvement, school security staff, mental health services, staff training, school disciplinary actions, and factors that limit the school's ability to reduce and prevent crime.

The SSOCS measures school crime incidents known to principals or administrators. There are questions about rape and attempted rape, sexual assault, physical attacks and fights with and without weapons, theft, possession of weapons, vandalism, and distribution/possession/use of alcohol and drugs. For each of these, respondents report the number of incidents during the current school year (as opposed to the number of victims or offenders) and the number reported to police or other law enforcement. Respondents also indicate how often (ranging from "happens daily" to "never happens") a range of problems occur at their school, including student bullying, sexual harassment, widespread disorder in classrooms, student verbal abuse of teachers, and gang activities.

As a survey of principals/administrators from a representative sample of schools, the SSOCS is particularly useful for understanding ongoing school policies, programs, and practices related to school crime and safety in the United States. That said, there are a number of limitations and research questions relevant to the study of school crime that it cannot address. First, the SSOCS only measures crime incidents known to the principal or administrator who completes the survey. Many incidents are unreported and therefore are absent from these data. Moreover, because crime incidents are aggregated in reporting by respondents, those involving more than one victim or perpetrator are not distinguished, thus undercounting the total number of students affected by the incidents. Finally, the SSOCS is a school-level dataset; it provides no information on students' individual experiences with crime or the risk and protective factors associated with in-school delinquent offending or victimization. Therefore, SSOCS is not useful for testing the individual-level offending and victimization theories reviewed in Chapter 2.

The National Longitudinal Study of Adolescent to Adult Health (Add Health)

The National Longitudinal Study of Adolescent to Adult Health (Add Health) is the largest and most comprehensive longitudinal study of adolescents. It addresses a congressional mandate to study adolescent health (Harris et al., 2009). Add Health surveyed a nationally representative sample of adolescent students in grades 7 through 12 during the 1994–1995 school year. The research team used systematic sampling methods with stratification to select the sample. A sample of 80 high schools and 52 middle schools were selected to be representative of U.S. schools in terms of region, urbanicity, school size, school type, and ethnicity (Harris et al., 2009). Follow-up interviews were conducted in home in 1995 (Wave I), 1996 (Wave II), 2001–2002 (Wave III), 2008 (Wave IV), and 2016–2018 (Wave V).

The first two waves are most relevant for our purposes of describing and explaining school-based crime. They focused on factors that may influence adolescent health and risk behaviors, such as individual traits, family, romantic relationships, peers, school factors, and neighborhood characteristics (Harris et al., 2009). In total, 12,105 adolescents made up the core sample interviewed during the Wave I in-home surveys. A parent, typically the resident mother when available, also completed a questionnaire during Wave I. In addition, Wave I data collection obtained information from school administrators on school policies and procedures, as well as teacher and student body characteristics. Add Health also includes geographic information about where the student lives at the block group, census tract, county, and state levels (Billy, Wenzlow, and Grady, 1998).

Features of the Add Health make it valuable for researchers seeking better understanding of adolescent health and risk behaviors, including crime. Notably, it is one of the few nationally representative longitudinal studies measuring an array of factors potentially relevant to understanding crime and victimization, including parental and peer relationships, individual traits, neighborhood factors, and so on. That said, unlike some of the other studies reviewed in this chapter, the Add Health study focus is not school crime and safety. Although it asks adolescents a range of questions about delinquency and victimization, most do not measure *school-based* behaviors and experiences. Exceptions include questions about being drunk at school, being high at school, carrying a weapon at school, feelings of safety at school, skipping school, suspension, and expulsion. Additional questions about assault, property crime, drug dealing, fighting, and sexual assault do not identify the location where these experiences occurred (e.g., in school, out of school).

National Education Longitudinal Survey of 1988 and the Education Longitudinal Study of 2002

The NELS:1988 is a nationally representative, longitudinal survey sponsored by the U.S. Department of Education's NCES (Curtin, Ingels, Wu, and Heuer, 2002). Participants were identified using a clustered, stratified national probability sample of 1,052 public and private schools with 8th graders. The initial student sample was 24,599 students in 8th grade during the spring of 1988. The NELS:1988 included data collected from the student, one parent, two teachers, and the school principal. A first follow-up data collection occurred in 1990 when the participants were in 10th grade, and a second follow-up occurred in 1992 during 12th grade. Follow-up data collection included participants who had dropped out of high school. Additional follow-up surveys occurred in 1994 and 2000 and aimed to capture the transition to adulthood among participants (e.g., employment, postsecondary access).

school, which we address in Chapter 5 (Schreck and Miller, 2003; Schreck, Miller, and Gibson, 2003).

A study conducted by Astor, Meyer, and Behr (1999) was designed to document when and where violence occurred within schools using the perspectives of students, teachers, staff, and administrators. Using a purposeful sampling methodology, the researchers selected five midwestern high schools embedded in a diverse set of school districts and communities. Data come from semi-structured interviews and focus groups with 78 students in grades 9 through 12, and 22 teachers. Principals, vice principals, hall monitors, and security guards from each school were also interviewed. Using maps of their schools, participants were asked to identify the places and times of violent events and dangerous areas in and around their school, as well as the offenders' and victims' demographics. Finally, participants were asked why they thought violent incidents occurred at specific places and times within school. We discuss the findings from this study in Chapter 7.

Finally, Welsh, Jenkins, and Greene (1997) collected Philadelphia middle-school data during the 1994–1995 school year as part of a study on school climate and culture. Their focus on middle schools stemmed from existing national survey data demonstrating that younger students ages 12 to 14 are more at risk for school-based violent victimization than are older students (see also Welsh, 2001). The researchers selected 11 of 43 Philadelphia middle schools in consultation with school district officials to ensure the sample included schools with varying levels of disorder, drawn from census tracts representing a range of income levels, and from all regions of the city (Welsh, 2001). Survey data were collected from 7,583 students and included information on student victimization, offending, misconduct, avoidance, peers, social bonds, school climate, and school culture. We review findings from these data related to student delinquency, student victimization, and school-level crime in Chapters 4, 5, and 7.

Conclusion

This chapter described key data sources researchers use to better understand variation in experiences of school crime and safety across people, places, and time. The particular data sources highlighted are the foundation of numerous studies exploring a wide range of research questions related to the nature and sources of school crime. In addition to these key sources, the research literature on school crime also includes numerous other smaller scale studies relevant for answering specific research questions, and these will be discussed in the coming chapters when relevant.

The problem analysis triangle points to a range of theories that can be used to understand school crime and safety, including theories of offending, theories of victimization, and theories of crime places. Our review above highlights the strengths and weaknesses that the reviewed data sources have for assessing the three sides of the triangle as a school crime and safety framework. In the chapters that follow, we will encounter key properties of these datasets as we review and discuss findings from individual-level, school-level, and multiple-level studies of student delinquency, victimization, and school crime prevention that use them.

4

Student Delinquency

The Motivated Offender

I n this book, we argue that crime is more likely to occur in schools when motivated offenders and suitable targets/victims converge in settings that facilitate crime. This chapter focuses specifically on the first of those dimensions: motivated offenders. It dives into factors influencing students' attraction to or aversion from criminal behavior on school grounds. Understanding school-based delinquent offending is important for both scientific and practical reasons. As crime scientists, criminologists develop theories and conduct research with a goal of accurately mapping the emergence of delinquent offending. They analyze empirical data to test the logic of theories and to identify modifications needed to improve their predictive and explanatory power. This process of developing and modifying our understanding of offending behavior is a fundamental part of advancing crime science.

Developing an understanding of offending is also important for practical reasons. It is an essential first step toward the prevention of the harms associated with school crime. Crime in schools has many obvious harms, including physical injury, psychological and emotional damage, monetary or property loss, and the destruction of school facilities or equipment. Less obvious but still important are harms to the learning environment. In schools with higher crime, students are likely to experience persistent fear of victimization, which detracts from their academic focus and may hinder their social-psychological development. Finally, understanding and preventing offending limits harms for those who are most at risk of involvement in delinquent behavior. While it is natural to think of crime's harms as limited to its victims, it often entails negative consequences for youths who engage in offending. For many, involvement in delinquent behavior reflects unmet needs for assistance, untreated trauma, or chronic exposure to adverse environments. It is a pathway filled with accumulating disadvantages, often culminating with criminal justice system contact, including incarceration. Far from being rehabilitative, criminal justice system contact commonly adds layers of negative consequences for delinquent youths. This includes weakening of family ties, increasing exposure to victimization, and transforming identity in ways that solidify rather than negate propensities for law violation. Thus, understanding offender motivation is important both because it helps to advance the scientific study of crime and because it helps create a prevention road map aimed at short-circuiting the myriad negative outcomes associated with crime.

To investigate and build a better understanding of school-based delinquent behavior patterns and motivations, we organize this chapter on offender motivation as follows. The next section briefly reviews data on trends and patterns of offending within schools, using information from both national and subnational/local surveys. Following that, we turn our attention to empirical research evaluating the criminological theories outlined in the first section of Chapter 2, which are the basis of most extant studies on school-based offending. We close with a short summary assessing the degree of empirical support each theory receives in our review of evidence from studies measuring school-based crime.

Prevalence and Trends in School-Based Offending

Nationwide Data on Offending

Nationally representative survey data provide valuable information on criminal offenses in schools or on school property within the United States. In the following sections, we discuss these data. Although the range of offense types measured in national datasets is somewhat limited, we present patterns and trends in several types of offending in schools: physical fighting on school property, weapon carrying on school property, and drug and alcohol use in school.

As detailed in Chapter 3, the Youth Risk Behavior Surveillance System (YRBSS) from the Centers for Disease Control and Prevention is a useful national-level source of information on criminal offending in high schools. The volume titled *Indicators of School Crime and Safety: 2018* (Musu et al., 2019) reports many statistical results from the YRBSS. We draw heavily from that volume in the discussion below.

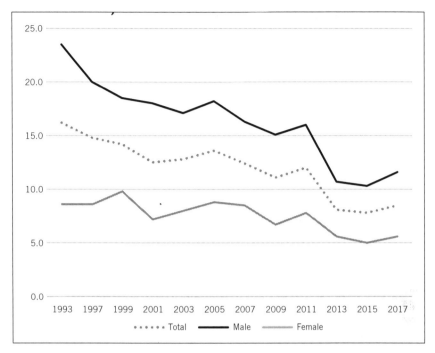

Figure 4.1 Percentages of students who reported physically fighting on school property

(Centers for Disease Control and Prevention, Division of Adolescent and School Health, Youth Risk Behavior Surveillance System [YRBSS], 1993 through 2017.)

Physical fighting at school. How common is physical fighting among students in schools? The YRBSS data suggest that involvement in fighting on school property is not exceptionally common, but neither is it rare.[1] As of 2017, estimates indicate roughly one in every eleven students reported being in a fight on school property (Musu et al., 2019). Hence, in a classroom of twenty students, roughly two had been involved in a physical fight at school within the previous year. Perhaps more interesting, the percentage involved in fighting has declined over the past quarter-century. As shown in Figure 4.1, 16.2% of students reported involvement in a physical fight on school property in 1993. A decade later, the percentage dropped by about one-fourth to 12.8%. It fell another third by 2017 (Musu et al., 2019).

---

1. Like many data sources, the YRBSS does not distinguish between the "offender" and "victim" in a fistfight.

Male students, on average, are about twice as likely to have been involved in fighting as female students. Prevalence estimates for both groups declined between 1993 and 2017. Fighting on school property also varies somewhat by race and age/grade level (Musu et al., 2019). The 2017 YRBSS indicates that the prevalence of fighting is highest among Black students at 15.3%, followed closely by Pacific Islanders at 14.2%. The lowest prevalence rate is for Asian American students, only 3.7% of whom reported fighting on school property in the past twelve months. White students have the second-lowest school fighting prevalence at 6.5%. Fighting is more common in the earlier grades of high school. For example, in the 2017 YRBSS, roughly 12% of 9th graders and 10% of 10th graders reported involvement in fighting on school property. Among high-school juniors and seniors, those percentages declined by one-half, falling to 6% and 5%, respectively (Musu et al., 2019).

Carrying of weapons at school. The Youth Risk Behavior Survey data also provide information on students' carrying of weapons on school property (Musu et al., 2019). In 2017, nearly 4% of students in grades 9 through 12 reported that they had carried a "gun, knife, or club" on school property during the past 30 days. Like fighting, carrying of weapons on school property has declined over time and is considerably more common among males than females (see Figure 4.2). In 2017, 5.6% of males reported that they carried a weapon on school property at least once in the preceding 30 days. For females, the corresponding prevalence of weapon carrying on school property was 1.9%. Although the gender difference persists over time, data indicate that the prevalence of weapon carrying on school property has declined since the early 1990s (Figure 4.2). In 1993, 11.8% of all students indicated they carried a weapon on school property on at least one of the preceding 30 days (Musu et al., 2019). That figure dropped by nearly half a decade later and fell to below 4% in 2017 (Musu et al., 2019).

Weapon carrying does not vary much by race or ethnicity. Similar percentages of White, Black, and Hispanic students (3.8%, 3.6%, and 3.5%, respectively) report weapon carrying on school grounds in the preceding month during 2017 (Kann et al., 2018). In contrast, there is evidence that weapon carrying varies by age. Unlike the pattern we observed for fighting, the prevalence of weapon carrying was higher in 2017 among 11th and 12th graders (5% and 4.2%, respectively) than among 9th (2.5%) and 10th graders (3.2%) (Kann et al., 2018).

Alcohol and marijuana use at school. Alcohol use is generally common among high-school students, but only small percentages of students indicate that they have used alcohol on school property at least once in the preceding 30 days. Data from 2011 indicates that 5.1% of all grade 9–12 students reported use on school property (Musu et al., 2019). Usage estimates vary only

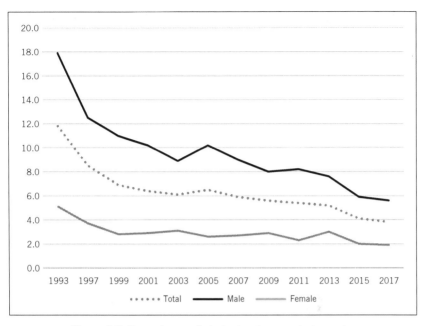

Figure 4.2 Percentages of students who reported carrying
weapons on school property

(Centers for Disease Control and Prevention, Division of Adolescent and School Health, Youth Risk
Behavior Surveillance System [YRBSS], 1993 through 2017.)

slightly by gender with the prevalence estimate for males at 5.4% and females at 4.7% (Musu et al., 2019). Small differences in school-based alcohol use are evident by race and ethnicity, with Hispanic students reporting slightly higher prevalence rates (7.3%) than Black students (5.1%) or White students (4.0%) (Musu et al., 2019). Alcohol use at school does not appear to vary systematically by age, with freshmen, sophomores, juniors, and seniors all reporting prevalence rates of roughly 4% to 5% (Musu et al., 2019).

Although the most recent YRBSS data do not measure marijuana use on school property, surveys taken between 1993 and 2011 asked students about preceding 30-day use on school property. Results from those data indicate that prevalence estimates ranged from a low of 4.5% to a high of 7.2% (Musu et al., 2019). There was no clear trend upward or downward in the percentage of students involved in this school-based drug use measure during the 1993–2011 period. Prevalence rates do vary somewhat by gender, with a higher percentage of males than females reporting preceding 30-day marijuana use on school property. In the most recently available year, 2011, the prevalence among males was 7.5% to 4.1% among females (Musu et al., 2019). White students reported estimates that ranged between 3.8% and 6.5% during the 1993–2011 period. Figures for Black students over the same years were slightly higher, ranging between 4.9% and 9.1% (Musu et al., 2019). Estimates of school-based marijuana use do not appear to vary systematically by age/grade level of students in the YRBSS data.

State-Specific Survey Data on School Offending

Along with national-level data, surveys of students sampled from schools in specific subnational geographic localities (e.g., city, state, or region) are a valuable source of additional information on school crime. Relative to national-level trend studies like the YRBSS, these datasets often provide data on a broader range of school-based offending behaviors and measure many of the potential correlates of school-based criminal offending. Moreover, they often provide information on how an individual's delinquent behavior and factors correlated with it change over time. The Rural Substance abuse and Violence Project (RSVP) is an example. As detailed in Chapter 3, RSVP began by surveying a panel of 7th-grade students in schools across the state of Kentucky. Those same students were administered surveys again in the subsequent three years (i.e., their 8th- through 10th-grade years). This longitudinal panel research design is valuable because of the range of research questions it supports. It enables researchers to investigate what differentiates youths who are crime-involved from those who are not at multiple points in time. Equally important, it facilitates investigation of why the same youths may transition from a non-offender in one year to an offender (or vice versa) in the next. Thus, local longitudinal panel studies complement and extend the information gleaned from broad national surveys, filling essential data gaps and facilitating exploration of additional and essential research questions.

Violent crime, property crime, and weapon carrying. Table 4.1 shows the percentage of students in the four waves of the RSVP reporting violent crime, property crime, and weapon carrying at school. Physically assaultive behavior is easily the most common of the four behaviors depicted in Table 4.1. About 21% of the student respondents reported some engagement in assaultive behavior at school during the recall period in the first wave of the RSVP. That is, when asked, "In the present school year, how often have you physically attacked someone at school (punched, slapped, kicked)?" these students registered a frequency of involvement above "never." The percentage reporting assaultive behavior declines in each of the subsequent years, falling to just below 12% in the fourth wave of the study (10th-grade year).

Of the violent and property crimes, robbery is least common of those reported in Table 4.1. The RSVP measured this behavior by asking, "In the

TABLE 4.1 PERCENTAGE OF STUDENTS REPORTING VARIOUS OFFENSES
AT SCHOOL

	Wave 1 (%)	Wave 2 (%)	Wave 3 (%)	Wave 4 (%)
Physical assault	20.90	17.50	12.60	11.80
Robbery	3.66	3.41	2.52	2.58
Sexual assault	6.17	7.68	6.30	6.47
Theft	6.80	6.92	5.99	5.38
Gun carrying	1.57	1.74	1.32	1.85
Explosive carrying	2.32	2.52	2.09	2.18
Non-gun weapon carrying (e.g., knife)	5.81	7.00	9.30	10.91
Source: Rural Substance abuse and Violence Project.				

present school year, how often have you forced someone at school to give up their money or property?" In the initial wave of the study, nearly 4% of the respondents reported this offense. Robbery involvement shows a general decline in subsequent waves of the study, falling to near 2.6% at wave 4. No clear time trend is apparent for the sexual assault offense, measured by a question asking students how often they have "touched someone in a sexual manner without their consent or against their will at school." The respective prevalence of students' involvement in this behavior ranged between 6.2% and 7.7% across the waves of the RSVP study. Theft at school ("stolen someone's money or property at school when they were not around") shows a similar prevalence, reaching its highest level in wave 2 (6.9%) and lowest level in wave 4 (5.4%).

The RSVP also collected data on students' involvement in carrying guns and non-gun weapons at school. Table 4.1 displays the percentage of Kentucky students surveyed who reported these behaviors in each of the study's four waves. Unsurprisingly, the percentage reporting the carrying of non-gun weapons such as a knife or brass knuckles is more common than the carrying of guns or explosives. Unlike the other school-based offending behaviors reviewed above, there is an upward trend in the carrying of "other weapons" across the four waves of the study. In the first wave of the RSVP data, 5.8% of students reported engaging in this behavior. The percentage increased to 7.0% in wave 2, to 9.3% in wave 3, and, finally, to 10.9% in wave 4. By contrast, the percentage of students reporting carrying explosives or guns to school is steady across the four waves of RSVP data. The percentage of students reporting carrying explosives to school varies in a narrow range between 2.1% and 2.5% over the four observation points. For gun carrying, the prevalence of student involvement is even lower, falling in a range between 1.3% and 1.9%.

TABLE 4.2 PERCENTAGE OF STUDENTS BY SELF-REPORTED FREQUENCY
OF SCHOOL-BASED DELINQUENCY

Frequency	Physical assault (%)	Robbery (%)	Sexual assault (%)	Theft (%)	Gun carrying (%)	Explosives carrying (%)	Other weapon carrying (%)
Never	83.99	96.91	93.32	93.68	98.37	97.71	91.91
Less than once a month	10.06	1.32	3.14	3.91	0.54	1.02	4.13
About once a month	2.66	0.66	1.38	1.16	0.30	0.39	1.17
About 1–2 times per week	1.52	0.44	0.97	0.56	0.30	0.30	0.75
Daily or almost daily	1.78	0.67	1.20	0.69	0.48	0.57	2.03

Source: Rural Substance abuse and Violence Project.

To gauge the share of respondents reporting high involvement in offending, it is instructive to look at variations in the relative frequency of offending at school in addition to prevalence. The RSVP study did not measure raw offense counts, but an ordinal scale was used to ask respondents to classify their behavioral frequency according to the following gradations: "never," "less than once a month," "about once a month," "about 1–2 times per week," and "daily or almost daily." In Table 4.2, we summarize this information by averaging the percentage of students in each response category across the four waves of the RSVP dataset. Notable here, almost all who reported committing an offense did so relatively infrequently, indicating the lowest category of less than once a month. In contrast, the percentages of respondents who reported high-frequency involvement occurring at least weekly is very small. For example, for the most prevalent offense, physical assault, only around 3% reported weekly or more frequent involvement. Less than 3% of respondents reported committing any of the other offenses on at least a weekly basis. Thus, frequent offenders are rare.

Differences in offending by gender. The RSVP data also provide evidence of substantial differences by gender in school-based offending. Consistent with differences in fighting observed in the national-level data, the RSVP data indicate that males are more likely to report physically attacking another student at school (see Table 4.3). On average, the prevalence is about twice as high for males than females. For both groups, the overall prevalence declines between the first and fourth waves of the study. For females, the decline appears consistent across observation points, whereas the direction of change reverses slightly for males between waves 3 and 4.

TABLE 4.3 PERCENTAGE OF STUDENTS REPORTING INVOLVEMENT IN OFFENSES AT SCHOOL BY GENDER

	Wave 1 (%)	Wave 2 (%)	Wave 3 (%)	Wave 4 (%)
Physical assault				
Females	14.44	12.70	9.46	7.64
Males	28.22	22.79	15.93	16.62
Robbery				
Females	1.42	1.22	0.82	0.87
Males	6.11	5.76	4.33	4.56
Sexual assault				
Females	2.74	3.07	3.09	2.67
Males	9.94	12.68	9.79	10.74
Theft				
Females	3.48	4.18	3.34	2.98
Males	10.47	9.91	8.87	8.11
Gun carrying				
Females	0.42	0.79	0.44	0.50
Males	2.79	2.79	2.23	3.35
Explosives carrying				
Females	0.47	1.01	0.44	0.62
Males	4.30	4.20	3.85	3.99
Non-gun weapon carrying (e.g., knife)				
Females	1.74	2.76	3.10	4.36
Males	10.34	11.69	16.14	18.45

Source: Rural Substance abuse and Violence Project.

Substantial gender differences are also evident for the other two violent offenses against persons—robbery and sexual assault—portrayed in Table 4.3. For robbery, the share of male students who reported engaging in the behavior averaged slightly above 5%, whereas it was only around 1% for female students. In comparison, sexual assault is more common among both gender groups, but the male-to-female prevalence ratio is slightly lower. The percentage of males reporting involvement in sexual assault averages about 3.7 times the percentage reported by females.

The overall prevalence of theft at school is similar to that of sexual assault. Moreover, as was true for the violent offenses, the RSVP data reveal a notable disparity between males and females in theft offending. Across the four waves of data, the percentage of males reporting school-based theft averages slightly above 9%. For females, the corresponding figure is only 3.5%. The percentage of students involved in theft shows evidence of decreasing prevalence for both gender groups as the students moved from middle- to high-school years.

Table 4.3 also shows that weapon carrying in school differs by gender. Carrying guns or explosives is generally uncommon, but it is especially so for female students. On average, female students are less than one-fifth as likely to carry a gun to school and one-sixth as likely to take an explosive item to their school as male students. The gender gap for carrying a nongun, nonexplosive weapon on school grounds is nearly as wide, with male students about 4.7 times as likely as females to report the behavior.

In sum, the evidence from the RSVP data indicates school-based criminal behavior varies considerably by the offense type, with physical fighting/assault between students constituting the most common infraction. Offenses including theft, robbery, sexual assault, and the carrying of guns or explosive weapons were less common. Notably, the self-reporting of all offense categories is more common for males than females. The gender discrepancy is smallest for the offense category of physical fighting/assault and is largest for carrying explosives and guns on school grounds.

Differences in offending by race. There is evidence of both similarity and difference in the school-based criminal behavior of racial groups in the RSVP data. The RSVP data contain few students of racial groups other than African Americans and Whites, so we limit our comparison to these two groups, as shown in Table 4.4. The data on physical assault at school indicates somewhat higher prevalence among African Americans than among Whites. In the first wave of data, the prevalence estimates are 1.17 times higher for African American students. This increases to between 1.5 and 1.6 times higher in each of the subsequent waves of data. However, for both groups, assaultive behavior is less prevalent in the 10th grade (wave 4) compared to the 7th grade (wave 1).

The reported prevalence of robbery, sexual assault, and theft offending among Black and White students is quite similar in the 7th-grade data. It differs more greatly in subsequent years. This is because prevalence rates among Black students increased on average, while those for White students remained stable or declined slightly. However, the year-to-year changes in percentage of students reporting the behavior varies across both the racial groups and the offense categories.

All of the weapon-carrying offenses are more common among White students during the 7th-grade year according to the RSVP data. This holds true for the carrying of non-gun, non-explosive weapons in the subsequent three years. However, the prevalence of gun- and explosives-carrying behavior is higher for Black students than for White students in the 8th-grade through 10th-grade years (waves 2–4) of the study. Nonetheless, both offenses are relatively rare for both groups.

TABLE 4.4 PERCENTAGE OF STUDENTS REPORTING INVOLVEMENT IN OFFENSES AT SCHOOL BY RACE

	Wave 1 (%)	Wave 2 (%)	Wave 3 (%)	Wave 4 (%)
Physical assault				
African Americans	23.67	25.71	18.87	16.33
Whites	20.30	16.46	11.65	11.03
Robbery				
African Americans	3.37	7.58	5.73	3.38
Whites	3.29	2.72	2.02	2.13
Sexual assault				
African Americans	6.73	10.00	9.43	11.49
Whites	5.67	7.20	5.96	5.81
Theft				
African Americans	6.25	9.48	11.95	10.14
Whites	6.20	6.52	5.32	4.59
Gun carrying				
African Americans	0.97	2.83	3.14	2.70
Whites	1.36	1.53	1.03	1.51
Explosives carrying				
African Americans	1.46	2.84	3.77	2.70
Whites	2.14	2.34	1.76	1.99
Non-gun weapon carrying (e.g., knife)				
African Americans	3.90	5.21	7.05	8.11
Whites	5.51	7.02	9.16	10.86

Source: Rural Substance abuse and Violence Project.

In summary, both national-level and local-level surveys provide useful data on crime in schools. Taken together, they indicate that violence, theft, substance use, and weapon-carrying offenses exhibit notable patterns of variation across time and demographic dimensions such as gender, race, and age (or, year in school). How can we account for these variations in offending? The major criminological theories reviewed in Chapter 2 generally view demographic variations as distal factors whose influence on offending may be explainable by key theoretical concepts such as social bonds, definitions favorable to law violation, differential association with delinquent peers, social strains, low self-control, and psychological traits. Whether those theoretical concepts account for demographic differences, and significantly affect school-based delinquent behavior as predicted, are empirical questions in need of answers. To find answers to these questions, we turn our attention to reviewing findings from the research literature on delinquent offending in schools.

Research on Explanations of
School-Based Delinquency

An ever-growing body of social science research examines explanations of school-based delinquent behavior. In the following paragraphs, we summarize findings from these studies, organizing our discussion around the major explanations of offending outlined in the first part of Chapter 2. This includes strain theory, social learning theory, social control/bonds theory, self-control theory, and biological/psychological trait perspectives.[2]

Strain and School Offending

As Chapter 2 describes, strain theories assert that individuals become motivated to commit crimes by negative emotions that arise when they experience blocked goals, poor or unfair treatment in social relationships, or a loss of relationships or other valued social or physical entities. Contemporary research in this theoretical tradition primarily focuses on Robert Agnew's (1985, 1992, 2006) version of the theory, called general strain theory. Most studies examine at least one of three central arguments in general strain theory: (1) strains are positively associated with offending, (2) strains affect offending indirectly by elevating negative emotional reactions (e.g., anger), and (3) the effects of strains on crime are moderated by various other factors, including individuals' personality traits, social supports, delinquent peer associations, and social bonds.

In early research, Agnew (1989) used a nationally representative dataset of male public high-school students to test the hypothesis that negative and painful stimuli encountered in school and family contexts led to criminal offending. He found that adolescents with greater exposure to teachers losing their temper, to teachers talking down to them, or to parents who screamed at, slapped, or threatened them were more involved in various acts of criminal offending including serious fighting at school, hitting a teacher, and damaging school property. Subsequent studies added empirical support for general strain theory's basic thesis, finding that strains and criminal offending (including school-based delinquency) are positively associated (Agnew and White, 1992; Agnew et al., 2002; DeCoster and Kort-Butler, 2006; Forster, Gower, McMorris, and Borowsky, 2020; Hoffman, 2006; James, Bunch, and Clay-Warner, 2015; Lee and Cohen, 2008; Mazerolle, Burton, Cullen,

---

2. While our main interest is explaining crime in schools, we note that many studies in the literature measure crime with scales that combine both in-school and out-of-school offending behavior. We included these studies in our review to ensure comprehensive coverage of the research linking social factors and individual traits to school-based offending.

Evans, and Payne, 2000; Paternoster and Mazerolle, 1994; Ousey and Wilcox, 2007; Ousey, Wilcox, and Schreck, 2015).

Since strains and crime can emerge within specific social institutions, a natural question centers on whether the link between strains and crime is institution-specific or general. For example, do strains emerging within school offer the best explanation of school crime? Or are strains in other social institutions, like the family, equally effective as school-based strains for explaining school crime? Research by DeCoster and Kort-Butler (2006) addresses these questions. It argues that school-specific strains should be more important for explaining school-specific crime than nonschool crime. This is because individuals are most likely to enact criminal behaviors within the institutional sphere where their strains are experienced. Yet, DeCoster and Kort-Butler (2006) also acknowledge the possibility that "spillover" effects may exist. For example, adolescents facing maltreatment within their family may socially withdraw in ways that elicit teasing from other students, producing school strains that motivate criminality. Results from their analysis of data from 400 middle-school students supported domain-specific effects. School strains had direct effects on school-related delinquency but did not directly affect family- or peer-related delinquency. Moreover, strains experienced within other institutional domains did not directly affect school-based delinquent behavior, but there was evidence of an indirect spillover effect, with family strains indirectly associated with delinquency occurring at school.

Other studies appear less consistent with the idea of domain-specific effects of strain. They suggest that strains within various social institutions including the family (Agnew et al., 2002; Forster et al., 2020; Hoffman, 2006; Marsh and Evans, 2007), the school (James et al., 2015), and the peer group (Goldstein, Young, and Boyd, 2008; Nansel, Overpeck, Haynie, Run, and Scheidt, 2003; Ousey and Wilcox, 2007; Paternoster and Mazerolle, 1994; Wallace, Patchin, and May, 2005; but see Agnew et al., 2002) directly affect school-related delinquency. Moreover, other studies indicate that witnessing violence or directly experiencing criminal victimization puts individuals at increased risk of engaging in various forms of school-based crime (Janosz et al., 2008; Kaynak, Lepore, Kliewer, and Jaggi, 2015; Ousey, Wilcox, and Schreck, 2015).[3] A major caveat in interpreting results of these studies, however, is many are predicting dependent variables combining items measuring in-school and out-of-school delinquency. Hence, the ability to draw strict

---

3. The correlation between victimization and offending, often referred to as the "victim-offender overlap" is the focus of Chapter 6, "Double Trouble: The Victim-Offender Overlap among Students."

conclusions about the domain-specific or institutional-spillover effects of strain from these is often limited.

A key part of general strain theory is the assertion that adolescents exposed to strains develop negative emotions like anger, which then spark involvement in criminal offending. Multiple studies measuring school-based crime test this hypothesis, arguing that strains affect offending indirectly through anger or other negative emotions. Findings from these studies are inconsistent (Mazerolle et al., 2000; Patchin and Hinduja, 2011; Wallace, Patchin, and May, 2005). Using data from students in a suburban high school in the midwestern United States, Mazerolle et al. (2000) examined whether anger mediates the effects of strain on a measure of school delinquency including school theft, school vandalism, and more minor school infractions such as skipping classes. Contrary to the theory, neither measures of strain nor of anger had a relationship with school delinquency. Patchin and Hinduja's (2011) study of middle-school students from 30 middle schools in one of the largest U.S. school districts found that several forms of strain—interpersonal-relationship problems, academic struggles, and money problems—had mostly direct effects on offending. Thus, anger did not substantially mediate the association between the measures of strain and offending as predicted. Finally, Wallace and colleagues' (2005) study of middle- and high-school students from four public school districts in a rural Southern county presents the best support for the mediating process predicted by general strain theory. Students with greater exposure to verbal and physical abuse by peers were more likely to experience two negative emotions—anger and frustration—and were more involved in delinquent acts at school (including thefts, threats, assault, and robbery). Nearly two-thirds of the total effect of peer victimization on school delinquency was direct, with another one-third mediated by the emotions of anger and frustration.

A final salient question raised by general strain theory focuses on whether the effects of strains on criminal offending are the same for all individuals. If not, why are there differences? The theory proposes that the relationship between strains and criminal offending may vary because individuals differ in their personality traits, social supports, coping resources, levels of social control, and delinquent peer associations. Some research supports this argument. Using data from the 2009 National Crime Victimization Survey's (NCVS) School Crime Supplement (SCS), James et al. (2015) found that greater social support from adults tempered the impact of teacher unfairness on two school-based measures of offending: weapon carrying and fighting. Likewise, adult social support weakened the magnitude of the relationship between perceived rule unfairness and carrying weapons at school. Agnew et al. (2002) used data from a national sample of individuals ages 12 to 16 to examine whether strains have greater effects on offending for students with personality traits of high negative emotionality and low constraint. They found that the association between a composite measure of strain and a delinquency index including a measure of school-based vandalism was stronger for individuals who ranked higher on the trait of negative emotionality and lower on the trait of constraint.

In contrast, other studies do not support the hypothesis that personal and social characteristics moderate the effect of strains on school-based offending (Ousey and Wilcox, 2007; Ousey et al., 2015). For example, based on analysis of data from middle- and high-school students in the RSVP, Ousey and Wilcox (2007) reported that the effect of exposure to peer bullying on delinquency does not materially differ across individuals with varying levels of impulsivity. Ousey et al. (2015) found that the impact of criminal victimization on both overall offending and the propensity for violent offending did not vary as a function of individual differences on a multidimensional risk index, which combined information on personality traits, social bonds, exposure to delinquent peers, and pro-crime attitudes.

In sum, it is clear that strain theory is relevant for explaining the criminal behavior of adolescents in middle and high schools. However, not all strain theory expectations receive consistent support in available research. We summarize major findings below:

- School-offending studies testing Agnew's general strain theory supported its most fundamental claim: individuals facing greater strains are more prone to criminal involvement.
- Evidence was inconsistent for the argument that strains affect crime indirectly by increasing negative emotions.
- Uneven evidence emerged from research examining the thesis that factors such as personality traits, social bonds, or delinquent peer associations moderate the effects of strains on crime. Some research supports this argument, but other research does not.

Social Learning, Subcultures, and School Offending

Social learning and subcultural explanations of offending propose that individuals are at risk of criminal offending when they have more associations with peers who engage in crime or greater exposure to crime within the social environments in which they carry on daily life activities. In a school setting, students with more friends who engage in crime or hold "definitions favorable" to crime/violence are at greater risk of adopting values and beliefs that frame illegal acts positively or frame them as useful for instrumental purposes. If this occurs, the students' likelihood of criminal behavior increases.

The subculture of violence is one popular perspective within the broader social learning theoretical framework. It argues that certain places such as neighborhoods or schools can develop shared subcultural values contradicting mainstream culture and conducive to violence. Individuals exposed to and immersed in these subcultures of violence internalize the values, condoning violence in an array of circumstances for both instrumental and symbolic purposes. Thus, the theory argues that motivation for acts of school violence arise from the pro-violent values shared among individuals within these school subcultures.

Felson, Liska, South, and McNulty, (1994) investigated this hypothesis with a national sample of high-school students. They examined whether students exposed to a school-based subculture of violence internalize values favoring violent behavior and thus act accordingly. In addition, they examined if the subculture of violence explanation applied only to violent behavior or to other criminal violations, including property offenses as well as minor, noncriminal, school-rule infractions. Consistent with the subcultural/social learning framework, they found students with beliefs that were more intolerant of nonaggressive responses to provocations exhibited greater involvement in violent behavior. However, subculture of violence values did not exclusively predict violent crimes. Variations in both property offenses and minor school delinquency also had associations with the subculture of violence values.

Subsequent research on data from students in Kentucky expanded inquiry on subcultural and social learning explanations of crime in schools (Johnson, Wilcox, and Peterson, 2019; McGloin, Schreck, Stewart, and Ousey, 2011; Ousey and Wilcox, 2005; Swartz et al., 2017; Wilcox Rountree, 2000). In a study of 7th-grade students in the first wave of the RSVP study, Ousey and Wilcox (2005) examined whether two concepts in the subculture/social learning theory tradition—values favorable to violence and association with violent peers—were predictive of an index of school-based violence, which included behaviors such as assault, robbery, and sexual assault. Findings supported the social learning/subcultural theory framework. Students scoring higher on a violent values index were more involved in violent offenses at school. In addition, involvement in violent behavior at school was higher among students who had more association with friends who engaged in violence.

Later studies extended this line of inquiry by assessing the generality, or explanatory scope, of the subculture of violence thesis. As its name implies, the subculture of violence theory developed as an explanation of violent crime, specifically. Thus, it arguably should discriminate between violent offenses and nonviolent offenses, predicting the former much better than the latter. McGloin et al. (2011) examined this issue by modeling the utility of subcultural values to explain two outcomes: (1) overall criminal offending, and (2) propensity for violent rather than nonviolent offending. Results revealed that while students with higher scores on subculture of violence values were more involved in school-based criminal offending (i.e., both violent and property), their propensity for violence was no higher than it was for individuals with lower scores of subculture of violence values.

Swartz et al. (2017) further expanded assessment of the theoretical scope of the subculture of violence theory by considering two issues: (1) whether subculture of violence values had similar effects on multiple types of violence (physical assault, robbery, and sexual assault), and (2) whether its effects on violent crime operated differently depending on the opportunity context—in school versus out of school. Their results also pointed to a broader explanatory scope of the subculture of violence. They found that effects of subculture values were remarkably similar for each type of violent offending. Moreover, effects were context-universal rather than context-specific. That is, students with higher scores on the subculture of violence measures had higher involvement in physical assault, robbery, and sexual assault both on school grounds and off school grounds.

Looking beyond the subculture of violence literature, numerous studies investigated whether school crime has a relationship with other concepts connected to social learning theory. This includes exposure to violent behavior, associations with delinquent peers, or gang involvement (Bradshaw, Rodgers, Ghandour, and Garbarino, 2009; Dijkstra et al., 2010; Estrada, Gilreath, Astor, and Benbenishty, 2014; Finigan-Carr, Cheng, Gielen, Haynie, and Simons-Morton, 2015; Furlong, Casas, Corral, Chung, and Bates, 1997; Gellman and DeLucia-Waack, 2006; Johnson et al., 2019; Ousey and Wilcox, 2007; Ousey et al., 2015; Sullivan, Ousey, and Wilcox, 2016). One key debate in this literature is concerned with unraveling the mechanism underlying the commonly observed association between delinquent peer associations and criminal offending. Using data on a sample of male adolescents recruited from two middle schools serving a predominantly Hispanic, low-income student body in northern New Jersey, Dijkstra et al. (2010) sought to decipher whether the tendency for similarity in weapon carrying among individuals and their friends resulted from either of two alternative processes. One is peer influence, which follows directly from social learning theory. It suggests that the actions of the peers with whom we associate influence our behavior. If our peers carry weapons, it raises the probability that we also will do so. An alternative thesis is peer selection. It suggests that peers who engage in similar behaviors attract one another. Hence, friendship networks of weapon-carrying adolescents will include many others who behave likewise because of the principle of homophily—attraction among those who think and act similarly. Findings from the Dijkstra et al. (2010) study supported the peer influence argument over the peer selection thesis. Specifically, adolescents tended to alter their weapon-carrying behavior to better imitate the behavior of their friends. Other studies also report evidence that individuals with delinquent friends in general, or weapon-carrying friends specifically, are more likely to carry weapons (Johnson et al., 2019; Wilcox Rountree, 2000; Wilcox and Clayton, 2001).

Street gangs are a particular peer group that criminologists have speculated may encourage individuals to engage in violence or other criminal acts at school. This is concerning, because data from the NCVS-SCS indicate that a substantial share of students report gangs are present in their schools. Indeed, from 2001 to 2009, between 20 and 24% of students aged 12 to 18 indicated that gangs were present at their schools (Musu et al., 2019). Moreover, percentages for Black and Hispanic students reached over 35 percent in several of the years studied. Percentages reporting gang presence at school have declined in more recent years, but nearly 10% of students reported the presence of gangs in school as recently as 2017 (Musu et al., 2019).

Is the concern justified? Does participation in a gang affect involvement in school crime? Using data from more than 275,000 9th- and 11th-grade California students, Estrada et al. (2014) examined whether and how gang membership affected the perpetration of school violence. They found that gang membership had no direct effect on violence but did affect school violence perpetration indirectly, via two pathways. First, gang membership had a relatively strong indirect effect through participation in "risky behaviors." Gang members were more likely to engage in risky behaviors—such as drug use or associating with friends who approved of drug use or weapon carrying—which were directly associated with an increase in violence perpetration. Second, gang membership had a much weaker indirect effect on violence perpetration that operated by reducing a student's "school protective factors," such as a sense of connectedness, belonging, and sense of safety at school. Collectively, these findings suggest that street gang membership increases the likelihood of school crime by increasing individuals' association with delinquent peers while simultaneously reducing prosocial connections to school.

Other studies yield additional evidence regarding the thesis that gang involvement places students at higher risk of school-based delinquent offending. Using data from 7th-, 9th-, and 11th-grade students from 16 school districts in a southern California county, Furlong et al. (1997) reported evidence that students participating in gangs were more involved in school-based offending. In an analysis of RVSP study data from Kentucky schools, Ousey et al. (2015) estimated the association between students' reported gang membership, overall offending, and violent crime propensity. Their analyses of wave 4 RSVP data revealed that students reporting gang membership exhibited greater involvement in overall levels of delinquency. However, students identifying as gang members did not have a significantly higher propensity for violent (rather than nonviolent) delinquent offending than students not reporting gang membership.

Although the influence of peers has received much attention in research on social learning theory and crime, the theory suggests that any direct exposure to violence in the environment may exacerbate the risks of learning violent behavior. One argument is that exposure to violence affects the probability of violent behavior because it affects the development of violence-conducive attitudes or alters patterns of information processing, cognitive-emotional associations, or interpretation of social cues in the environment (Bradshaw et al., 2009; Gellman and DeLucia-Waack, 2006). For example, in their study of high-school students from a suburban school in New York, Bradshaw et al. (2009) argue, "Exposure to violence and aggression likely influences the formation of scripts and beliefs about the use, appropriateness, and effectiveness of aggressive responses to threat" (p. 207). Findings from their study indicated that students with greater exposure to community violence were more likely to develop negatively biased social information–processing styles—hostile-attribution biases, aggressive responses to social situations, perceptions of aggression as legitimate—that were associated with increased participation in violent behavior at school. Other research supports the argument that exposure to violence and its deleterious effects on cognitive and emotive processes contribute to greater involvement in violent behavior (Gellman and DeLucia-Waack, 2006).

In sum, a growing body of school crime research suggests that students' risk of violent behavior increases if they have higher exposure to community violence or greater associations with peers who model violent behaviors and attitudes. The major findings from our review of this literature indicate that:

- Studies on school-based offending yield consistent support for the social learning and subcultural explanations as general explanations of student offending.
- Evidence supports the argument that students with greater association with delinquent peers are more involved in delinquent behavior in school.
- Exposure to violence or holding beliefs/values supportive of violence also appear to put students at heightened risk for both violent and nonviolent offending at school.

- Evidence indicates that gang involvement adds to the risk of school-based delinquency.

Social Bond and School Offending

As we outlined in Chapter 2, Travis Hirschi's social bond theory attributes criminal offending to a weakening or breakdown in relationships or social ties that connect individuals to conventional social institutions, such as families and schools. Multiple studies of school crime test the merit of this theory (Jenkins, 1995; Jenkins, 1997; Johnson et al., 2019; Kirk, 2009; Kodjo, Auinger, and Ryan, 2003; Malecki and Demaray, 2003; Marsh and Evans, 2007; McGloin et al., 2011; Ousey and Wilcox, 2005, 2007; Ousey et al., 2015; Payne, 2008; Peguero, 2011a; Peguero et al., 2011; Peguero and Jiang, 2014; Wilcox and Clayton, 2001; Wilcox et al., 2006; Wilcox Rountree, 2000). In general, these studies examine if school-based offending relates to one or more of the social bond dimensions: attachments to students, teachers, and parents; commitments to educational goals; involvement in academic and extra-curricular activities; and beliefs in the fairness and legitimacy of school rules.

In an early school-based study examining social bond theory, Jenkins (1995) examined data from 7th- and 8th-grade students in a desegregated urban-suburban middle school in Delaware to test whether students' school commitment was predictive of an index of school crime, which included items measuring substance use, violence against teachers or students, damaging school property, and weapon carrying. Results from path analysis indicated support for the theory. Specifically, Jenkins (1995) reported a strong inverse association between school commitment and school crime. Students who placed more importance on school and academic success were less involved in crime at school.

In subsequent work using the same data, Jenkins (1997) extended her investigation of social bond theory, testing the effects of each of the four theory elements—attachment, commitment, involvement, and belief—on school crime. She found mixed evidence regarding the effects of the social bond on school crime. In support of the theory's logic, measures of educational commitment and belief in the fairness and consistent enforcement of school rules were inversely associated with school crime, as the theory predicts. Contrary to the theory, however, neither a measure of school attachment nor a measure of school involvement had significant independent effects on school crime. Mixed support for the theory is also evident in Welsh's (2001) study of students from 11 Philadelphia middle schools. Counter to social bond theory, involvement in school activities was associated with increased offending. However, students with greater belief in school rules, school effort, and positive peer associations offended at lower levels, as Hirschi's theory would suggest.

Several studies using data from the RSVP have examined the effects of social bond elements, including parental attachment and school attachment, on student offending. Evidence from these studies consistently report that individuals with stronger attachment to school are less involved in offending (Ousey and Wilcox, 2005; Ousey et al., 2015; Swartz et al., 2017). Results are more inconsistent, however, regarding effects of parent attachment on school offending, with significant effects observed in some analyses (Ousey and Wilcox, 2007; Ousey et al., 2015) but insignificant effects in others (Ousey and Wilcox, 2005; Swartz et al., 2017). This variation in findings may occur because effects of parental attachment are not the same across types of offending. Significant negative effects appear in analyses predicting general delinquency indices, but not in analyses predicting violent offending.

School delinquency also appears affected by students' bond to religious institutions. In their analysis of data from middle- and high-school students from a rural Southern county, Wallace, Moak, and Moore (2005) report that school delinquency varies as a function of the bond to three distinct institutions: school, family, and church. Specifically, school delinquency was lower among students reporting greater educational commitment, stronger emotional attachment to parents, and higher levels of religious commitment and involvement.

While much of the evidence supporting social bond theory derives from studies of students from individual cities, counties, or states, studies using national-level data on school offending concur (Payne, 2008; Peguero and Jiang, 2014; Peguero et al., 2011). For example, Payne's (2008) investigation of data from more than 13,000 student participants in the National Study of Delinquency Prevention in Schools (NSDPS) indicated that three measured elements of the school social bond—attachment, commitment, and belief—had significant negative relationships with school delinquency.

Alongside research examining general school delinquency, there is a steadily growing body of research exploring social bond theory's usefulness as an explanation of student weapon carrying (Johnson et al., 2019; Kodjo et al., 2003; Malecki and Demaray, 2003; Marsh and Evans, 2007; Wilcox and Clayton, 2001; Wilcox, May, and Roberts, 2006; Wilcox Rountree, 2000). Findings from these studies indicate that weapon carrying is lower among students who experience greater interpersonal connectedness and social support (Kodjo et al., 2003; Malecki and Demaray, 2003) and who are more attached to teachers and school (Marsh and Evans, 2007; Wilcox and Clayton, 2001, Wilcox et al., 2006). However, there are nuances and caveats in research findings. Some research finds that effects of social bonds on weapon carrying vary by demographic characteristics such as gender or by geographic regions (Kodjo et al., 2003; Johnson, Wilcox, and Peterson, 2017; Wilcox Rountree, 2000). Other studies report evidence that does not support social bond theory, with measures of peer attachment, parent attachment, and religious involvement not significantly affecting weapon carrying (Johnson et al., 2019; Wilcox and Clayton, 2001; Wilcox Rountree, 2000).

One salient issue in school crime research is whether the social bonds affect crime similarly across racially and ethnically diverse samples. Peguero and his colleagues (Peguero, 2011b; Peguero and Jiang, 2014; Peguero et al., 2011) have addressed it by investigating whether the effects of the school-based social bond on school misconduct vary across students in relation with their race/ethnicity (Peguero et al., 2011) or their "immigrant generation" (Peguero, 2011b; Peguero and Jiang, 2014). Using national-level data on students in public high schools from the Education Longitudinal Study (ELS:2002), Peguero et al. (2011) reported evidence of interesting differences by race/ethnicity. For White students, all four social bond elements had significant negative effects on school misconduct. By comparison, the misconduct-suppressing effects of attachment and commitment are significantly weaker for Black/African American students. Likewise, the effects of commitment and involvement are significantly weaker for Asian American students than for White students. For Latino/a Americans, higher school involvement was actually associated with higher rather than lower school misconduct. Of all social bond elements, only the effects of "belief" on school misconduct did not significantly differ by race/ethnicity.

In their comparison of effects across immigrant generations, Peguero and Jiang (2014) found that most social bond dimensions affected student misconduct similarly, with a few notable exceptions. For example, the effect of attachment on misconduct was significant and positive for 1st-generation immigrants, but it was negative for 2nd- and 3rd- or higher-generation immigrants. In addition, the association between sports involvement and misconduct, which was unexpectedly positive, was larger for 2nd-generation students than for 3rd-plus-generation students. This means that students with greater involvement in school sports are more prone to offending, especially 2nd-generation students.

In total, the research evidence suggests that social bond theory adds value to our understanding of variations in individuals' likelihood of engaging in school crime. However, research findings contain some important nuances and caveats as indicated in the summary below:

- School-based offending is lower, in general, among students with stronger commitment to school.

- Individuals with greater attachment to school and a stronger belief in the fairness and legitimacy of school rules are less prone to criminal behavior.
- Evidence regarding the effects of school involvement generally contradict the theory, showing that greater involvement in school activities is associated with higher participation in criminal behavior. As discussed further in Chapter 5, this may be because involvement in extracurricular activities, while an important aspect of bonding, also provides criminal opportunity.
- The effects of parental attachment yield mixed support for the theory, with the evidence somewhat dependent on the type of criminal behavior considered.
- A bond to other social institutions, such as religion, appears to impact school delinquency, but research on this issue is limited.

Self-Control and School Offending

The self-control explanation suggests that due to failures in early-life parent-child socialization processes, some individuals will not develop sufficient levels of self-control by the time they reach elementary-school age. Consequently, they are impulsive and have difficulty resisting short-term pleasures along with an inability to make associations between their present-moment actions and negative long-term consequences. As students lacking self-control enter into their middle- and high-school years, their impulsive gratification-seeking behavior produces higher risks of engaging in all forms of school-based delinquency.

Since its introduction, Gottfredson and Hirschi's (1990) self-control theory has become one of the leading individual-level explanations of criminal offending. Not surprisingly, a growing body of research examines the impact of self-control on crime in schools (McGloin et al., 2011; Moon and Alarid, 2015; Ousey and Wilcox, 2005, 2007; Ousey et al., 2015; Swartz et al., 2017; Unnever, Pratt, and Cullen, 2003; Vogel and Barton, 2011). These studies investigate several questions. First, do students with lower levels of self-control commit more offenses at school than those with higher self-control? Second, is low self-control associated with multiple types of offending, or is it limited to specific offense categories (e.g., violence)? Finally, does low self-control affect school crime independent of, or in combination with, causal factors identified in other criminological perspectives, such as general strain, social learning, and social bonds?

Unnever and colleagues (2003) examined whether lower levels of self-control were associated with greater involvement in delinquent behavior, including damaging school property and hitting or threatening a teacher or other adult at school. They investigated whether, as Gottfredson and Hirschi (1990) argued, parental management affects the development of self-control, which in turn affects delinquent behavior. Their analyses of data from a sample of middle-school students from six schools in a Virginia metropolitan area yielded results generally supporting the theory. As the theory outlines, students with parents who engaged in greater monitoring and more consistently punished misbehavior were more likely to develop effective levels of self-control. Moreover, as expected, students with lower levels of self-control were significantly more involved in delinquency, including school-based offending.

Studying middle-school students from two schools in a large urban area in the southwestern United States, Moon and Alarid (2015) examined how low self-control and four "opportunity" factors (i.e., parental supervision, peer associations, negative school environment, and teacher discipline) affected involvement in violent offending. Measures of offending included items such as "hit or pushed other students," "shoved or provoked other students," "threatened or took other students' money with force," and "physically attacked other students." Results of the Moon and Alarid (2015) study support self-control theory. As predicted, students with lower self-control were more involved in violent offenses relative to those with higher self-control. Self-control was not the only important predictor of violent offending, however. Factors reflective of social bond and social learning theories, such as parental supervision, associating with delinquent peers, and teacher discipline practices, also exerted significant effects on violent offending among students.

Several studies of RSVP data have examined the relationship between impulsivity, a key component of self-control, and school-based offending (Johnson et al., 2019; McGloin et al., 2011; Ousey and Wilcox, 2005, 2007; Ousey et al., 2015; Swartz et al., 2017). These studies reported results consistent with the theoretical expectations of self-control theory. Indeed, impulsivity is associated with several measures of school-involved criminal offending including general delinquency (Ousey and Wilcox, 2007; McGloin et al., 2011), violence (Swartz et al., 2017; Ousey and Wilcox, 2005; Ousey et al., 2015), and weapon carrying (Johnson et al., 2019).

While the preceding discussion documents evidence supporting the argument that low self-control is an important risk factor for criminal offending in schools, the studies are limited geographically, focusing only on students within schools in a single state. Do the findings replicate in a broader, nationally representative data? The answer appears to be yes. Vogel and Barton (2011) used data on high-school students in the National Longitudinal Study of Adolescent to Adult Health to investigate if a measure of impulsivity predicted several infractions, including being under the influence of alcohol at school, being high on drugs at school, and carrying a weapon at school. In accord with Gottfredson and Hirschi's (1990) contention that self-control is explanative of a wide array of criminal offenses, Vogel and Barton (2011) report impulsivity has a significant positive association with both substance use and weapon carrying at school.

Although school crime research offers substantial evidence supportive of self-control theory, there is also some nuance in the findings reported in prior work. Our summation of major findings is below.

- Students with lower levels of self-control (or higher impulsivity) are more prone to committing delinquent behaviors in school.
- Consistent with Gottfredson and Hirschi's (1990) claims, low self-control appears to be a general explanation of offending in school. It predicts varied forms of delinquency including violence, theft, substance use, and weapon carrying.
- Some research suggests the effect of low self-control on school delinquency varies with an individual's associations with delinquent peers or with the opportunity context of the school itself. However, the impact of impulsivity is unmoderated by individual variation in social bonds or strains (Ousey and Wilcox 2007).

Biological/Psychological Traits and School Offending

A less prominent but emerging body of research examines empirical relationships between school-based criminal behavior and biological or psychological traits. Trait arguments assert that individuals differ in terms of stable characteristics rooted in biology or early-life psychosocial development. Some traits, including stable features of human personality, give individuals differential propensities for crime. Self-control theory, discussed earlier, is sometimes classified as a trait argument because levels of self-control are conceptualized as stable beyond early points in the life course. Yet, Gottfredson and Hirschi (1990) rejected the notion that self-control was biologically or genetically determined. Research by Unnever et al. (2003) argued an alternative position. They surmised that low self-control was partly a result of ineffective parental socialization (as posited by Gottfredson and Hirschi, 1990) but also partly due to a genetically influenced neurobehavioral, attention deficit hyperactivity disorder (ADHD). Further, they proposed that ADHD affects both an individual's level of self-control as well as their involvement in delinquent behavior. Their study results indicated that low self-control was more common among kids with ADHD. Moreover, students with ADHD reported greater involvement in offending, including vandalism and violence at school. Effects of ADHD on self-reported crime were indirect, operating through low self-control. Thus, findings were generally consistent with a trait perspective in that a condition with a heavy biogenetic basis—ADHD—affected an individual's involvement in criminal offending by curtailing their development of self-control.

Emphasis on the contributions of personality traits to delinquent offending is also part of Agnew and colleagues' (2002) research on general strain theory. They hypothesized that two stable personality traits—negative emotionality and low constraint—were central factors in shaping how individuals respond to strains. Students with personalities featuring higher negative emotionality and lower constraint should be more likely to respond to strains by committing delinquent acts. Analysis of data from the National Survey of Children indicated that the personality traits had important effects on delinquent behavior in two ways. First, those individuals with higher scores on a negative-emotionality/low-constraint personality scale exhibited more involvement in delinquent behavior. Second, the measures of strain and negative emotionality/low constraint interacted in their effect on offending. More specifically, the personality traits amplified the effects of strains on crime, and vice versa.

Wilcox and colleagues (2014) extend the research linking traits to school crime by exploring how personality traits and situational opportunities converge to affect both school-based offending and victimization. Using RSVP data, they explored whether two personality traits from the Big Five personality model, "agreeableness" and "conscientiousness," affected school-based criminal offending as well as victimization. Agreeableness refers to a person's tendency to be flexible, forgiving, and cooperative in interpersonal relationships. Conscientiousness is the tendency to plan, organize, and not react impulsively. Wilcox et al. (2014) developed an integrated propensity-opportunity framework that proposes multiple routes by which these two traits may relate with offending (and victimization). First, they offered that agreeableness and conscientiousness directly affect offending by influencing uncooperative and impulsive behavior in daily social interactions. Second, they suggested that situational opportunity factors serve as mediators of the effect of the traits on school offending. Finally, they posited that variations in criminal opportunity modify the strength of the association between the personality traits and offending. Results of their analyses suggest that traits affect crime through all three routes. Agreeableness had a direct negative effect on offending as well as indirect negative effects through delinquent peer associations and access to illicit goods (i.e., agreeableness was negatively associated with delinquent peer associations and access to illicit goods, which were both positively associated with offending). Conscientiousness did not affect crime directly, but it had an indirect negative effect through delinquent peer associations. Finally, both traits reduced offending more strongly in conditions of greater opportunity—that is, when individuals had greater exposure to delinquent peers and to illicit goods.

Other research has posited that mental illness or psychological difficulties may influence involvement in particular school-based offenses, such as weapon carrying (Johnson et al., 2019; Muula, Rudatsikira, and Siziya, 2008). Findings from these studies are somewhat mixed. Using data from the 2005 YRBSS, Muula et al. (2008) examined correlates of weapon carrying on school grounds. They found that two measures of psychological difficulties, depression and suicidal ideation, were associated with greater odds of weapon carrying at school. Odds of weapon carrying at school increased by a factor of 1.4 for students who experienced depression and by 1.6 for students who experienced suicidal ideation. With data from the RSVP, Johnson and colleagues (2019) examined whether several measures of psychological difficulties—family history of mental illness, experiencing anxiety and depression, being fearful of crime, and low self-control—contributed to weapon carrying at school. Initial models indicated that weapon carrying was elevated for students with a family history of mental illness, fearfulness about crime, and low self-control, but not for anxiety or depression. The effects of all psychological difficulties, except low self-control, were nonsignificant when controlling for variation in factors including gender, delinquent associations, victimization experience, and school attachment.

In sum, the research literature explicitly linking school crime to biological or psychological traits is a somewhat small but emerging area of work. Our review of this literature yields several major findings:

- To date, school-based studies testing trait perspectives are less common than studies of other major criminological theories.
- Available evidence suggests that personality traits such as low conscientiousness, low agreeableness, and the combination of high negative emotionality/low constraint increase the likelihood of school delinquency either directly or indirectly.
- Individual characteristics including ADHD and psychological difficulties are associated with increased risks of school-based delinquent offending.

Conclusion

In this chapter, we considered the "motivated offender" side of the crime triangle framework first presented in the opening chapter of the book. Using national and state/local survey datasets, we traced patterns in several kinds of criminal offending, including assault, robbery, theft, sexual assault, and weapon carrying at school. Those data indicated temporal variation in many school-based delinquent offenses, with prevalence rates for several trending lower in more recent years. We also observed variation across demographic characteristics, with gender differences most prominent and race differences somewhat less so.

After reviewing data patterns and trends, we examined school crime research evidence. More specifically, we reviewed results from studies testing whether several major criminological theories were explanative of school-based measures of criminal offending. We examined research evidence for strain, social bonds, social learning/subculture, self-control, and individual trait theoretical perspectives. These criminological theories clearly have merit in ongoing efforts to gain understanding of variations in criminal offending in schools. Our assessment is that the evidentiary foundation for the theories of offending outlined in Chapter 2 falls somewhere between "promising" (trait perspective) to "compelling" (social learning). Findings revealed at least some support for all perspectives considered. Moreover, in no case did we see a pattern of evidence arguing for an outright rejection of the core arguments proffered in the general strain, social learning, social bonds, self-control, or trait theories. Rather, each perspective contributes productive value toward understanding students' motivation to engage in, or refrain from, crime at school.[4]

Despite the clear importance of the theories, it is worth noting that in many of the studies reviewed, demographic differences in school delinquency remained significant when controlling for the impact of the major criminological theories discussed in this chapter. This is especially true for gender differences and to a more limited degree for racial and ethnic variations. Thus, although school crime studies have identified some salient mechanisms leading individuals to vary in their levels of school-based delinquency, they have not yet effectively unpacked all social processes explaining the effects of gender and race on school-based offending.

Given that major criminological theories help explain variation in students' motivation for delinquent offending, they are a necessary part of efforts at school crime prevention. Ameliorating some factors that influence offending may seem especially challenging to address within school settings (e.g., strains or weak bonds within family life). Yet, obstacles are removable.

---

4. While of differing scope than our work in key ways, a recent meta-analysis focused on school violence (Turanovic et al., 2019) reports concepts associated with social learning, general strain, self-control, and social bond theories are related to aggressive/delinquent behavior in the direction predicted by theory. Moreover, while social learning effects appear strongest and social bond effects are weakest, all have important and statistically discernible effects on school-based violent offending.

School crime prevention will likely not succeed if particular sides of the "crime triangle" are not incorporated. Therefore, we need strategies to mitigate the criminogenic impact of strains, weak bonds, antisocial peer associations, low self-control, and personality traits. We discuss some of the prevailing strategies employed in schools in Chapter 8, "School Zone: Strategies in Search of Safety."

5

Student Victimization

The Suitable, Unguarded Target

As noted previously, we argue that crime results from the convergence of a motivated offender and an unguarded, suitable target/victim in a particular place or setting. Therefore, to understand crime in schools, we must examine what makes a student motivated to commit crime; what makes a student a suitable, unguarded target for victimization; and what makes a school setting more or less favorable for crime. This chapter addresses the second of these questions, reviewing and assessing the empirical validity of the explanations for victimization introduced in Chapter 2. In particular, it examines research addressing whether these general theories of victimization explain the specific problem of *school-based student victimization.*

It is important to note that the *harm* of victimization often extends well beyond the event itself. Thus, developing a comprehensive understanding of school crime helps inform efforts to reduce student victimization and its extended consequences. For example, data from the Education Longitudinal Study of 2002 (ELS:2002) demonstrate that exposure to violence and victimization at school increases the likelihood of dropping out of school among African American and Latino American students (Peguero, 2011a). Experiencing victimization at school also increases fear among students, a topic we specifically address later in this chapter (Tillyer et al., 2011). More broadly, victimization in adolescence is linked to series of negative outcomes, including depression and substance use in adolescence and income deficits, criminal offending, substance use problems, risky sexual behavior, depression, suicide ideation, and hospitalization in adulthood (Macmillan, 2001; Menard, 2002; Pinchevsky, Fagan, and Wright, 2014; Turanovic and Pratt, 2014; Turner, Finkelhor, and Ormrod, 2010). In short, the range of potential harms associated with victimization makes the understanding of its causes and the routes to its prevention more pressing.

We present this chapter in three major sections. The initial section describes several patterns in data on school-based student victimization. First, we describe victimization prevalence, or the proportion of the student population estimated to have experienced it. Next, we review victimization trends, or changes over time in student victimization. Then we focus on victimization concentration, which illustrates how much victimization experiences cluster among a relatively small group of students.

The second major section systematically reviews research evidence on the correlates of student victimization and evaluates whether the general explanations presented in Chapter 2—including lifestyle-routine activities, target congruence, low self-control, and other forms of criminal propensity—are useful for understanding *school-based student victimization*. In addition, it considers the correlates of recurring victimization, investigating whether available theories help explain why some students are more prone to repeated victimization at school.

The third section of the chapter looks beyond actual victimization experiences. It focuses on related outcomes including worries about crime at school, assessments of victimization risk at school, and behaviors employed to reduce victimization risk at school. Using theories of victimization and the broader problem analysis framework presented in Chapter 2, this section describes and seeks explanation of variation in these salient phenomena.

The Nature and Consequences of Student Victimization

Prevalence and Trends

Recall from Chapter 3 that researchers draw from a range of data sources to understand variations in school crime and safety, including school-based student victimization. The National Crime Victimization Survey's (NCVS) School Crime Supplement (SCS) and the Centers for Disease Control and Prevention's (CDC) Youth Risk Behavior Surveillance System (YRBSS) are particularly useful for understanding prevalence and trends in student victimization for a number of reasons. Each study: (1) collects data from nationally representative samples of students in the United States, (2) asks about school-based victimization experiences, and (3) administers surveys every two years, allowing an observation of national trends over time. Moreover, researchers can also use data collected from school-aged participants (12–18 years old) as part of the routine NCVS household data collection in conjunction with the SCS, because NCVS participants who report a criminal victimization are asked for the location of the incident, with options including "inside school building" and "on school property (school parking area, play area, school bus, etc.)." This allows measurement of more serious forms of school-based student victimization not captured on the SCS.

Data from the 2017 NCVS indicate that the majority of victimizations experienced by students ages 12–18 in the preceding six months occurred at school, with student participants reporting 827,000 total victimizations at school compared to just 503,800 total victimizations away from school. In short, the school context is very much relevant for understanding the victimization experiences of this population. Data from the NCVS and SCS indicate that the six-month prevalence rate of any *school-based* student criminal victimization in 2017 was 2.2% among students ages 12–18 (Musu-Gillette et al., 2018; Yanez and Seldin, 2019). About 1.5% of students reported being a victim of theft at school in the preceding six months, and 0.7% reported any violent victimization at school in the preceding six months (including serious violent crime and simple assault). About one-half of 1% of students reported simple assault, and 0.2% reported experiencing serious violent victimization (including rape, sexual assault, robbery, and aggravated assault) at school in the preceding six months (Yanez and Seldin, 2019).

General school-based criminal victimization varied by student characteristics (Yanez and Seldin, 2019):

- Male students reported higher prevalence rates (2.6%) relative to female students (1.8%).
- Black students reported higher prevalence rates (2.6%) relative to White (2.2%) and Hispanic or Latino (2.0%) students.
- Sixth graders reported the highest rate (3.1%), which declined steadily to 2.6% among 7th graders and 1.8% among 8th graders. Prevalence then increased as students entered high school, with 2.7% of 9th and 10th graders reporting school-based victimization, and then declined again for 11th and 12th graders (1.4%).
- Students from urban schools reported higher rates of victimization (2.7%) relative to students in suburban (2.1%) and rural (1.6%) schools.

As Figure 5.1 displays, the 2017 prevalence rates reflect a recent low point following a substantial and steady decline in school-based criminal victimization over the previous two decades. In 1995, the six month prevalence

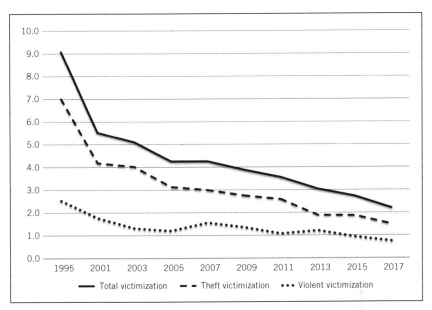

Figure 5.1 Percentages of students ages 12–18 who reported criminal victimization at school during the preceding 6 months (1995–2017)

(U.S. Department of Justice, Bureau of Justice Statistics, School Crime Supplement [SCS] to the National Crime Victimization Survey, 1995 through 2017.)

rate of total criminal victimization was approximately 9.1% among students ages 12–18, with approximately 7% reporting theft victimization and 2.5% reporting violent victimization. Declines in school-based criminal victimization were observed across student gender, race, ethnicity, and grade level.

The YRBSS provides another piece of information on student victimization in schools. Specifically, 9th- through 12th-grade students were asked if they were threatened or injured with a weapon on school property in the 12 months before the survey. As Figure 5.2 illustrates, 7.3% of students reported being threatened or injured with a weapon on school property in 1993. This increased to 9.2% in 2003, and then decreased to a low of 6.0% of students in 2017. The YRBSS prevalence rates are notably higher than the prevalence rates observed in the NCVS. This is not surprising because they measure different types of victimization experiences (e.g., the YRBSS question includes threats), cover different time frames (i.e., events in the preceding 12 months versus 6 months) and age ranges (i.e., ages 12–18 versus grades 9 through 12).

Note that both the NCVS and YRBSS data presented above measure criminal victimization. The SCS also asks about specific bullying experiences, but only some rise to the level of *criminal* victimization that would appear in the NCVS figures reported above. As Figure 5.3 demonstrates,

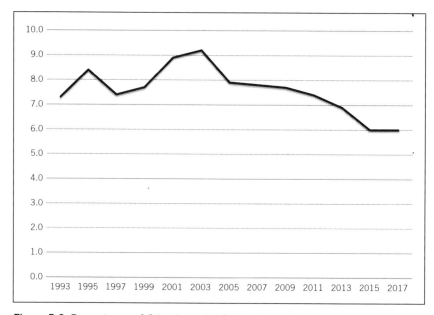

Figure 5.2 Percentages of 9th- through 12th-grade students threatened or injured with a weapon on school property during the preceding 12 months (1993–2017)
(Centers for Disease Control and Prevention. Trends in the Prevalence of Behaviors That Contribute to Violence on School Property, National YRBSS: 1991–2017.)

bullying is much more common than criminal victimization, with 20.2% of students ages 12 to 18 reporting some form of bullying victimization in 2017. Yet, three of the four most common forms of bullying victimization reported in 2017 (i.e., subject of rumors; made fun of, called names, or insulted; and excluded from activities on purpose) do not constitute criminal offenses. Similar to criminal victimization, the prevalence of school-based bullying has declined in recent years, after peaking at 31.7% in 2007.

School-based bullying victimization varies by student characteristics:

- Unlike school-based *criminal* victimization, which male students were more likely to report relative to their female counterparts, school-based *bullying* victimization was more common among female students (23.8%) than male students (16.7%).
- Black and White students reported bullying victimization at similar rates (22.9% and 22.8%, respectively), while Hispanic students were less likely to report being bullied (15.7%).
- Bullying victimization also declined with age, with 29.5% of 6th-grade students reporting some form of bullying, compared to 25.3% of 8th-grade students, 18.9% of 10th-grade students, and 12.2% of 12th-grade students.

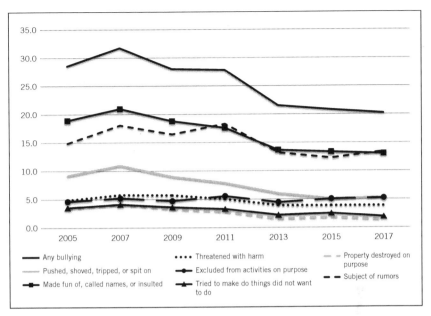

Figure 5.3 Percentages of students ages 12–18 who reported being bullied at school during the school year (2005–2017)

(U.S. Department of Justice, Bureau of Justice Statistics, School Crime Supplement [SCS] to the National Crime Victimization Survey, selected years, 2005 through 2017. Note that there was a significant redesign in the bullying measures in 2005, so prior years are not reported here. For the "any bullying" category, students who reported more than one type of bullying were counted only once.)

- Unlike criminal victimization, bullying victimization was more common among students in rural (26.7%) schools relative to suburban (19.7%) and urban (18.3%) schools.

Homicides of children and adolescents at school remain rare, accounting for a small fraction of the overall number of homicides of youths ages 5–18 during each school year. As Figure 5.4 displays, the total number of homicides for this age group peaked at 3,253 during the 1993–1994 school year, with only 29 of these deaths occurring at school. Similar to national crime trends for all age groups, the rate of homicide for this group declined steadily in the 1990s, and homicide at school remained very rare.

School-Based Victimization Concentration: Recurring Victimization among Students

An important and consistently reported finding in victimization studies is the phenomenon of recurring victimization, with a relatively small propor-

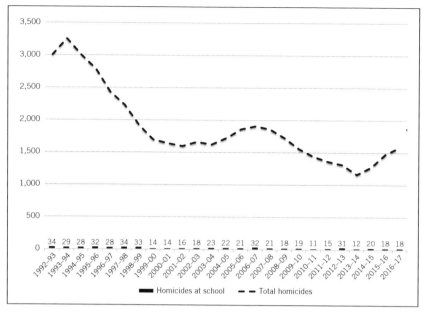

Figure 5.4 Homicides of youth ages 5–18 by location
(Centers for Disease Control and Prevention [CDC], 1992–2017 School-Associated Violent Death Surveillance System [SAVD-SS]; and CDC, National Center for Health Statistics, 1992–2017 National Vital Statistics System [NVSS].)

tion of the population suffering a large proportion of all criminal victimizations due to repeated experiences (Farrell, 1992).[1] For example, Farrell and Pease's (1993) analysis of data from the British Crime Survey found that more than 80% of all crime incidents were perpetrated against victims who experienced more than one incident. Moreover, 4.3% of respondents reported experiencing *five or more* victimizations with these high frequency victims accounting for 43.5% of all criminal victimization incidents.

Victimization appears even more concentrated among American adolescents. Lauritsen and Davis Quinet (1995) examined the concentration of crime incidents among adolescents using the first wave of the National Youth Survey, a longitudinal study aimed at examining drug use and delinquency among American adolescents aged 11–17. Participants were asked about assault, robbery, larceny, and vandalism victimization frequency in

---

1. Though early work in this area used the term "repeat victimization" broadly, scholars now distinguish between different forms of recurring victimization. Repeat victimization typically refers to recurring victimization of the same crime type, while multiple victimization is recurring victimization of different crime types.

the past year. For all crime types, the majority of youths reported no victimizations, but most crime incidents were perpetrated against repeat victims as opposed to one-time victims. For example, 68.9% of participants reported no assault victimization in the past year, 12.9% reported one assault victimization, accounting for only 10.4% of all assault incidents reported by participants. The remaining 89.6% of assault incidents affected individuals experiencing repeated victimization. Indeed, 5.2% of study participants suffered five or more victimizations in the past year, accounting for 63.2% of the total reported assault victimizations described in the data.

Why does victimization reoccur for some individuals? Scholars have used both risk heterogeneity and state dependence explanations to account for repeated victimization. The former, also known as "flag theory," suggests that some individuals have stable characteristics or behaviors that continuously place them at risk for victimization over time (Farrell, Phillips, and Pease, 1995). Examples include risky routine activities that create opportunities for criminal victimization (Eck, 2001; Wittebrood and Nieuwbeerta, 2000) and low self-control (Schreck, Stewart, and Fisher, 2006). The latter, also known as "boost theory" or "victim labeling," suggests that victimization may increase the risk of future victimization (Farrell et al., 1995; Ousey, Wilcox, and Brummel, 2008). This explanation relies on a rational choice theory of offender decision making, in which offenders gain knowledge about risks and rewards during their previous events (Farrell et al., 1995). For example, an offender has a better understanding of the victim's suitability and potential guardianship after an initial attack. Offenders also may tell others about the initial incident, alerting additional potential offenders about vulnerable or attractive targets.

Victimization scholars have argued that studying repeat victimization is essential for understanding and preventing crime. Descriptions and investigations of victimization that do not account for how risk is highly concentrated among the few are misleading (Farrell, Tseloni, and Pease, 2005; Planty and Strom, 2007). Moreover, because experiencing victimization in the past is a relatively good predictor of future victimization risk, interventions targeting those previously victimized represents an effective and defensible use of prevention resources (Farrell, 1995; Farrell and Pease, 1993).

What about repeat victimization in schools? Understanding how *school-based* crime incidents are concentrated among students is important for developing a more accurate description of risk among students, as well as identifying a subset of individuals most in need of intervention. As discussed in Chapter 3, the Rural Substance abuse and Violence Project (RSVP) asked students in Kentucky about the frequency with which they experienced several victimization types in the current school year. Table 5.1 summarizes the victimization frequencies, as reported in two studies examining repeat victimization in the RSVP (Tillyer, Gialopsos, and Wilcox, 2016; Tillyer et al., 2018).

Across all crime types, a majority of students reported zero victimizations in the current school year. But among those experiencing a particular victimization type, repeated victimization events are more common than single victimization events. For example, 11.1% of students reported physical assault a single time in the current school year, while 27.2% of students reported being physically assaulted two or more times in the current school year. Tillyer et al. (2018) note that the 27.2% of students reporting multiple assault victimizations accounted for 92.7% of all the physical assaults reported by students. Moreover, "chronic victims," who reported 10 or more physical assaults in the current school year, accounted for 40.6% of all physical assaults, despite representing only 6.2% of students (Tillyer et al., 2018).

In addition to studies focused on short-term repeat victimization within a single academic year, researchers analyzing the RSVP data examined the extent to which there is cross-year stability in school-based victimization and what accounts for within-student variation in victimization across years. Latent class analysis of all four waves of the RSVP by Sullivan, Wilcox, and Ousey (2011) revealed considerable stability year to year in school-based victimization. Specifically, they reported four distinct victimization trajectories, with the majority (80%) of students experiencing little to no

TABLE 5.1 FREQUENCY OF SCHOOL-BASED VICTIMIZATION IN THE CURRENT SCHOOL YEAR: FINDINGS ON SHORT-TERM REPEAT VICTIMIZATION FROM THE RURAL SUBSTANCE ABUSE AND VIOLENCE PROJECT

Frequency	Sexual harassment (%)	Sexual assault (%)	Physical assault (%)	Robbery (%)	Weapon pulled (%)
Zero	56.20	69.10	61.70	92.70	90.50
1	8.80	7.00	11.10	2.70	3.10
2	6.50	4.80	6.70	1.30	1.90
3	4.90	3.70	4.80	0.80	0.80
4	3.60	2.40	3.00	0.50	0.60
5	3.80	2.40	2.90	0.50	0.40
6	2.00	1.40	1.60	0.20	0.40
7	1.60	1.30	1.00	0.20	0.20
8	1.20	0.60	0.60	0.20	0.10
9	0.80	0.70	0.40	0.10	0.20
10 or more	10.60	6.60	6.20	0.80	1.80

Source: Rural Substance abuse and Violence Project.

victimization during the study period (see Figure 5.5). Another group (16.1%) experienced a moderate amount of victimization at a fairly consistent rate over time. A small group of students (<4%) experienced rather sharp increases or decreases in victimization over the four-year study period.

In sum, school-based student victimization appears to be highly concentrated, with some students repeatedly suffering a disproportionate number of victimizations. To build further understanding of phenomenon, the next section delves into research examining correlates of school-based victimization, including recurrent victimization.

The Correlates of School-Based Student Victimization

In Chapter 2, we introduced several theories—including lifestyle-routine activities, target congruence, low self-control, and other forms of criminal propensity—developed to help explain why individuals are at risk for criminal victimization. We view these theories as more compatible than competing. In brief, lifestyle-routine activities theory suggests that crime is more likely when a suitable, unguarded target is exposed to a motivated offender (Cohen and Felson, 1979). Individual lifestyles and routine activities provide individuals with varying degrees of exposure and guardianship, thus helping to shape opportunities for crime (Cohen et al., 1981). Target congruence theory (Finkelhor and Asdigian, 1996) extends the concept of target suitability, positing that individuals whose characteristics align with an of-

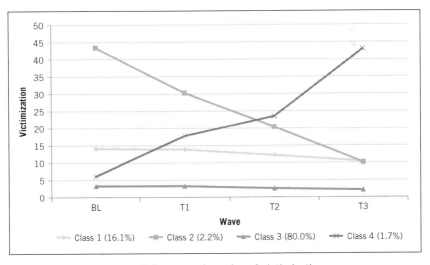

Figure 5.5 Four trajectories of victimization
(Rural Substance abuse and Violence Project; Sullivan, Wilcox, and Ousey [2011]).

fender's needs, motives, or reactions are more likely to become victims. This includes vulnerability, or characteristics making it difficult for them to deter an attack; characteristics that gratify specific desires of the offender; and characteristics that antagonize offenders and arouse reactions. Finally, victimization risk is assumed to be elevated among those lacking in self-control, both because they are more likely to engage in risky routine activities without precautions, and because they are more likely to be antagonistic, displaying behaviors that provoke aggression from others (Schreck, 1999).

In Chapter 2, we briefly presented evidence demonstrating that these explanations have enjoyed some degree of empirical support in general studies of victimization. But are they useful in understanding the specific problem of *school-based student victimization*? In this section, we examine research applying traditional explanations of victimization to help identify individual correlates of student victimization at school. Understanding variations in risk for victimization requires the identification of factors providing guardianship (or lack thereof) to students as well as the characteristics affecting their suitability as crime targets for motivated offenders. The empirical research on school-based victimization of middle- and high-school students is reviewed below, with a focus on factors that correlate with violent, property, and sexual victimization, as well as the serious forms of physical bullying that rise to the level of criminality.

Attachment to Parents, School, and Peers

A considerable body of research has examined the influence of students' attachments to parents, school, and peers on their victimization risk in schools. Attachments, which refer to the degree of emotional closeness individuals have for others (Hirschi, 1969), have the potential to shape student lifestyles and routine activities by limiting exposure to motivated offenders and/or providing guardianship (Schreck and Fisher, 2004; Wilcox et al., 2009). For example, a student who shares a strong bond with his mother may be more inclined to disclose he is bullied at school. His mother can use this information to help reduce her son's victimization risk by contacting the school and/or counseling him on how to respond effectively. A caring, supportive teacher may provide guardianship during conventionally risky times at school, monitoring vulnerable students on the playground or allowing students to eat their lunch in the classroom to avoid the school cafeteria. Strong peer attachments may provide guardianship to students during times that are "unguarded" by adults at school, such as after school before extracurricular activities begin. In short, conventional social attachments may serve to protect students from school-based victimization, as they may limit exposure to motivated offenders and/or offer a potential source of guardianship.

While the NCVS-SCS does not directly measure parental attachment, researchers using those data to understand student school-based victimization have examined the importance of other family variables that may tap guardianship. For example, Burrow and Apel (2008) report that students living in a household with an intact family structure were at lower risk for assault victimization at school; there was no relationship between intact family structure and larceny victimization. Family size and having a sibling at school were unrelated to both assault and larceny victimization at school. Gerlinger and Wo (2016) found that students with a single mother are more likely to experience physical bullying.

Researchers analyzing the effects of parental attachment using the RSVP data draw on 24 items asking about respondents' relationships with their parents. Findings from these studies indicate that the effect of parental attachment on student victimization may vary by gender and crime type (Wilcox et al., 2009; Tillyer et al., 2016, 2018; Tillyer, Wilcox, and Gialopsos, 2010). Key findings include:

- Higher parental attachment was associated with lower risks for physical assault, theft, and sexual harassment victimization for female students, but not male students.
- The effects of parental attachment on sexual assault were significant for both male and female students.
- Greater parental attachment also appears to be protective against some repeated attacks among students who experienced a prior victimization. Parental attachment was negatively associated with repeat sexual assault and harassment victimization, but not repeat physical assault victimization.

Beyond the protection provided by a healthy parent-child relationship, strong bonds to school—evidenced by academic achievement and/or affective attachment—may also provide guardianship to students. Wynne and Joo (2011) analyzed NCVS-SCS data from 2003 and found that academic achievement, measured using students' grades, was negatively associated with criminal victimization (see also Burrow and Apel, 2008). Gerlinger and Wo (2016), using NCVS-SCS data from 2005, 2007, 2009, and 2011, found student grades to be negatively associated with physical bullying victimization. Higher grades were also associated with a lower risk of becoming a victim of violent crime in or around school among 7th through 12th graders according to the 1994 Metropolitan Life Survey of the American Teacher (Fitzpatrick, 1999). Similarly, studies analyzing data from the ELS:2002 reported a significant negative association between academic achievement, measured using standardized test scores, and both violent and property victimization among students (e.g., Peguero, 2009; Peguero, Popp, and Koo, 2015; Popp and Peguero, 2011). In a study of Philadelphia middle-school students, Welsh (2001) reported that school effort—measured as how much care and effort the student devotes to schoolwork—was associated with lower victimization. Finally, research on data from the RSVP indicated that the effect of student grades also varies by gender and crime type, with higher grades associated with a lower risk of theft victimization for girls but not boys, and higher grades associated with a lower risk of assault victimization for boys but not girls (Wilcox et al., 2009). However, grades were not significantly associated with short-term repeat violent or sexual victimization risk (Tillyer et al., 2016; 2018).

Researchers using the RSVP data measure school attachment with six items about students' relationships to their teachers, the importance of education, and their attitude toward school. Similar to the RSVP findings on parental attachment, these studies suggest that a student's bond to school is important, but the effects of student grades and school attachment vary by gender and crime type:

- Kulig, Cullen, Wilcox, and Chouhy (2019) report that school attachment was significantly and negatively associated with a measure of general school-based victimization that includes physical assault, robbery, theft, and having a gun or weapon pulled.
- Additional studies reveal that the effect varies by crime type, with school attachment significantly and negatively associated with more serious forms of violent victimization (e.g., robbery and weapons offenses), but not more minor forms of assault or theft (Tillyer et al., 2011; Wilcox et al., 2009).
- The relationship between school attachment and *sexual* victimization appears to be gendered, with a school attachment leading to a lower risk of sexual assault and harassment victimization for male students, but not female students (Tillyer et al., 2010).
- School attachment, however, was not significantly associated with *short-term* repeat violent or sexual victimization risk (i.e., repeated attacks within the same school year) (Tillyer et al., 2016, 2018).
- An additional study examining year-to-year changes in physical assault victimization at school using the four waves of RSVP data indicates school attachment was negatively associated with school-based victimization over time (Ousey et al., 2008).

Beyond measures of school attachment and achievement, research also suggests that students who have negative thoughts and feelings toward school are more likely to experience school-based victimization. For example, the belief that rules are unfair was significantly associated with both violent and theft victimization among students in grades 6 through 12; alienation from school was significantly related to theft victimization only (Schreck et al., 2003). Similarly, NCVS-SCS data indicate that students who report often feeling rejected at school were more likely to experience criminal victimization (Wynne and Joo, 2011).

Finally, there is evidence to suggest that strong peer attachments may serve to reduce some forms of school-based victimization, though there are some differences between male and female students. Researchers who analyze the RSVP data rely on six items that ask students about their attitudes toward and expectations of their closest friends to measure the quality of peer attachments. Students with strong peer attachments were less likely to experience both serious violent victimization and more minor forms of assault (Tillyer et al., 2011; Wilcox et al., 2009). For sexual harassment and assault victimization, the effect was significant for male students only (Tillyer et al., 2010), whereas peer attachment was associated with lower risk of theft victimization among female students only (Wilcox et al., 2009). Finally, peer attachment reduced the likelihood of a repeated violent victimization attack (Tillyer et al., 2018) but was unrelated to repeat sexual victimization (Tillyer et al., 2016). Beyond the quality of students' attachment to their peers, research also indicates that the mere quantity of friendships may also be important. Wang, Iannotti, and Nansel (2009) analyzed data from the Health Behavior in School-Aged Children 2005 survey and reported that students in grades 6 through 10 with more friends were less likely to experience physical bullying.

Involvement in School Sports and Activities

Several studies have examined how students' participation in extracurricular activities may influence their risk for victimization. While involvement in conventional social attachments is thought to provide guardianship and limit exposure to motivated offenders, involvement in conventional activities at school may do the opposite, increasing students' risk of personal and property victimization. Such routine activities may expose students to potential offenders—and perhaps multiple potential offenders who are more likely to offend in the presence of accomplices—in the absence of adult supervision (Felson, 1986). This is because extracurricular activities often happen after school and on weekends, when much of the school is unmonitored. Students may store their property in locker rooms or gym bags, leaving them vulnerable to theft. Limited resources require sports teams to maximize use of facilities. The junior varsity basketball team may practice as soon as school dismisses, leaving the varsity team unsupervised until the court becomes available later in the afternoon. In short, students' involvement in conventional extracurricular activities exposes them and their property to opportunities for victimization.

Data from the NCVS-SCS indicate that participation in extracurricular activities significantly increases the risk of physical bullying victimization and larceny victimization (Gerlinger and Wo, 2016; Burrow and Apel, 2008).[2] Data from the ELS:2002 also confirms that participation in extracurricular activities influences risk of school-based victimization, though different activities' effects vary by student race, ethnicity, and gender (e.g., Peguero, 2009; Peguero and Popp, 2012; Peguero et al., 2015; Peterson et al., 2018; Popp and Peguero, 2011). For example, involvement in school sports was associated with an increased risk of violent victimization among racial and ethnic minority male students but a decreased risk among female students and White male students (Peguero and Popp, 2012). Participation in intramural sports was associated with an increased risk for girls but not boys, while participation in clubs increased risk for boys but not girls (Popp and Peguero, 2011). Finally, Welsh (2001) found participation in extracurricular activities (e.g., athletics, band, drama, and other clubs) was associated with higher levels of victimization among middle-school students in Philadelphia.

Findings from studies utilizing RSVP data suggest that the effects of extracurricular activities on school-based victimization vary by type of activity, gender, and crime type (Tillyer et al., 2010, 2011, 2016, 2018; Wilcox et al., 2009):

- Participation in school sports was associated with an increased risk of serious violent victimization, while participation in other school activities was not significantly associated with serious violent victimization.
- For more minor physical assault, both school sports and school activities increased risk for girls; for boys, participation in school sports was associated with a lower risk of assault victimization, while participation in other school activities was associated with an increased risk.
- Participation in school sports increased theft victimization risk among both male and female students, while participation in school activities was associated with increased risk for girls only.
- Participation in school sports was associated with a greater risk of sexual harassment and sexual assault victimization risk for both

---

2. Extracurricular activity participation was also significantly associated with assault victimization (Burrow and Apel, 2008) and overall criminal victimization (Wynne and Joo, 2011) but was nonsignificant in models controlling for school and family characteristics.

genders; participation in other school activities was associated with an increased risk of sexual harassment victimization among boys only, with no effect on sexual assault victimization for either gender.

- School sports and other school activities increased the risk of repeat sexual assault victimization, but not the risks of repeated violent or sexual harassment victimizations.

Low Self-Control and Other Personality Traits

Individuals lacking in self-control are self-centered, have volatile temperaments, prefer physical as opposed to mental tasks, are impulsive, and have rule-breaking tendencies (Gottfredson and Hirschi, 1990; Schreck, 1999). There is a growing body of literature suggesting that low self-control elevates a student's victimization risk in a number of ways. First, students lacking self-control may be less inclined to take precautions to reduce their risk for victimization, failing to lock up unattended property at school, for example. Second, the rule-breaking tendencies of students with low self-control may lead other students to see them as suitable targets unlikely to report their own victimization to school authorities. Third, those lacking in self-control antagonize their peers, creating conflicts leading to victimization. In sum, students with lower levels of self-control are less likely to take reasonable precautions to protect themselves, more likely to be perceived as suitable victimization targets by motivated offenders, and more likely to provoke attacks from their peers.

A recent study by Peterson, Lasky, Fisher, and Wilcox (2018) found that low self-control was associated with increased violent victimization risk among students in the ELS:2002. In addition, low self-control indirectly affected both violent and property victimization. Students with lower levels of self-control were more likely to engage in school misconduct, which in turn elevated risk for both forms of victimization. Data from other sources also suggest that low self-control and impulsive personality traits place students at increased risk for school-based victimization. Analyzing data from the 1997 Kentucky Youth Survey,[3] Campbell Augustine, Wilcox, Ousey, and Clayton (2002) found that an impulsive personality significantly increased violent and property victimization for both middle- and high-school students.

---

3. The Kentucky Youth Survey, which preceded the RSVP, includes data from 26,687 middle- and high-school students in 40 schools across 15 Kentucky counties. For their study, Campbell Augustine et al. (2002) drew a 20% random subsample of 5,364 students, with listwise deletion resulting in a final sample of 3,183 for analysis.

School-based student victimization studies using the RSVP data to measure low self-control and/or impulsivity rely on 11 survey items assessing frustration, temper control, attention span, and restlessness (Wilcox et al., 2009). These studies consistently report that male and female students lacking self-control are at greater risk for school-based victimization, including minor physical assault, theft, sexual assault, sexual harassment, and serious violent victimization (Tillyer et al., 2010, 2011; Wilcox et al., 2009). Moreover, once a student experiences sexual or violent victimization, those with lower levels of self-control are significantly more likely to suffer a repeated attack in the same school year (Tillyer et al., 2016, 2018); low self-control is also associated with repeat physical assault victimization in subsequent school years (Ousey et al., 2008). Beyond the items used to measure low self-control in the RSVP, Kulig et al. (2019) explored whether personality traits known as the Big Five—extraversion, neuroticism, agreeableness, conscientiousness, and openness—help explain victimization risk among students. They report that neuroticism (that is, feelings of being anxious, nervous, sad, or tense) was positively and significantly associated with school-based victimization, net of low self-control, risky behaviors, and school attachment.

Delinquent Peers

Research on adolescent victimization, and school-based victimization in particular, has examined the effects of delinquent peer associations on the risk for victimization. Scholars note that having friends who engage in delinquency has the potential to expose adolescents to motivated offenders, weaken guardianship, and enhance one's attractiveness as a target in the eyes of potential offenders (Schreck and Fisher, 2004). Given that crime often unfolds during normal, routine activities of offenders, students who associate with them may become targets. Schreck and Fisher (2004) argue that the *delinquent* peer group can undermine the guardianship potential of peer attachment in a number of ways. Delinquent peers presumably lack self-control, making them more impulsive, selfish, and less diligent. These qualities make them unlikely to come to the defense of the vulnerable. Moreover, friends who are also engaged in their own delinquency may be less inclined to consult parents, teachers, and other authorities when their friends face the threat of victimization. Finally, given the common group nature of crime, associating with a delinquent peer group—independent of one's own involvement in crime—may invite retaliation. In short, students with delinquent peer associates may be at elevated risk for victimization because they are accessible targets for their associates, such associates offer little protection in the way of guardianship, and their associates' delinquent activities may even provoke attacks on the group at large.

Though the NCVS-SCS does not include a measure of delinquent peers, other studies indicate that associating with delinquent peers affects school-based student victimization. Schreck, Miller, and Gibson (2003) analyzed data from the 1993 National Household Education Surveys Program (NHES), measuring delinquent friends using an index of items asking students if any of their friends smoke cigarettes, drink, smoke marijuana, or take any other illegal drugs. They report a positive and significant relationship between delinquent friends and overall victimization, as well as violent and theft victimization. In an analysis of data collected from Philadelphia middle-school students, Welsh (2001) measured positive peer associations, which indicated the extent to which students' friends value school and avoid trouble (as opposed to disliking school and getting into trouble). Consistent with findings from other studies, students with more positive peer associations experienced significantly lower levels of school-based victimization.

Peterson et al.'s study (2018) further examines how peer characteristics—including the degree to which one's friends are prosocial—might influence student victimization risk by structuring lifestyles and routine activities at school. Using data from the ELS:2002, they found that having prosocial peers reduces one's likelihood of engaging in school misconduct, which in turn reduces risk for violent and property victimization. In addition, having popular friends also increased victimization risk via increased school misconduct, though the relationship was stronger for male students. Having opposite-sex friends increased the risk for victimization through school misconduct for female students only.

Research using RSVP data reveal findings on the effects of delinquent peers that are similar to those reported above. Both male and female students with more delinquent peer associations were at greater risk for all forms of victimization, including physical assault, theft, sexual assault, sexual harassment, and serious violent victimization (Kulig et al., 2019; Tillyer et al., 2010, 2011; Wilcox et al., 2009). While delinquent peer associations were significantly associated with repeat sexual assault and harassment victimization in the same school year (Tillyer et al., 2016), association with delinquent peers was not significantly associated with repeated physical assault victimization in the same year (Tillyer et al., 2018). Ousey et al.'s (2008) study examining year-to-year changes in physical assault victimization at school using the four waves of RSVP data indicates that delinquent peer associations partially mediate the relationship between prior and subsequent physical assault victimization.

Risky Lifestyles and Activities

In addition to the variables described above, researchers studying school-based student victimization have also examined the effects of risky lifestyles and other activities that potentially expose students to motivated offenders in the absence of guardianship. Also considered are factors that shape offenders' perceptions that students are suitable targets. Included here are substance use, access to illicit opportunities (i.e., contraband), and activities that create victimization opportunities (e.g., long commute to school, skipping class, etc.). Data from the 1988 National Education Longitudinal Survey (NELS:1988), for example, indicate that cigarette use and heavy drinking were associated with increased risk of victimization among students (George and Thomas, 2000). Tillyer and colleagues' (2010) analysis of RSVP data found that tobacco, alcohol, and marijuana use was associated with increased risk for sexual harassment and assault for female students, but not male students. In contrast, another study using RSVP showed that substance use was unrelated to repeated incidents of sexual assault and sexual harassment (Tillyer et al., 2016).

Findings from the NCVS-SCS indicate that access to illicit drugs, alcohol, and guns is significantly related to physical peer victimization at school (Cho, Hong, Espelage, and Choi, 2017). Data from the RSVP reveal a similar relationship, with access to illicit opportunities—measured as how easily the student can obtain drugs, alcohol, cigarettes, or guns during a typical school day—positively and significantly associated with school-based victimization (Kulig et al., 2019; see also Ousey et al., 2008). In addition, the NCVS-SCS data highlight other activities that are associated with school-based victimization risk. Skipping class increased the risk of both assault and larceny victimization; leaving school for lunch was associated with an increased risk of larceny victimization, while a long commute to school was associated with an increased risk for assault victimization (Burrow and Apel, 2008). In addition, students who walk or take a bus to school were more likely to report physical peer victimization compared to those who take a car or bike (Cho et al., 2017). George and Thomas (2000) report similar findings from the 1988 NELS data: their lifestyle composite measure, which includes items such as skipping classes and in-school suspension, was significantly associated with greater victimization risk.

Delinquent Behavior

Beyond substance use, there is a considerable body of research demonstrating that those who engage in other criminal or delinquent activities as offenders are also at an increased risk for victimization. Interpreted through an opportunity perspective, some scholars have argued that delinquent behavior represents a risky routine activity that creates opportunities for criminal victimization by exposing individuals to other motivated offenders in contexts lacking guardianship (e.g., Jensen and Brownfield, 1986; Lauritsen et al., 1991; Wilcox et al., 2009). Indeed, numerous studies on school-based student victimization report a significant association between delinquent behavior and victimization risk for various crime types when analyzing data from a range of sources (e.g., Campbell Augustine et al., 2002; Nofziger, 2009; Ousey et al., 2008; Peguero et al., 2015; Tillyer et al., 2010, 2011; Wilcox et al., 2009; Zaykowski and Gunter, 2012).

The argument that delinquency creates opportunities for victimization is important for understanding school-based victimization. Yet, research suggests that the victimization-offending relationship is complex. Studies examining varied crime types with data collected from different populations demonstrate that victims and perpetrators are often overlapping, rather than distinct, populations (Jennings et al., 2012; Lauritsen and Laub, 2007). This "victim-offender overlap" is a common criminological finding and warrants greater theoretical and empirical scrutiny. Consequently, in Chapter 6, we place sustained attention on the victim-offender overlap among students in schools, including an exploration of explanations for the phenomenon.

Other Student Characteristics

As we reported above, the NCVS-SCS indicates that criminal victimization among students varies by gender, race, ethnicity, and age (Yanez and Seldin, 2019). Studies of school-based victimization have examined the effects of these and other student characteristics such as socioeconomic status, immigrant status, LGBTQ identification, and disabilities. How might student characteristics influence victimization risk? Some may be associated with increased exposure to potential offenders in the absence of guardianship (Cohen et al., 1981) and/or they may align with offenders' perceptions of target vulnerability, gratifiability, and antagonism (Finkelhor and Asdigian, 1996; Campbell Augustine et al., 2002). Higher socioeconomic status may increase risk for property victimization, for example, as material gains will gratify offenders, whereas younger students and students with disabilities may be viewed as more vulnerable to physical attack relative to other students. A student's race, ethnicity, or LGBTQ identification may serve to antagonize the homophobia, racism, and/or prejudice of other students.

Consistent with an opportunity model of victimization, findings from some multivariate analyses suggest that some demographic characteristics influence school-based student victimization indirectly through other risk factors tapping exposure, guardianship, and target congruence. That is, demographic effects often are nonsignificant in multivariate models that include individual, family, and school risk factors for victimization. Using the NCVS-SCS data, Burrow and Apel (2008) found no significant gender effects in their multivariate analyses estimating school assault and school larceny victimization. Also using NCVS-SCS data, Wynne and Joo (2011) report no significant race or ethnicity effects net of controls for other individual, family, and school characteristics. Conversely, both studies report a significant and negative relationship between age and victimization net of controls (Burrow and Apel, 2008; Wynne and Joo, 2011).

Multivariate studies analyzing other data sources, however, still observe significant effects of race, ethnicity, and gender. Popp and Peguero (2011), for example, found that female students were significantly less likely to experience violent victimization relative to male students net of controls (see also Kulig et al., 2019; Nofziger, 2009; Schreck et al., 2003; Tillyer et al., 2011; Zaykowski and Gunter, 2012). Nofziger (2009) reports that Black students were significantly *more* likely to experience both sexual assault and physical assault at school relative to White students, while Peguero (2013) found that Black students had *fewer* reported incidents of school-based violent victimization relative to White students.

The effects of variables tapping socioeconomic status vary across studies. Data from the NCVS-SCS indicate that family income is significantly associated with increased risk for assault and larceny victimization (Burrow and Apel, 2008), though poverty was not significantly related to physical bullying (Gerlinger and Wo, 2016). The RSVP data indicate that SES—measured as parent educational attainment—is significantly associated with increased theft victimization risk for both male and female students, and assault victimization for male students only (Wilcox et al., 2009). Data from other studies, however, report nonsignificant effects of family income on violent, theft, and sexual assault victimization (Nofziger, 2009; Schreck et al., 2003).

Research suggests that immigration status may influence victimization risk by structuring students' lifestyles and routine activities. Data from the ELS:2002 indicate that first- and second-generation students are *less* likely to experience violent victimization at school relative to third-generation-plus adolescents, a finding that may be partially explained by increased involvement in activities and misbehavior as generations assimilate (Peguero, 2013). Consistent with Finkelhor and Asdigian's (1996) concept of target congruence, research suggests that other characteristics are associated with increased risk for school-based victimization. A recent meta-analysis, for example, reported a moderate effect of LGBTQ identification on school-based victimization (Myers, Turanovic, Lloyd, and Pratt, 2020). Additionally, school victimization risk was higher among transgender students relative to other LGBTQ students, LGBTQ students were at greater risk for crimes motivated by homophobia than general bullying, and the relationship between LGBTQ identification and school victimization was stronger among students in the western United States. Data from the Special Education Elementary Longitudinal Study and the National Longitudinal Transition Study-2 indicate the rate of bullying victimization among students with disabilities is higher than the national rates of bullying for students without disabilities (Blak, Lunch, Zhou, Kowk, and Benz, 2012). Once bullying begins, repeated victimization is more likely among students with disabilities. Students with disabilities such as emotional disturbance, autism spectrum disorders, orthopedic impairment, and other health impairments are especially at risk.

In sum, there is evidence to suggest that some student characteristics are associated with increased risk of school-based victimization. Many of these effects are consistent with an opportunity perspective that identifies lifestyle-routine activities and target congruence as important concepts for understanding victimization risk. That said, it is difficult in many cases to empirically identify the one or more mechanisms by which some of these characteristics influence risk.

Summary

As the above review indicates, researchers analyzing data from several different sources have generally found support for variables consistent with concepts from lifestyle-routine activities, target congruence, low self-control, and other forms of criminal propensity that are used to explain adolescent school-based victimization. In addition, several of the RSVP studies cited above noted differences in effects by gender and crime type. Given that these studies relied on a single data source, we are cautious about drawing firm conclusions about how these theoretical mechanisms may operate differently based on crime type and gender—or race and ethnicity, for that matter—without evidence from multiple data sources.[4]

---

4. As noted in Chapter 4, a recent meta-analysis by Turanovic et al. (2019) examines correlates of school violence, including student violent victimization. Among the individual correlates for violent victimization at school, Turanovic et al. (2019) report positive effects for prior victimization, peer rejection, sex (male), antisocial behavior, LGBT status, and deviant peers. In contrast, social competence, bonds to school, school performance, self-control, and age were negatively associated with violent victimization. The scope of the meta-analysis is not directly comparable with this book, as the former focuses on students as young as kindergarten age, includes data collected from both international and American samples, and assesses effect sizes from bivariate relationships. In contrast, our review considers evidence from multivariate analyses focused on middle-school- and high-school-aged students in U.S. schools.

The Threat of Victimization: Perceptions of Risk, Feelings of Fear, and Constrained Behaviors

In addition to direct experiences of victimization, students differ in assessments of their risk of future victimization, in feelings of fear about crime at school, and in precautionary behaviors taken to limit victimization risk faced at school. Rader (2004) argues the threat of victimization manifests in three distinct components (see Figure 5.6 below). The first is a cognitive component involving one's subjective perceptions of risk or their assessment about the likelihood of victimization (see also Ferraro and LaGrange, 1987). A student may assess, for example, that the risk of having property stolen at school is greater than the risk of a school shooting. The second is an emotive component, which describes one's fear or worry about crime. Students may feel fearful, for example, about the possibility of a school shooting after hearing about several such cases in the media. The third component is behavioral and describes constrained behaviors that people take or avoid to protect themselves from the threat of victimization. Students may avoid certain areas of the school property unsupervised by school officials, or skip school entirely to avoid victimization.

Figure 5.7 presents the prevalence of student fear and avoidant behaviors over time among U.S. students ages 12–18. The percentage of students who reported being afraid of attack or harm has declined over the past two decades, from 11.8% in 1995 to 3.3% in 2015, with a slight increase to 4.2% in 2017. This trend mirrors changes in the prevalence of actual school-based victimization (see Figure 5.1 above), which fell from 9.1% in 1995 to 2.2% in 2017. As for avoidant behaviors, students were more likely to report avoiding places in school because of fear of attack or harm than avoiding school ac-

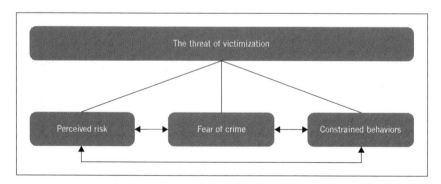

Figure 5.6 The three components of threat of victimization

(Adapted from N. Rader [2004]. The threat of victimization: A theoretical reconceptualization of fear of crime. *Sociological Spectrum, 24,* 689–704.)

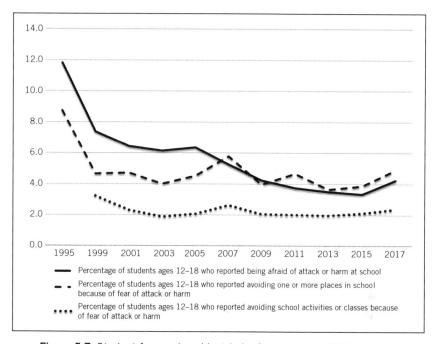

Figure 5.7 Student fear and avoidant behaviors at school (1995–2017)
(U.S. Department of Justice, Bureau of Justice Statistics, School Crime Supplement [SCS] to the National Crime Victimization Survey, 1995 through 2017.)

tivities or classes altogether. In 2017, 4.9% of students avoided one or more places in school, compared to 2.4% of students who avoided school activities or classes because of fear of attack or harm.

Understanding Perceptions of Risk and Fear of Crime

What shapes students' cognitive perceptions of risk for school-based victimization? And what causes feelings of fear at school? Researchers studying perceived risk and fear of crime often rely on a risk assessment framework to answer these questions. This framework suggests that a range of environmental and personal characteristics influence subjective cognitive assessment of one's risk for victimization, which in turn influences fear of crime (Ferraro, 1995). Perceived risk for victimization is informed by the same factors thought to create criminal opportunity: motivated offenders, suitable targets, and lack of guardianship (Melde and Esbensen, 2009). In other words, individuals develop cognitive perceptions of risk by taking stock of their environment, prior experiences, behaviors, and personal characteristics to assess their exposure to motivated offenders, their vulnerability as a suitable target, and the availability of guardianship to protect them. In their assessments, students may include the school environment and various security measures, past personal and vicarious victimization experiences, their own risky routine activities, and relationships with teachers and peers.

Researchers use a variety of data sources to understand students' thoughts and feelings about school crime. The NCVS-SCS asks students "How often are you afraid that someone will attack or harm you on the way to and from school?" This allows researchers to examine the correlates of students' fear of crime, or what Rader (2004) refers to as the emotive component. Although the NCVS-SCS does not directly measure cognitive perceptions of risk, findings from studies using it suggest that fear of crime has associations with factors that presumably could elevate students' perception of victimization risk. Alvarez and Bachman (1997), for example, reported that prior victimization, gang presence at school, violence against teachers, and the availability of illicit substances are associated with increased fear among students. Conversely, the presence of empathetic adults at school—whom students may consider guardians against victimization—can reduce fear of crime in school (Gutt and Randa, 2014). Experiences online can also shape students' emotional fear and worry at school. Randa (2013) found that students who experienced cyberbullying reported significantly higher levels of fear of victimization at school.

Although some evidence indicates that students' fear of crime *levels* does not vary significantly by race or gender (Alvarez and Bachman, 1997), the effects that some *predictors* have on fear of crime at school do vary by race. For example, the presence of security guards was associated with higher levels of fear among White students, but not African American students (Bachman, Randolph, and Brown, 2011). Data from the ELS:2002 suggest that race and ethnicity should be examined in combination with immigrant generational status, as first-generation Latino students were significantly more likely to believe their school is unsafe (Peguero, 2009). Research using data collected from students in a single state suggest there may be additional nuanced race and gender effects, with potential regional variation:

- May and Dunaway (2000) analyzed data from 742 high-school students from a southeastern U.S. state and report that Black male students were more fearful than White male students, but that no significant racial differences were observed among female students. Moreover, prior victimization was associated with fear of crime for female students, but not male students.
- Wallace and May (2005) used data from 2,136 public-school students from a rural southern state to examine the impact of parental attachment and feelings of isolation on adolescent fear of crime

at school. They found that students who had been previously victimized, lower levels of attachments to parents, and higher levels of isolation were more fearful. The effect of attachment to parents was stronger among male students, while the effect of isolation was stronger among White students.

Researchers have also explored whether high-profile events such as school shootings increase student fear of crime. Addington (2003) analyzed NCVS-SCS data to examine whether fear of victimization at school changed post-Columbine. Students were only slightly more fearful following the Columbine school shooting, with 3.8% more students reporting fear at school; most students (77%) were not fearful at school. Addington (2003) suggests students may adapt to reduce fear, assessing as low their risk for homicide at school and perceiving victims of school shootings as distant from themselves. While there have been a number of high-profile school shootings since Columbine, the data reported in Figure 5.7 above suggests that fear of crime at school has generally declined in the past two decades. Indeed, analyzing statewide survey data collected from high-school students in a single state, Fisher, Nation, Nixon, and McIlroy (2017) found no significant effect of the 2012 Sandy Hook school shooting on students' feelings of safety at school.

The RSVP is another useful data source for understanding students' subjective experiences with school crime. Not only does the RSVP ask students about how often they are afraid of or worried about experiencing specific forms of victimization in the current school year, it also asks about perceptions of risk, or the chance that they will experience specific forms of victimization while at school. Crime types include assault, robbery, theft, sexual harassment, sexual assault, and having a gun or other weapon pulled. The fear of crime questions asks students how often they are afraid or worried they will experience a specific form of victimization in the current school year, with responses ranging from never (1) to always (5). The perceived risk questions ask students what the chance is that they will experience a specific form of victimization in the current school year, with responses ranging from very low (1) to very high (5). The RSVP also asks students about the number of times they actually experienced these crime types as victims in the current school year. Figure 5.8 below displays students' mean scores on crime-specific fear, perceived risk, and victimization measures.

The crime-type specific data reveal that students' actual victimization experiences vary considerably by crime type, as do their perceptions of risk and feelings of fear. As Wilcox, Campbell Augustine, Bryan, and Roberts (2005, p. 22) report, "More serious acts of violence, including robbery and weapon/gun threats, receive a lot of attention from the media, concerned parents, and responsive administrators, yet they appear to comprise the smallest school-

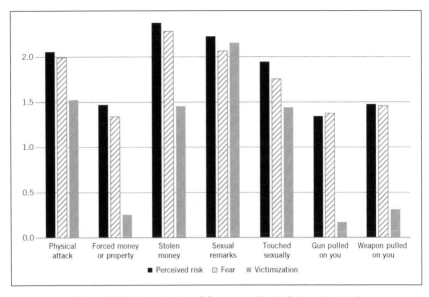

Figure 5.8 Mean levels of fear, perceived risk, and actual
victimization among students in the RSVP
(Rural Substance abuse and Violence Project)

crime problem *in terms of both objective and subjective experiences."* Rather, students report feeling most at risk and fearful of less serious, but more common, forms of victimization, such as theft, unwelcome sexual remarks, and physical attacks in the form of punching, shoving, or kicking. Multivariate analyses predicting students' perceived risk and fear of victimization suggest that these subjective experiences appear to be rational: prior victimization is consistently associated with increased perceived risk, and both prior victimization and perceived risk are related to heightened levels of fear (Wilcox et al., 2005; see also Gialopsos, 2011, and Tillyer et al., 2011). Moreover, Wilcox et al. (2005) found substantial "crossover" effects whereby victimization of one crime type increased students' perceived risk for, and fear of, other crime types. For example, those who experienced physical attack victimization had significantly higher perceived risk for and fear of physical attack, as well as theft and unwelcome sexual remarks.

Studies analyzing RSVP data also provide some support for the idea that opportunities for victimization (i.e., target vulnerability and lifestyle/routine activities) shape students' perception of risk for and fear of victimization at school. For example, male students and students with stronger peer attachments have significantly lower perceptions of risk and fear for both sexual and nonsexual victimization in school, while students with lower levels of self-control have higher levels of risk and fear (see Gialopsos, 2011; Til-

Iyer et al., 2011). Involvement in delinquent activities and access to illegal items at school are also associated with greater perceived risk among students (Gialopsos, 2011; Tillyer et al., 2011). Students who attend schools with high rates of delinquency report higher perceptions of risk (Tillyer et al., 2011), while those who attend schools where teachers intervene to stop violence report lower perceptions of risk (Gialopsos, 2011).

That said, there is also evidence from the RSVP and other data sources that students' perceptions of risk and feelings of fear may not always align with actual risk factors. Though peer delinquency was associated with increased risk for actual victimization, it was not directly related to perceived risk. Moreover, students who reported associating with delinquent peers reported significantly *lower* levels of fear (Tillyer et al., 2011). Melde and Esbensen (2009) found similar effects in an analysis of longitudinal data from students in grades 6 through 9 from 15 schools across 9 cities in the United States. Delinquent lifestyle—a measure including minor delinquency, serious delinquency, substance use, and peer delinquency—significantly increased school-based victimization, but it did not directly influence perceptions of risk, and it was negatively associated with fear of victimization at school. As Melde (2009) notes, adolescents may view victimization risk as deterministic, rather than a result of their own behavior, making it important for prevention efforts to clearly communicate factors increasing risk for school-based victimization.

Finally, findings on the effects of school security practices—such as metal detectors, security guards, locker checks, and so forth—on students' perceptions of risk and feelings of fear at school are mixed. Research using the RSVP data provides little support that such measures are significantly related to students' perceptions of risk and fear of serious violence at school. Police presence, metal detectors, locker checks, and backpack and book bag bans were all unrelated to students' perception of risk, and only metal detectors were significantly associated with lower levels of fear of crime (Tillyer et al., 2011).

Other studies report security measures have deleterious effects, increasing perceptions of risk and making students feel more fearful. For example, Mowen and Freng (2019) analyzed data from the ELS:2002 and found more school security was associated with lower perceptions of safety. Specifically, they measured school security by counting up to 15 potential security measures implemented by a school (e.g., controlled access to the building, metal detectors, security cameras to monitor students, paid security officers, etc.). Greater numbers of security measures were associated with *lower* perceptions of safety among parents and students. Perumean-Chaney and Sutton's (2013) analysis of the National Longitudinal Study of Adolescent to Adult Health (Add Health) suggests similar results; students felt *less* safe in schools with metal detectors and more visible security measures. Data from the 1993 NHES-School Safety and Discipline Component (SSD) suggest students are significantly *more* likely to worry about some forms of crime at school when various forms of school security—such as metal detectors, locked doors, restroom limits, hallway supervision, and drug education—are in place (Schreck and Miller, 2003). Other practices, including the use of guards, visitor sign-ins, locker checks, and hall passes, were unrelated to student worrying (Schreck and Miller, 2003). Bachman et al. (2011), analyzing NCVS-SCS data from 2005, report that metal detectors were associated with an increased fear of crime at school; the presence of guards increased fear among White students only. The presence of cameras and locked doors were unrelated to student fear.

In contrast, a recent study by Connell (2018) indicated that safety measures reassure students and promote feelings of safety. Using data collected from students across 10 high schools in a mid-Atlantic state in 2008–2010, Connell finds that students who are aware of more safety protocols at school—including supervised hallways, locked doors during the day, locker checks, badge requirements, visitor sign in, security cameras, and a student code of conduct—reported feeling significantly safer. What accounts for the divergent findings on school security measures? Inferring causality from such studies is tenuous, as security measures are not randomly assigned to schools and may be implemented in response to existing crime problems in a school. Moreover, how students think and feel about security measures may vary across contexts and time. Connell (2018) argues that student perceptions of school security measures may have changed in recent decades due to increased awareness of bullying, school shootings, and so on. Many of the studies reviewed above rely on data collected in the 1990s and early 2000s. In the last couple of decades, as students became sensitized to the need to focus on school safety, the presence of security measures may have gained greater acceptance.

Constrained Behaviors

Students may change their behaviors in response to the threat of victimization at school. Numerous studies analyzing the NCVS-SCS data have examined how objective and subjective student experiences with victimization relate to avoidance behaviors in the form of staying home, skipping classes, or avoiding certain places at school. Several studies show bullying victimization is positively associated with staying home or skipping classes to avoid attack or harm (e.g., Howard, 2019; Randa and Reyns, 2014; Randa and Wilcox, 2010), as well as with place-specific avoidant behaviors (DeVoe, 2007; Hutzell and Payne, 2012; Randa and Wilcox, 2010). Experiencing cyberbullying online is also associated with avoidance behaviors (Randa and

Reyns, 2014).[5] Beyond these objective victimization experiences, students' perceptions of gangs at school increased general and place-specific school avoidance (Howard, 2019; Randa and Wilcox, 2010). Finally, fear of victimization is associated with both general and place-specific avoidant behaviors among students (Barrett, Jennings, and Lynch, 2012; Howard, 2019; Randa and Reyns, 2014; Randa and Wilcox, 2010).

Studies examining how avoidant behaviors changed among students following the Columbine school shooting reveal mixed findings. Addington's (2003) study using data from the NCVS-SCS found no significant changes in students' avoidance of school entrances, hallways, cafeterias, restrooms, parking lots, or other areas at school or on school grounds. However, data from the YRBSS suggest that there were general avoidance effects following Columbine: students who completed the 1999 survey *after* the Columbine incident were significantly more likely to report missing school because of feeling unsafe during the 30 days preceding the survey compared to those who completed the survey *before* the Columbine incident (10.2% compared to 3.9%) (Brener et al., 2002).

In Chapter 4, we reviewed the literature on a range of delinquent behaviors at school, including the carrying of weapons by students. Here, we revisit student weapon carrying as a possible reaction to the threat of victimization at school. Data from the NCVS-SCS indicate that students who reported bullying victimization were significantly more likely to report weapon carrying at school (DeVoe, 2007). May's (1999) analysis of data from approximately 8,000 public high-school students from a southeastern state reports that even when accounting for differential association and social control explanations for weapon carrying, fear of criminal victimization is related to gun carrying at school. Meyer-Adams and Connor (2008), analyzing data collected from middle-school students in Philadelphia public schools, found that both bullying perpetration and victimization are associated with students reporting more negative psychosocial school environments, which in turn is related to student weapon carrying. That said, these studies relied on cross-sectional data, making causal order uncertain. Wilcox, May, and Roberts (2006) analyzed longitudinal data from the RSVP and found little evidence that prior victimization and fear of crime at school increased subsequent weapon carrying among students. Moreover, perceptions of risk were

---

5. Studies focusing on single school districts also confirm that bullying victimization is associated with avoidant behaviors. For example, data analyzed from the School Culture, Climate, and Violence: Safety in Middle Schools of the Philadelphia Public School System found that bullying victimization is associated with students reporting more negative psychosocial school environments, which in turn was associated with avoidance (Meyer-Adams and Connor, 2008).

negatively associated with subsequent weapon carrying. Alternatively, they found that weapon carrying (both guns and other weapons) was associated with *increases* in subsequent victimization, fear, and perceived risk. They surmised that weapon carrying may embolden students to engage in riskier activities than they otherwise would, thus increasing criminal opportunity and their objective and subjective experiences with crime.

Conclusion

This chapter highlighted the "victim" side of the problem analysis triangle, guided by the premise that understanding student victimization can provide additional avenues for school crime prevention beyond tackling student motivation to offend. The empirical research on school-based victimization among adolescents in the United States reveals a multidimensional portrait of students' experiences. The majority of nonfatal criminal victimizations experienced by adolescents ages 12–18 in the United States occurs at school, making it the primary context in which to consider adolescent victimization. Yet, data from the NCVS-SCS indicates that school-based criminal victimization has been trending down for over two decades, with prevalence rates as low as 2.2% among students ages 12–18 in recent years. While relatively few students experience serious victimization at school, those who are victimized are at heightened risk for repeated victimization. Data from the RSVP reveal that all forms of serious victimization are highly concentrated among relatively few students who may experience cumulative consequences. Indeed, the victimized are at risk for a range of harmful consequences, including subsequent fear of crime while at school, increased perceptions of risk, and school avoidance.

Given the range of deleterious outcomes associated with adolescent victimization, what should guide its prevention? First, efforts should target the subpopulation of students who suffer repeatedly, from both the actual victimization experiences and the subsequent consequences. As victimization scholars have long noted, focusing on individuals previously victimized is an efficient and humane way to allocate crime prevention resources. One barrier to this approach, however, is the low reporting rates by students to school officials. Data from the NCVS-SCS indicate that less than 40% of students who are bullied at school report the bullying to an adult (Lessne and Harmalkar, 2013). Campaigns to encourage disclosure of student victimization to a trusted adult, coupled with messaging that an initial victimization may lead to repeated attacks if left unaddressed, may be a necessary first step for effective intervention (Tillyer et al., 2018).

Second, research on the correlates of school-based victimization among students is largely consistent with an opportunity framework that identifies the importance of lifestyle-routine activities, target congruence, low self-control, and other forms of criminal propensity in creating victimization risk. In short, victimization risk is not random but rather is a function of a range of risk and protective factors that should inform the development of interventions. Far from victim blaming, we must view victimization—especially repeat victimization—through a lens of criminal opportunity and make efforts to enhance protective factors and mitigate risk factors for students. We provide further discussion and evaluation of some school-based approaches to the prevention of victimization in Chapter 8.

6

Double Trouble

The Victim-Offender Overlap among Students

C riminologists observe a small number of empirical relationships with such regularity they become accepted facts. The most famous example is the curvilinear relationship between age and crime. Referred to as the age-crime curve, rates of crime generally increase with age beginning around the onset of adolescence, peak in later adolescence/early adulthood, and decline from the middle twenties onward (Hirschi and Gottfredson, 1983). Increasingly, the correlation between victimization and offending—that is, the victim-offender overlap—is also becoming an accepted empirical fact in criminology. Wolfgang's (1958) famous study of homicide cases in Philadelphia, Pennsylvania, provided one of the earlier recognitions of the victim-offender overlap. In his analysis, Wolfgang observed that homicide victims and homicide offenders were similar in terms of their demographic and social class profiles. Moreover, he noted many of the homicide victims in his study also had arrest records for serious crimes. This suggested the victim-offender overlap was more than just a coincidence wherein the populations of victims and offenders had similar sociodemographic characteristics. Rather, it indicated that in many cases "victim" and "offender" roles coincide within the same people.

Although scholars have documented the existence of the victim-offender overlap for many decades (Gottfredson, 1984; Lauritsen and Laub, 2007; Reiss, 1981; Wolfgang, 1958), research aiming to explain the phenomena has been relatively sparse. This is changing in recent years with a growing research literature seeking understanding of mechanisms underlying the association between victimization and offending (for detailed review, see Berg and Mulford, 2020). Despite the growing interest, studies of the victim-offender overlap within schools is in short supply. This is unfortunate because schools bring together large numbers of adolescents in settings that can be conducive for the co-occurrence of victimization and offending. Thus, they are fertile ground for research aimed at better understanding the victim-offender overlap; schools provide an arena where the knowledge gained can be directly applied toward crime prevention efforts.

In Chapters 4 and 5, we discussed research examining patterns and explanations of delinquent offending and victimization in schools, respectively. In this chapter, we discuss their overlap. To explore research on the victim-offender overlap in schools, we organize the chapter as follows. In the next section, we present data on the victim-offender overlap in schools using both national-level data from the National Crime Victimization Survey-School Crime Supplement (NCVS-SCS) and subnational data from the Rural Substance abuse and Violence Project (RSVP). We follow that by outlining potential explanations of the victim-offender overlap. Finally, we review school-based studies that examine the victim-offender overlap and investigate the validity of those explanations.

Evidence of the Victim-Offender Overlap in School Crime Data

The Victim-Offender Overlap in the NCVS-SCS

National data on the victim-offender overlap within schools is sparse, but the NCVS-SCS provides some information on the matter. In general, it confirms the relationship between victimization and offending among students in schools. According to a report by Yanez and Lessne (2018), an estimated 97.3% of students were not victims of crime at school, while 2.7% experienced criminal victimization at school during the preceding six months. Importantly, the prevalence of fighting in school is considerably higher for crime victims than for nonvictims. As seen in Table 6.1, only 2.7% of nonvictims reported engaging in any physical fights at school. In contrast, the percentage multiplies fivefold to 13.7% among students reporting any crime victimization. Yanez and Lessne's (2018) report further suggests that risks of involvement in fighting vary by type of crime victimization. Specifically, while only 6.2% of theft victims were involved in physical fighting at school, 30.9% of violent crime victims reported involvement in fighting.[1]

---

1. Violent crime refers to rape, sexual assault, robbery, aggravated assault, and simple assault. Theft includes purse snatching, pickpocketing, and other thefts excluding motor vehicle theft.

TABLE 6.1 PERCENTAGE OF STUDENTS AGES 12–18 REPORTING PHYSICAL FIGHTING AT SCHOOL, BY REPORTED CRIMINAL VICTIMIZATION EXPERIENCES AT SCHOOL, NCVS-SCS DATA 2014–2015

	No victimization (%)	Any victimization (%)	Theft victimization (%)	Violent victimization (%)
Engaged in physical fight(s) at school	2.7	13.7	6.2	30.9

Source: Yanez and Lessne (2018).

A recent study by Kurpiel (2020) analyzes NCVS-SCS data from 1999 through 2015. It investigates the connection between criminal victimization at school and two delinquency measures: (1) fighting at school and (2) weapon carrying at school. With regard to fighting, Kurpiel's analysis shows that criminal victimization in school—including rape, robbery, assault, and theft—is associated with increased risk of involvement in fighting at school. Table 6.2 shows that among students reporting any criminal victimization at school, 16.2% reported engaging in physical fighting, compared to only 4.3% of those experiencing no criminal victimization. Moreover, the risk of fighting is higher among repeated victims: 28.2% of students experiencing multiple victimizations at school reported engaging in fighting, compared to 14.4% of students with a single victimization at school. Weapon carrying at school also varied by victimization experiences. Among nonvictims, 1.7% reported carrying a weapon at school, while among victimized students, 2.6% carried a weapon at school. The prevalence of weapon carrying increased further among students who experienced multiple victimizations at school (3.7%) relative to those who experienced a single victimization at school (2.5%).

The Victim-Offender Overlap in the RSVP

While the NCVS-SCS provides valuable national-level information on the victim-offender overlap, it measures delinquent offending with the two items, fighting and weapon carrying, noted above. RSVP data from students in middle and high schools in Kentucky permit further exploration of the victim-offender overlap across several specific types of school-based crimes. As reported in Table 6.3, we used these data to categorize the percentage of students falling into four different groups—victim only, offender only, victim and offender, and nonvictim/non-offender (i.e., no involvement)—based on their experiences with four school-based crimes (physical assault, robbery, theft, and sexual assault). For each offense category, the majority of

TABLE 6.2 PERCENTAGE OF STUDENTS AGES 12–18 REPORTING PHYSICAL FIGHTING AND WEAPON CARRYING AT SCHOOL, BY REPORTED CRIMINAL VICTIMIZATION EXPERIENCES AT SCHOOL, NCVS-SCS DATA 1999–2015

	No victimization (%)	Any school victimization (%)	One school victimization (%)	Multiple school victimizations (%)
Physical fighting	4.3	16.2	14.4	28.2
Weapon carrying	1.7	2.6	2.5	3.7

Source: Adapted from Kurpiel (2020).

TABLE 6.3 PERCENTAGE OF STUDENTS IN VICTIM AND OFFENDER CATEGORIES BY CRIME TYPE

	No involvement (%)	Victim only (%)	Offender only (%)	Victim-offender (%)
Physical assault	58.4	25.9	3.4	12.3
Robbery	91.1	6.1	1.7	1.0
Theft	50.9	43.0	1.5	4.6
Sexual assault	66.8	26.8	2.4	4.0

Source: Rural Substance abuse and Violence Project.

student respondents were not involved in crime incidents, though percentages falling into this category varied notably by crime type. On the low end, just over one-half reported no involvement in theft, whereas on the high end, over 90% reported no involvement in robbery. Of the three "crime-involved" categories, the most common role is "victim only," which ranges from 6.1% for robbery to 43% for theft. The "victim-offender" category is next-most common for all crime types except robbery. It ranges from 1% for robbery to 12.3% for physical assault. Finally, the "offender only" category is least common for physical assault, theft, and sexual assault. The percentage of students falling into this category ranges from a low of 1.5% for theft to a high of 3.4% for physical assault.

Exploring the overlap between victimization and offending further, we considered differences in the likelihood of school-based delinquent offending between students who were nonvictims and victims of school crime. Figure 6.1 shows the results. For all crime types, students experiencing criminal victimization were more likely to be offenders than students who were nonvictims. For physical assault, the percentage of victims who also committed assault in school (32.2%) is nearly six times the percentage of nonvictims who committed assault (5.5%). For robbery, the disparity is even greater,

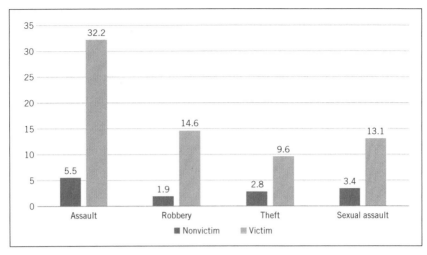

Figure 6.1 Percentage of students committing physical assault, robbery, theft, or sexual assault at school, by school victimization experience
(Rural Substance abuse and Violence Project)

with the percentage of robbery victims committing a robbery (14.6%) nearly eight times the percentage of nonvictims who committed a robbery (1.9%). For theft and sexual assault categories, students who were victims were more than three times as likely to be delinquent offenders as students who were nonvictims.

Figure 6.2 shows differences in the likelihood that students experienced a school-based victimization based on whether or not they were delinquent offenders. Among students who reported committing a physical assault, 78.5% also reported being a physical assault victim at school. In contrast, the percentage of non-offenders indicating that they endured a physical assault victimization in school (30.7%) is less than half of that for offenders. For robbery, students who were offenders were nearly six times as likely to have been robbery victims (37.7%) at school as were non-offenders (6.3%). Lastly, for theft and sexual assault, students who committed those offenses were 1.65 (75.5% vs. 45.8%) and 2.21 (63.1% vs. 28.6%) times, respectively, as likely to be victims.

In sum, both national-level data from the NCVS-SCS and state-level data from the RSVP study of Kentucky schools provide evidence of the victim-offender overlap. While the overall share of students who reported both offending and victimization at school is relatively small, victims were much more likely to commit acts of delinquency at school than nonvictims were. Likewise, those who committed delinquent offenses at school were far more likely to be crime victims than those who refrained from delinquency.

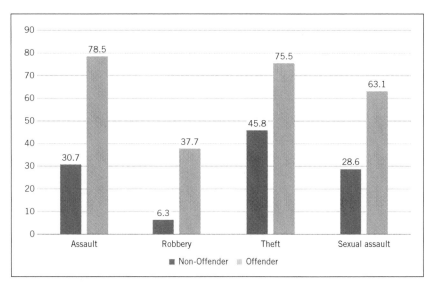

Figure 6.2 Percentage of students experiencing physical assault, robbery, theft, or sexual assault victimization at school, by school offending experience
(Rural Substance abuse and Violence Project)

Thus, these data confirm the victim-offender overlap is a phenomenon highly relevant in the study of school crime. The question needing explanation is why does the overlap exist? In the sections to follow, we discuss criminological efforts to address this question. We begin by briefly describing some alternative explanations developed by criminologists to explain the victim-offender overlap. Next, we review the small but developing body of empirical research evaluating potential explanations of the victim-offender overlap in schools.

Explaining the Victim-Offender Overlap in Schools: Two Frameworks

In the decades following Wolfgang's initial observations of the victim-offender overlap, criminologists have called for the development of theoretical and research efforts aimed at explaining the etiology of the victim-offender overlap (Gottfredson, 1984; Lauritsen and Laub, 2007). In their review of this literature more than a decade ago, Lauritsen and Laub (2007) noted that the victim-offender-overlap literature had stalled because it posited few novel theoretical or empirical insights explaining the victimization-offending correlation. Since that assessment, research interest in the victim-offender overlap has grown notably, and two types of explanations, *causal* and *noncausal*, have emerged in efforts to understand the victim-offender overlap.

Causal Explanation Framework

Causal explanations claim that victimization and offending cause each other. The mechanics of this can vary, however. Some explanations assert that victimization is the cause of subsequent offending, others contend that offending causes subsequent victimization, and still others posit reciprocal causal effects between victimization and offending. Generally, these arguments all *make assertions that the causal impact of victimization (offending) on offending (victimization) operates indirectly via the changes in cognition, emotion, or social relationships* that they produce. Figure 6.3 depicts the genesis of the victim-offender overlap as proffered by the causal explanation framework.

Numerous crime theories suggest mechanisms by which criminal victimization and offending causally affect each other. General strain theory is one such theory. To illustrate its argument, imagine a scenario in which two teenage students, John and Roy, are playing a game of one-on-one basketball in gym class. John is beating Roy badly at the game and incessantly "trash talks" about his awesomeness and Roy's lack of basketball skills. When Roy tells John to stop the trash talking, John slams him against the wall and punches him in the stomach. Several others in the class laugh at Roy, who doubles over in pain. The gym teacher quickly stops the skirmish and checks that Roy

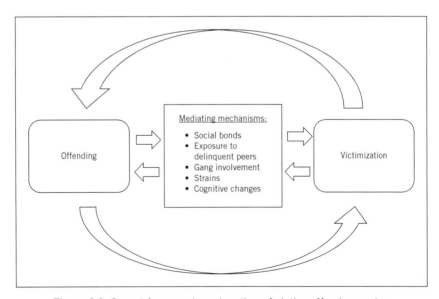

Figure 6.3 Causal framework explanation of victim-offender overlap

is not seriously hurt but does not discipline John for his actions. Roy is angered and embarrassed by the events. He wants to get even. Later in the week, he waits in a corridor off the main school hallway. When John walks past, he jumps out and attacks him, landing several punches to John's face, bloodying his nose and knocking him down. Roy spits on John and walks away, leaving him bleeding and dazed on the hallway floor.

General strain theory explains that Roy's victimization experience causes his delinquent behavior. His victimization is a "strain," a significant and unwarranted aversive experience that arouses intense negative emotions. Roy copes with those emotions through delinquent behavior, a retaliatory assault on John. Meanwhile, John's offending behavior—the initial assault of Roy—is the cause of his subsequent assault victimization. By creating a strain for Roy, John's delinquent offending increased his own subsequent victimization risk.

Cycles of retaliatory violence neatly illustrate how the victim-offender overlap results from reciprocal, dynamic causal sequences whereby violent victimization causes subsequent violent offending, and offending causes subsequent victimization. Yet, many other examples are imaginable and explained via other theoretical traditions in criminology. For instance, imagine that in the preceding scenario, Roy does not retaliate against John but is upset that classmates laughed at him. He loses trust in others and withdraws socially from his friendship network. Increasingly isolated from others, his behavior becomes bizarre. Former friends and classmates start viewing him as strange. They exclude him from activities and he sits by himself at lunch. At home, Roy disengages from his family relationships, and his parents have difficult, contentious communications with him. His behavior becomes increasingly unpredictable, and one day he steals a small bottle of his dad's whiskey and grabs his hunting knife, taking both to school. In between his morning classes, he drinks the whiskey in the bathroom. When two other students walk into the bathroom and see him drinking, he flashes his knife and threatens to cut them if they say anything about what he is doing. An hour later, all the whiskey is gone and Roy is unconscious on the floor of a bathroom stall. Max walks in, sees Roy lying there with an empty liquor bottle beside him. Seizing on the opportunity, Max checks Roy's wallet and finds 20 dollars, which he takes. He then leaves the bathroom and reports the scene to his teacher, who quickly responds to the situation.

Social bond theory instructs us that Roy's experience of victimization causes his delinquent offending by weakening his sense of trust in, and bonds to, significant others. Without those relationships providing important guardrails, he drifts toward destructive behavior. Ultimately, he breaks not only the school rules but also legal codes, committing several delinquent offenses in the school setting. Moreover, his delinquent behavior exposes him to additional victimization. His drunkenness exposes him to the thievery of a fellow student.

While these vignettes are fictional, they illustrate how causal connections between victimization and offending may operate via mechanisms specified in two prominent criminological theories. They illustrate potential causal explanations of the victim-offender overlap but are far from exhaustive. Numerous additional examples drawing on other theoretical traditions are plausible.

Noncausal Explanation Framework

As an alternative to causal explanations of the victim-offender overlap, *noncausal explanations* suggest that the association between victimization and offending is spurious. This means that offending is not the cause of victimization and/or vice versa. Rather, victimization and offending vary together (i.e., are correlated), because both are caused by a "third" variable (or set of variables). This third variable is often a background variable specific to individuals (e.g., personality traits) or social environments (e.g., high levels of community economic disadvantage) determined well prior to the occurrence of victimization or offending. Figure 6.4 depicts the victim-offender overlap as imagined by the noncausal framework.

Gottfredson and Hirschi's (1990) self-control theory—introduced in Chapter 2 and linked to student offending and victimization in Chapters 4 and 5, respectively—is an instructive example of the high-risk-personality-trait version of the noncausal framework. Due to inadequate socialization and the lack of sanctioning of wrongdoing in early childhood, some individuals develop little self-control. As a result, they behave impulsively to attain short-term pleasures, with little consideration given to potentially del-

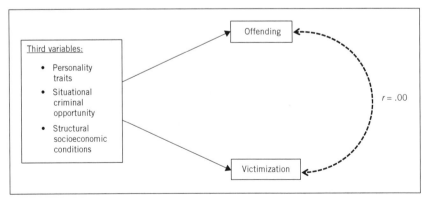

Figure 6.4 Noncausal framework for explaining victim-offender overlap

eterious longer-term consequences of their actions. Criminal opportunities are fleeting opportunities for immediate gain, carried out by taking advantage of others' vulnerabilities. Individuals with low self-control are especially attracted to and unrestrained from such opportunities. Indeed, a large body of research reports that low self-control is predictive of many types of criminal offending (Hay and Meldrum, 2016; Pratt and Cullen, 2000). But the same trait that makes an individual more likely to respond to a criminal opportunity—low self-control—is also likely to make an individual behave in risky ways. Research indicates that individuals with low self-control tend to be at greater risk for many "dangers." They are more prone to accidents (DeRidder, Lensvelt-Mulders, Finkenauer, Stok, and Baumeister, 2012), early mortality (Kern and Friedman, 2008), risky financial moves (Reisig, Pratt, and Holtfreter, 2009), and, most pertinent for our work, are more likely to become crime victims than individuals with high self-control (Pratt et al., 2014; Schreck, 1999).

Applied to a hypothetical school context, the high-risk-personality-trait version of the noncausal victim-offender overlap goes something like follows. Jane is a high-school student with neglectful parents who rarely supervise her behavior. Because they infrequently corrected or sanctioned misbehavior, she entered school lacking self-control. In elementary school, she was often disruptive in class, not staying seated at her desk and speaking out of turn during instructional time. She was easily distracted and did not like reading books or working to solve math problems. On the playground, she had trouble following game rules and taking turns, causing conflict with other students. In middle and high school, she increasingly got into trouble, fighting with other students and taking things not belonging to her. Her impulsive and selfish behaviors also placed her in situations of high victimization risk. For example, she often skipped out on classes and wandered around unmonitored areas of the school with other students with similar personality traits. Once, another student physically assaulted her after the two exited the lunchroom early and goofed around in an unmonitored auditorium. In sum, Jane's lack of self-control causes her to have higher propensity for both delinquent offending and victimization.

Another noncausal explanation argues that correlations between victimization and offending are a result of exposure to risky environments. Risky environments expose individuals to criminogenic conditions that elevate risks of involvement in crime, both as offenders and victims. Schools experiencing extreme resource deficits, poor supervision by instructional and administrative staff, higher access to illicit goods (e.g., alcohol, drugs, weapons), or physical designs that hinder effective guardianship may set the stage for higher rates of crime. Individuals exposed to these school environments are therefore more likely to offend and be crime victims. Thus, this explanation offers that the correlation between victimization and offending results from school-environment conditions, not because victimization causes offending or vice versa.

Research on the Victim-Offender Overlap in Schools

Research investigating the victim-offender overlap appeared in the early 1990s (Lauritsen et al., 1991) and grew rapidly in the 2000s (Barnes and Beaver, 2012; Berg and Felson, 2020; Berg and Loeber, 2011, 2015; Berg, Stewart, Schreck, and Simons, 2012; Felson, Berg, Rogers, and Krajewski, 2018; Jennings, Higgins, Tewksbury, Gover, and Piquero, 2010; Piquero, MacDonald, Dobrin, Daigle, and Cullen, 2005; Reisig and Holtfreter, 2018; Schreck, Stewart, and Osgood, 2008; Schreck, Berg, Ousey, Stewart, and Miller, 2017; Tillyer and Wright, 2014; Zavala and Spohn, 2013; Zaykowski and Gunter, 2013). In general, this body of research addresses several issues: (1) whether patterns and predictors of variation in offending and victimization are similar, (2) whether victimization and offending are causally or noncausally related, and (3) whether the causal relationship between victimization and offending, if any, is unidirectional or reciprocal. Much of this work does not focus on school crime, but as we document below, research on the victim-offender overlap in school contexts is gradually expanding.

Is There Similarity in the Predictors of School-Based Victimization and Offending?

One research area on the victim-offender overlap focuses on similarity in patterns and predictors of variation in delinquent offending and victimization. Studies not specific to school settings yield evidence of similarity, with measures of strain, school commitment, parental monitoring, violent peer associations, and self-control found related to both outcomes (Berg et al., 2012; Jennings et al., 2010; Schreck et al., 2008; Zavala and Spohn, 2013). However, research on intimate partner violence (IPV) suggests more nuance, with factors related to IPV victimization differing from those related to IPV perpetration (Tillyer and Wright, 2014). It is unclear whether findings from the preceding studies inform understanding of the victim-offender overlap in school contexts. Several studies using RSVP data partly address this limitation, investigating similarities in victimization and offending among a panel of more than 3,000 students in middle schools and high schools in Kentucky (Sullivan et al., 2016; Wilcox, Sullivan, Jones, and van Gelder, 2014).

Using waves 3 and 4 of the RSVP study, Wilcox et al. (2014) evaluated how measures of individual personality and situational opportunity affected both delinquent behavior (both school and nonschool-based) and criminal victimization experiences in school. They explored if two personality traits (conscientiousness and agreeableness), along with measures of situational opportunity (access to illicit goods, exposure to delinquent peers), affected delinquency and victimization outcomes. Their findings indicated much similarity in the process by which personality and opportunity affect delinquency and victimization, as well as noteworthy differences. In terms of similarity, Wilcox et al. (2014) reported that exposure to delinquent peers and exposure to illicit goods have similar significant and positive associations with both offending and victimization. Moreover, the agreeableness trait has significant negative total effects on offending and victimization, but there are nuances in how those effects play out for each outcome. For offending, the effect comprises two components: a significant direct effect and a significant indirect effect via criminal opportunity measures. For victimization, the total effect operates primarily through the significant indirect effects via criminal opportunity; the direct effect is not significant. In addition, conscientiousness has a significant negative total effect on victimization, but its total effect on offending was not significant. However, for both offending and victimization there is a significant negative indirect effect of conscientiousness operating through exposure to delinquent peers.

Wilcox et al. (2014) also observed differences when examining personality-by-opportunity effects on offending and victimization. For offending, they found evidence of significant interactions. Higher agreeableness and conscientiousness suppressed crime most for individuals experiencing higher criminal opportunity (i.e., greater exposure to illicit good and delinquent peers). In contrast, they found no significant personality-by-opportunity interaction effects for victimization. Finally, Wilcox et al. (2014) reported some differences in the effects of social bonds on offending and victimization. For offending, school bonds had a significant negative effect, but mother bonds and peer bonds were not significant. For victimization, the pattern of significant effects was opposite, with significant negative effects reported for mother bonds and peer bonds, but not for school bonds.

Despite providing useful comparative analyses of predictors of offending and victimization, the Wilcox et al. (2014) study does not consider how individuals' experiences of offending and victimization change over time and what factors might explain those changes. Subsequent research by Sullivan et al. (2016) extends the literature by using all four waves of the RSVP study to examine two central issues in the comparative study of offending and victimization in schools.[2] First, they examined whether offending and

---

2. The measures of victimization in the Sullivan et al. (2016) study refer specifically to victimization on school grounds or at school-related activities. The measures of offending include assault, robbery, and weapon use items both at school and away from school.

victimization exhibited similar patterns of variation in between-person mean scores and within-person growth over time. Second, they examined if observed variation matched patterns predicted by the noncausal or causal victim-offender explanations reviewed earlier.

Findings indicated some similarity in patterns of offending and victimization, but also some divergence. For both victimization and offending, mean levels varied systematically between individuals. However, offending and victimization also differed systematically over time for individuals. One key difference between the victimization and offending outcomes was the direction of growth over time. Whereas levels of offending increased slightly as students moved between 7th and 10th grades, levels of victimization decreased during the same time window. Sullivan et al. (2016) concluded that the observed variations in delinquent offending and victimization provided some support for both the noncausal and causal perspectives on the victim-offender overlap. Specifically, they found that a key personality trait (impulsivity) predicted between-individual variations in offending and victimization. Moreover, changes in delinquent peer associations predicted within-individual over-time variations in offending and victimization.

In sum, extant studies yield initial support to the argument that there are similar patterns of variation in offending and victimization between individuals and over time. There is also evidence that some key predictors have similar effects on victimization and offending in schools (e.g., impulsivity, exposure to delinquent peers). However, the effects of other key correlates on victimization and offending are different (e.g., bonds to school, peers, and mother). Importantly, the number of available studies is small, making clear the need for additional inquiry addressing this "similarity" dimension of the victim-offender overlap.

Does Victimization Cause Offending?

Another important area of investigation on the victim-offender overlap in schools evaluates the nature of the relationship between victimization and offending. This work addresses whether the victimization-offending relationship is causal or noncausal and if it is unidirectional or reciprocal. We begin our discussion of this body of research by reviewing studies investigating the argument that experiencing victimization in school is an important cause of school-based delinquent offending.

Criminal victimization is an unpleasant, traumatic experience. As a result, it is easy to imagine victimization as having many behavioral consequences for individuals. From the perspective of general strain theory, victimization is a severe strain that engenders delinquent behavior as a means of coping with the trauma of victimization. If this theory is valid, the victim-offender overlap, at least in part, is the result of the causal effects of victim-ization experiences on offending.

Research on crime in schools provides general support to the argument that victimization has an effect on offending (Kaynak et al., 2015; Ousey et al., 2015). For example, Ousey, Wilcox, and Schreck (2015) used data from wave 4 of the RSVP study to examine whether experiences with violent vic-timization contributed to a student's involvement in general delinquent of-fending as well as a specific tendency for violent delinquency. Importantly, their analysis also controlled for the impact of impulsivity/low self-control, a salient personality trait that may produce the correlation between victim-ization and offending, according to the noncausal perspective on the vic-tim-offender overlap. Their findings indicated that impulsivity/low self-control is predictive of both overall delinquent behavior as well as a propen-sity for violent delinquency. However, impulsivity does not explain away the association between victimization and offending. Net of the effects of im-pulsivity, students reporting more violent crime victimization at school were significantly more involved in both general and violent delinquency than students without such exposure to violent crime victimization were.

Other research concurs that the victim-offender overlap is not simply the result of personality traits affecting victimization and offending. In their com-parative study of the effects of personality and opportunity on victimization and offending in the RSVP data, Wilcox et al. (2014) estimated the residual correlation between victimization and offending after the effects of personal-ity traits (agreeableness and conscientiousness) and situational crime oppor-tunities (exposure to illicit goods, exposure to delinquent peers) were con-trolled. They found a significant positive association between victimization and offending, suggesting that neither the measures of personality traits nor the measures of situational opportunity explained why students who were vic-tims of crime at school were more involved in delinquent offending in school.

While this literature is sparse, findings are consistent with the thesis that victimization exerts causal influence on offending. However, it is notable that the available evidence comes from studies measuring offending and vic-timization contemporaneously. Hence, temporal ordering of victimization and offending is not possible, which weakens causal claims. Better evalua-tions of this relationship ideally would specify prior victimization as a cause of subsequent offending, while controlling for personality traits, criminal opportunity, and the like.

Does Offending Cause Victimization?

An alternative causal argument reverses the causal sequence noted above, specifying delinquent offending as a cause of criminal victimization in schools.

As noted in our earlier fictional vignette, this relationship may occur for several reasons. For example, an individual who commits offenses may elicit subsequent retaliation. Alternatively, their offending behavior may cause others to pull away, leaving them without the protective cocoon against victimization established by positive social relationships. Numerous other mechanisms linking offending to victimization but not enumerated here are plausible.

Several studies using data from both national- and state-specific samples have examined whether students' delinquent offending is predictive of their school-based victimization experiences. Using national data from the Education Longitudinal Study of 2002 (ELS:2002), Peguero and his colleagues (Pegureo 2013; Peguero et al., 2015) investigated factors related to school-based victimization. Included in these studies were estimates of the effects of school-based misbehavior—a construct combining relatively minor school-rule violations and involvement in physical fighting—on measures of in-school violent crime victimization and property crime victimization. Peguero (2013) found that students involved in school-based misbehavior had significantly more experiences with both violent victimization and property victimization. Likewise, Peguero et al. (2015) reported that students with higher scores on school-based misbehavior had significantly greater odds of violent victimization and property victimization. Of note, both of these studies included controls for both person-specific and context-specific measures of criminal opportunity (school-based routine activities: participation in academic, athletic, and club activities; school size, diversity, and poverty; location in urban/rural area). Consequently, they estimated the effect of offending on victimization while accounting for some of the possible factors that could produce a spurious or noncausal association between victimization and offending. However, noticeably absent are controls for other potential confounding variables, such as low self-control or other personality traits that research shows are associated with both offending and victimization.

Research on RSVP data from students in Kentucky investigated the impact of school-based delinquent behavior on school-based criminal victimization while controlling for salient personality traits, students' routine activities, and/or their exposure to risky situations or guardianship (Wilcox, Tillyer, and Fisher, 2009; Schreck, Ousey, Fisher, and Wilcox, 2012). Pooling all four waves of RSVP data, Wilcox et al. (2009) examined whether students' self-reported criminal behavior was associated with two types of in-school victimization, assault, and theft. Their findings indicated that students with higher levels of delinquent behavior had greater odds of theft and assault victimization. Higher impulsivity, association with delinquent friends, and participation in school sports were also associated with higher odds of both victimization types. Nonetheless, the effect of offending on victimization was significant even accounting for measures of personality, criminal opportunity, and attachment to parents and school. Similarly, in their study investigating the factors related to overall victimization levels as well as latent propensity for violent victimization, Schreck et al.'s (2012) analysis of each wave of the RSVP study yielded a consistent pattern of results. In each wave of data, a measure of the students' self-reported violent behavior had a statistically significant, positive relationship with overall victimization and the propensity for violent victimization. Those findings were net of the impact of impulsivity, school-based guardianship, associations with violent friends, and holding of attitudes associated with a violent subculture. In sum, because these RSVP-based studies estimate the effects of offending on victimization while accounting for several "third variables," they offer support for the causal framework contention that delinquent behavior causes elevated victimization risk.

Interestingly, some research evidence indicates that the victim-offender overlap may vary by demographic characteristics of the study participants. More specifically, Peguero (2013) found that the effects of offending on violent and property victimization were significantly weaker for second-generation immigrants than for nonimmigrants. Peguero et al. (2015) found the effects of school-based delinquency on violent victimization was strongest for White students and significantly weaker for Black, Latino, and Asian American students. The effect of offending on property victimization was similar for White, Black, and Asian American students but significantly lower for Latino students. Using RSVP data, Wilcox et al. (2009) examined whether the correlates of two forms of victimization, assault and theft, had differing effects for female and male students. Controlling for measures of personality and opportunity, they found evidence that self-reported criminal behavior had a positive association with victimization for both gender groups. However, the effects of delinquent offending on school-based assault and theft victimization were significantly greater for females than males. These findings complement research on nonschool samples, which report variability in the victimization-offending association by factors such as age (Schreck et al., 2015), neighborhood disadvantage (Berg and Loeber, 2011), and neighborhood cultural processes (Berg et al., 2012).

Are Victimization and Offending Reciprocal Causes?

In light of the preceding research, it is clear that victim-offender overlap is evident in research on school crime. Moreover, the causal process appears to work in both directions: (1) victimization causes offending, and (2) offending causes victimization. Thus, there is support for the thesis that the relationship between victimization and offending in schools is reciprocal. To date, research has typically focused on just one side of this causal equation, with comparatively few studies attempting to estimate bidirectional effects. However, two studies using RSVP data investigate bidirectional or reciprocal effects between victimization and offending in schools.

In their study of causal process by which student weapon carrying is linked to other school-crime experiences such as victimization and fear of crime, Wilcox, May, and Roberts (2006) specified structural equation models that estimated the effects of wave-1 victimization on two measures of subsequent offending: wave-2 weapon carrying and wave-3 general delinquent offending. Their findings indicated that wave-1 victimization had a significant positive effect on both wave-2 non-gun-weapon carrying and wave-3 general delinquent offending. Wave-1 victimization had no effect on wave-2 gun carrying, however. They also reported causal effects running from offending to victimization. Specifically, both wave-1 general delinquent offending and wave-2 weapon carrying had significant positive effects on wave-3 victimization. These findings clearly support the reciprocal-effects argument, but with limitations. First, the Wilcox et al. (2006) analysis does not account for any of the personality traits and few of the situational or school contexts (e.g., routine activities, guardianship, socioeconomic disadvantage) that other studies reported as associated with both victimization and offending. Second, the study measures few of the factors theorized to mediate victimization-offending relationships, such as strains and social bonds. Consequently, while the analysis generally supports the thesis asserting reciprocal victimization-offending effects, it does not effectively rule out the "noncausal" explanations, neither does it effectively test the "causal" explanations of the victim-offender overlap.

Partially addressing the noted limitations, Ousey, Wilcox, and Fisher (2011) used all four waves of the RSVP study to examine the possibility of reciprocal effects between victimization and offending occurring over a one-year time period (e.g., prior-year victimization on current-year offending; prior-year offending on current-year victimization). Their analysis included measures of personality (e.g., impulsivity) and social bonds, as well as exposure to risky situations and relationships (access to illicit goods, exposure to delinquent friends, and gang membership). Moreover, their statistical model accounted for other sources of population heterogeneity that may produce noncausal associations between victimization and offending. Their findings suggest that, net of all controls (impulsivity, social bonds, exposure to delinquent peers, access to illicit goods, and gang membership), the effect of prior-year victimization on current-year offending was statistically significant; likewise, prior-year offending on current-year victimization was significant. However, estimates of the effects of victimization on offending, and offending on victimization, were negative, rather than positive. Ousey et al. (2011) suggest that one possible interpretation of these effects is that after accounting for noncausal explanations, prior-victimization experiences may exert causal effects that suppress subsequent offending, and vice versa. Alternatively, some scholars argue that reciprocal relationships between victimization and offending play out across shorter time intervals—hours, days, weeks—and may be distorted by analyses of longer time frames, such as one-year time intervals (Berg and Mulford, 2020; Wilcox et al., 2009). This alternative argument, and the general topic of reciprocal effects between victimization and offending, involve complexities that warrant additional research attention.

In sum, research on the victim-offender overlap in schools offers intriguing preliminary evidence supporting the argument of reciprocal causal effects. Yet, the paucity of empirical studies leaves salient theoretical and empirical questions unanswered. Consequently, understanding of the causal processes connecting victimization and offending in schools remains limited, with more research required.

Conclusion

The victim-offender overlap is an important topic in criminology. Although still under-researched, it is gaining increasing attention from scholars. As we have shown in this chapter, the victim-offender overlap appears in school crime data. However, constraints in available data somewhat limit our documentation of the phenomena. Data constraints notwithstanding, the study of the victim-offender overlap in school settings is a high-value activity. This is because schools compel the physical proximity of higher-risk populations (e.g., adolescent males) in crowded spaces where adult supervision is uneven. Hence, they are settings where elevated temptations and provocations for delinquency can occur in situations with varying levels of guardianship. This makes schools salient venues for the study of who commits offenses, who suffers victimization, and why there is a co-occurrence of offending and victimization for some individuals. Moreover, because a substantial share of students in schools remain "crime-free" (i.e., nonvictim, non-offenders), there is ample opportunity to understand the personal, social, and environmental characteristics of these individuals as well.

The research reported in this chapter suggests that both noncausal and causal frameworks may be relevant to understanding the victim-offender overlap. Evidence suggests that stable, predetermined characteristics of individuals and environments are important pieces of the victim-offender overlap puzzle. Yet, causal mechanisms linking victimization and offending are important as well. Unfortunately, at present, the research literature is insufficient to do more than broadly verify that noncausal and causal frameworks gain some empirical support. Precisely specifying theories and explanatory variables that account for the victim-offender overlap is a task that will require additional research inquiry. At present, the limited evidence suggests that well-established correlates of both offending and victimization, such as low self-control and delinquent peer association, are contributors to the association between victimization and offending. Nevertheless, the unexplained portion of the victimization-offending relationship remains far greater than the explained portion. This fact demands great caution in efforts to derive crime prevention prescriptions from the present state of victim-offender-overlap research. Still, we believe that the potential for advances emerging from this area of research is great. Thus, the expansion of school-based research aiming to improve knowledge of the victim-offender overlap is an essential task for criminologists to take up.

7

The School Environment

A Place for Crime

The previous three chapters provided in-depth analyses of the individual-level correlates of delinquent offending, victimization, and the victim-offender overlap in schools. Collectively, those chapters focused on
the offending and victimization sides of the problem analysis triangle. This
chapter considers its third side—the *places* or *settings* where offenders and
victims converge and school crimes take place. Across the entire set of U.S.
secondary schools, variability of crime rates is striking. Research reveals that
some schools host a disproportionate share of offending and victimization,
whereas others experience almost none. The first major section of this chapter details the between-school variation in crime incidents. The subsequent
section reviews evidence from studies seeking explanation of that variation.

Explanations of differences in rates of crime across schools fall into two
major categories: *compositional* and *contextual*. The first category argues that
cross-school variability in rates of crime is due to differences in the characteristics of the individuals in the student body, or *compositional* differences.
For example, if schools have higher crime rates because they contain more
students who are motivated to offend or more students with a propensity for
victimization, their high crime rate is a result of the (high-propensity) composition of the student body. If compositional differences are at work, we
can understand between-school differences in crime rates simply by identifying the important individual-level correlates of offending and victimization (reviewed in Chapters 4, 5, and 6) and determining in which schools
those correlates are more common. Alternatively, the *contextual* explana-

tion for differences in rates of crime across schools offers that crime rates are at least partly the result of variations in characteristics of school contexts, net of aforementioned individual differences (compositional effects). In other words, schools with exactly the same student body composition may differ in their crime rates due to variations in the features of the school. These school-level features may directly affect crime, or they may moderate the effects of salient individual-level factors on offending or victimization.

Given attention already devoted to individual-level explanations of offending and victimization, the primary focus of this chapter is empirical research addressing how school contexts exert causal influence on crime. In line with the crime-place perspectives discussed in Chapter 2, our review focuses on empirical research examining three conceptual domains: (1) social (dis)organization, (2) culture, and (3) situational opportunity. We provided evidence in Chapter 2 that these concepts are important for understanding crime in general, and we briefly discussed their relevance for understanding school crime specifically. Our objective here is to address in more detail whether school-based research supports the importance of these concepts. In addition, we consider the effects of other school characteristics—school size (enrollment), socioeconomic status of students' families (i.e., percent impoverished), student racial composition, and location (i.e., inner-city, suburban, rural)—on crime in schools. However, these aspects are largely beyond the control of schools, and theory suggests they impact school crime indirectly by affecting more proximal, and more malleable, school-level processes, including school organization, school culture, and situational opportunity (Gottfredson, Gottfredson, Payne, and Gottfredson, 2005).

Variation in School Crime across Time and Place

Conceptual Background

As noted in Chapter 2, studies of crime settings in the United States date back to the important work by Shaw and McKay and colleagues in early twentieth-century Chicago (Shaw, 1929; Shaw and McKay, 1942). That work showed that rates of delinquency varied substantially across areas of the city, with crime concentrating heavily in certain neighborhoods. Moreover, crime concentration in particular communities was stable across multiple decades despite substantial changes in the racial and ethnic composition of residents living in these areas. This led Chicago School criminologists to conclude that high rates of crime were not attributable to the traits of individual residents but were instead due to the features of crime-ridden communities, including their physical spaces, social relationships, and cultural processes.

The study of variation in crime rates across neighborhoods continues to be an important area within criminology; contemporary work reiterates that crime is experienced unevenly across neighborhoods because they differ in key ways that impact crime rates (for recent review, see Wilcox et al., 2018; see also Chapter 2). Moreover, a complementary line of scholarship—referred to as "the criminology of place"—examines crime across smaller-scale geographic units *within neighborhoods*, including street blocks and addresses. It illustrates convincingly that certain street segments within a given neighborhood are crime-ridden "hot spots," whereas others are crime-free (e.g., Groff, Weisburd, and Yang, 2010; Sherman et al., 1989; Weisburd et al., 2012). Overlapping with research on hot spots, some work shows that crime also concentrates at the facility level. Eck et al. (2007, p. 226) suggest that "for any group of similar facilities (for example, taverns, parking lots, or bus shelters), a small proportion of the group accounts for the majority of crime experienced by the entire group." These "risky facilities," according to Eck and colleagues (p. 226), "might show up as hot spots in a city's crime map . . . hospitals, schools, and train stations are well-known examples." Comparing risky facilities with non-risky ones "could reveal many important differences between them, which account for the differences in risk and which might provide important pointers to preventive action" (Eck et al., 2007, p. 226).

The study of variation in school crime draws on both the neighborhood disorganization and the criminology of place paradigms. This is because schools are community-like settings, with ever-changing sets of students, teachers, and staff members that resemble the residents in a neighborhood. At the same time, schools are also distinct places (facilities) within neighborhoods. Crime within schools might be relatively high or low at any point in time, influenced by characteristics of the school itself rather than the characteristics of the broader community in which it is situated. Moreover, within the entire set of U.S. schools, crime is likely to be highly concentrated such that many schools experience relatively little crime, whereas other "risky facilities" experience a far greater share. We document these patterns of variation in crime across schools next. Then we follow with a review of the school-level features linked to variations in school crime in the research literature.

School Crime Incidents in Historical Context

Recall from Chapter 3, that the School Survey on Crime and Safety (SSOCS) is an important source of school-level data in the United States. Sponsored by the U.S. Department of Education's National Center for Education Statistics (NCES), the SSOCS has been administered regularly to public-school principals since 1999–2000.[1] It asks them to report on the number of known incidents of crime and other forms of misconduct (i.e., classroom disruptions); the incidents of *crime* are most pertinent to this book's focus. While the number of "known incidents" of crime likely undercounts actual incidents, the SSOCS data are nonetheless helpful for understanding changes over time in the overall rates of crime in schools. The SSOCS data are particularly valuable for highlighting variation in crime *across school contexts.* That said, the data should be used in conjunction with student self-reports on offending and victimization (see Chapters 4 and 5) for a complete view of school crime.

As of this book's publication, the most recently available SSOCS data collected information in 82,300 schools during the 2017–18 academic year. During that year, those schools reported a total of 962,300 incidents of violence, 132,500 thefts, and 343,700 other crime incidents.[2] Focusing only on sampled middle schools and high schools (N=27,700), there were 493,000 incidents of violence, 96,200 theft incidents, and 254,200 other crime incidents. Thus, adjusting for student population size, 29.6 violent crimes, 4.2 thefts, and 8.6 other crimes occurred per 1,000 students in middle schools. In high schools, there were 16.0 violent crimes, 4.3 thefts, and 13.3 other crimes per 1,000 students (Wang, Chen, Zhang, and Oudekerk, 2020, p. 144).

The rates of violence, theft, and other crime incidents in 2017–18 were generally lower than in previous years, especially compared to a decade ago. Figure 7.1 demonstrates over-time trends by comparing rates of violence, theft, and other incidents, as reported in the SSOCS, in the years 2009–10, 2015–16, and 2017–18. The figure indicates that rates for all three types declined in both middle schools and high schools between 2009–10 and 2015–16. The decline in violent incidents in middle schools was particularly dramatic, dropping from 40 (per 1,000 students) in 2009–10 to 27.1 in 2015–16. In high schools, violent incidents dropped from 21.4 to 16.2 per 1,000 students. Thefts also declined roughly 40 percent between the two time points in both middle and high schools, dropping from 7.4 to 4.4 (per 1,000 students) in middle schools, and declining from 10.1 to 6.4 in high schools. From 2015–16 to

---

1. While the SSOCS is generally administered every two years, there have been exceptions to that pattern since its inception in 1999–2000 (i.e., recently, it has been administered annually). See Chapter 3 for a review of specific details about survey administration.

2. The SSOCS includes the following as "violent incidents": rape or attempted rape, sexual assault other than rape, physical attack or fighting with or without a weapon, threat of physical attack with or without a weapon, robbery with or without a weapon. Theft is defined as "taking things worth over $10 without personal confrontation" (Wang et al., 2020, p. 42). "Other incidents" include possession of a firearm, explosive, knife, or sharp object; possession, use, or distribution of alcohol or illegal drugs; inappropriate distribution, possession, or use of prescription drugs; sexual harassment; and vandalism.

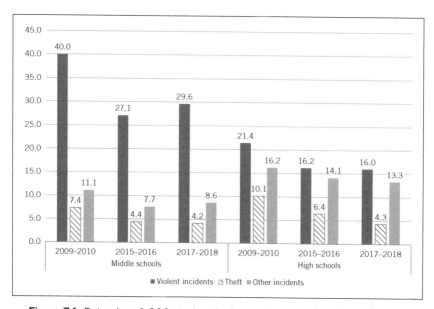

Figure 7.1 Rates (per 1,000 students) of recorded crime incidents in public middle and high schools, 2009–2010, 2015–2016, and 2017–2018

(U.S. Department of Education, National Center for Education Statistics, 2009–10, 2015–16, 2017–18 School Survey on Crime and Safety [SSOCS], 2010, 2016, 2018)

2017–18, crime rates (violence/property/other) slightly increased in middle schools, but there were small, continued declines in high schools. Overall, the trends in school-level crime incidents observed over time in the SSOCS data coincide with the general declines in student-reported offending and victimization from the mid-1990s to 2015, with stabilization since 2015 (described in Chapters 4 and 5).

Crime Incidents across Schools

Although temporal variation in school crime is important, our major focus in this chapter is between-school variation in crime. Regardless of year, some schools experience no crime, while others experience a great deal. Figure 7.2 illustrates this school-level variation, displaying a sampling of results from the SSOCS administered during 2017–18. The bar chart depicts the distribution of the number of violent incidents of crime reported by the principals in sampled middle and high schools, with response categories (shown along the x-axis) ranging from "none" to "20 or more incidents." The bars reflect the percentage of schools reporting a particular number/range of violent incidents. Keeping in mind that the SSOCS only counts incidents known to principals, the figure illustrates variation in the frequency of violent inci-

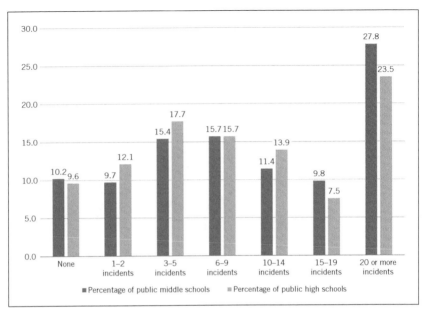

Figure 7.2 Percentage of public middle and high schools recording violent incidents of crime, by number of incidents (2017–2018)

(U.S. Department of Education, National Center for Education Statistics, 2017–18 School Survey on Crime and Safety [SSOCS], 2018)

dents across our nation's schools. At one end of the spectrum, 10.2% of public middle schools and 9.6% of public high schools reported no violent incidents during 2017–18. Another 9.7% of middle schools and 12.1% of high schools reported "1 or 2" incidents of violence. Thus, in approximately one in five of the surveyed middle/high schools, violence was comparatively rare (two or fewer violent incidents per year). However, at the other end of the spectrum, approximately a quarter of sampled middle schools and high schools reported "20 or more" incidents of violence during 2017–18. Thus, a sizeable percentage of U.S. public schools experience a violent incident, on average, at least every other week. The discrepancies in school experiences with crime illustrated in Figure 7.2 are thus consistent with the idea of crime concentrating in "risky facilities." Observed discrepancies imply that a subset of all U.S. secondary schools account for a disproportionate share of all school crime. This pattern of crime concentration in a small share of schools is not a new one. In fact, the government report summarizing the inaugural SSOCS (1999–2000) indicated that just 7% of sampled schools accounted for 50% of all reported crime incidents, and 18% of sampled schools accounted for 75% of all reported crime incidents (Miller, 2003).

The Rural Substance abuse and Violence Project (RSVP) illustrates variability in crime incidents across schools within a single state and therefore is a useful complement to the school differences observed in the SSOCS data. One might think public schools within a single state, especially a heavily rural state like Kentucky, would be homogenous. However, data from 108 middle and high schools in the RSVP study suggest there is observable variation. Table 7.1 reports the number of middle and high schools in the RSVP where physical assault and theft prevalence are low, medium-low, medium-high, and high, respectively, based on students' self-reports of victimization (i.e., the percentage of students reporting any assault/theft victimization).[3] Importantly, across the 108 schools, prevalence rates for physical assault ranged from as low as 14% to as high as 72%. For theft, prevalence rates ranged between 23% and 83%.[4] Despite the width of the ranges, Table 7.1 suggests that most schools fell in the two middle categories for both assault and theft prevalence. However, three schools experienced particularly low assault prevalence (below 20%). At the other end of the spectrum, two schools had assault prevalence rates above 60%, and ten schools had theft prevalence rates above 60%. Prior statistical analyses of RSVP data indicated that the differences in prevalence rates of victimization across the sampled schools are statistically significant, meaning they are greater than one would expect to occur just by random chance alone (Tillyer et al., 2011, 2018).

Interestingly, the schools in the RSVP data with unusually high levels of theft or physical assault are not homogeneous. Rather, they run the gamut from rural or small-town schools enrolling just a few hundred students to schools in the state's largest metropolitan area, enrolling around 1,000 students each. Thus, the variability in school crime observed in the RSVP data is not simply a function of the rural versus urban settings of schools. To further illustrate this point, Table 7.2 presents the physical assault and theft prevalence rates for nine public middle and high schools sampled for RSVP from Kentucky's most metropolitan city, Louisville. It is evident that assault prevalence ranges widely, from 14% to 54% across these nine schools. Variation in theft prevalence is also quite large, from 24% to 65%. In sum, there is important variation in crime incidents across schools. This variation is observable when comparing schools sampled from the entire United States, when comparing schools sampled from a single state, or when comparing schools selected from a single city/district within a state.

---

3. In total, 111 schools participated in RSVP over the course of the 4 years of the study. However, 3 of those schools contained fewer than 10 student participants. Because prevalence rates based on a small sample size can be misleading, we elected to drop those schools from the descriptive analysis presented here.

4. Physical assault victimization was measured in RSVP by asking students to report whether they (in the current school year) had been "physically attacked (example: punched, slapped, kicked)" on school grounds or during school-related activities.

TABLE 7.1 THE FREQUENCY DISTRIBUTION OF RSVP MIDDLE AND HIGH SCHOOLS BY PHYSICAL ASSAULT AND THEFT VICTIMIZATION PREVALENCE

Victimization prevalence	Number of schools by physical assault prevalence	Number of schools by theft prevalence
Low (< 20%)	3	0
Medium-low (20–39%)	53	22
Medium-high (40–59%)	50	76
High (≥ 60%)	2	10

Source: Rural Substance abuse and Violence Project, 2001–2004.

TABLE 7.2 PHYSICAL ASSAULT AND THEFT PREVALENCE RATES ACROSS NINE SCHOOLS IN ONE METROPOLITAN DISTRICT

RSVP largest-city schools	Physical assault prevalence rate (%)	Theft prevalence rate (%)
School 1	27	35
School 2	14	24
School 3	22	50
School 4	54	60
School 5	37	54
School 6	54	54
School 7	48	50
School 8	54	65
School 9	44	40

Source: Rural Substance abuse and Violence Project, 2001–2004.

School Structure and School Crime

The extent to which schools experience crime incidents, as reported in the SSOCS, varies according to structural characteristics of the schools. However, as implied in the discussion of wide-ranging prevalence rates in the RSVP data, patterns do not always support common preconceived notions regarding the distribution of crime according to (1) school size, (2) school locale, (3) school-community economic disadvantage, and (4) minority-student enrollment.

School size. It is often assumed that larger schools have more crime problems than smaller schools, but the SSOCS data reveal a more nuanced pattern. In 2017–18, the largest schools (those with more than 1,000 students) actually had the lowest rates of violent incidents. Moving across schools of varying size, changes in violence rates are not linear: the rate was

20.3 in schools with fewer than 300 students, 22.7 in schools with 300–499 students, 19.9 in school with 500–999 students, and 16.3 in schools with 1,000 or more students (Wang et al., 2020, p. 144). Relationships between school size and thefts and other crime incidents were different, though also nonlinear. For thefts and other crime incidents, the largest schools (1,000+ students) had the highest incident rates, but the smallest schools (fewer than 300) had the second-highest rates. Schools in the middle-size categories (300–999) had relatively low rates of theft and other crime in comparison to both large and small schools (Wang et al., 2020, p. 144).

School locale. Another common assumption is that city schools are more problematic than suburban and rural schools. Again, however, the SSOCS data suggests nuance in the relationship between school location and crime. During 2017–18, rates of violence per 1,000 students was highest in urban schools (26.2), followed in turn by small-town schools (21.1), and rural schools (18.3). The lowest rates (14.9) occurred in suburban schools (Wang et al., 2020, p. 144). With respect to theft and other crimes, rates were similar in city, small-town, and rural schools (e.g., 7.2–8.4 other crimes per 1,000), all of which were moderately higher than in suburban schools (e.g., 5.9 other crimes per 1,000).

School-community economic disadvantage. Vast inequality in educational experiences across schools in communities of varying levels of economic deprivation is well-documented (e.g., Kozol, 1991). In contrast, the link between economic disadvantage and school crime experiences is not quite as clear-cut. To illustrate, Table 7.3 examines rates of crime incidents reported in the 2017–18 SSOCS across four categories of economic deprivation, based on the percentage of students eligible for free or reduced-price lunches. It indicates that violent crime rates increase incrementally as percentage poor increases in the student body. Thus, there is a stark contrast in the rate of violence among schools in the lowest quartile of economic deprivation (7.0 per 1,000) versus the rate among schools in the highest quartile of economic deprivation (29.6 per 1,000). A somewhat different pattern emerges when considering rates of theft and other crime incidents. While rates of theft and other crime incidents were lowest among schools with the fewest poor students, rates were quite similar across schools in the remaining three quartiles (Wang et al., 2020, p. 144). Thus, the extent to which rates of crime are associated with levels of economic disadvantage (among the student body) appears dependent on type of crime.

Minority enrollment. Patterns of community-level economic disadvantage overlap with persistent patterns of racial segregation in the United States. Thus, community-school economic depravity is experienced, disproportionately, by racial and ethnic minorities. As such, we would expect the bivariate relationships between the percent minority enrollment and rates

TABLE 7.3 CRIME INCIDENT RATES BY PERCENTAGE OF STUDENTS ELIGIBLE FOR FREE OR REDUCED-PRICE LUNCH, AY 2017-18

Percent of students eligible for free or reduced-price lunch (%)	Violence rate per 1,000 students (%)	Theft rate per 1,000 students (%)	Other incident rate per 1,000 students (%)
0–25	7.0	1.8	4.8
26–50	15.2	2.9	7.2
51–75	22.0	3.0	7.9
76–100	29.6	2.8	7.6

Source: Adapted from Wang, K., Chen, Y., Zhang, J., and Oudekerk, B. A. (2020). *Indicators of school crime and safety: 2019* (NCES 2020-063/NCJ 254485). National Center for Education Statistics, U.S. Department of Education, and Bureau of Justice Statistics, Office of Justice Programs, U.S. Department of Justice. Washington, DC (p. 144).

of school crime to be similar to the relationships between school disadvantage and school crime.[5] SSOCS data from 2017–18 support this expectation. Rates of violence (per 1,000) in schools with 0–25% minority, 26–50% minority, 51–75% minority, and 75–100% minority were 12.6, 18.3, 24.7, and 25.1, respectively (Wang et al., 2020, p. 144). In contrast, rates of theft and other crime incidents were not much different across levels of minority enrollment. For example, the rate of other crime incidents was 6.7 per 1,000 students in schools composed of 0–25% minority students; the rate was 7.3 per 1,000 in schools with 75–100% minority population.

Summary

Crime incidents vary a great deal across school contexts. Some of the variability may be due to schools' structural characteristics, such as their size and location or their economic or racial composition. Yet, evidence indicates that observed relationships between these characteristics and school crime are not straightforward or consistent with common assumptions. The recent SSOCS data suggest that school size and location appear to have a minimal association with school crime rates, and although school-community disadvantage and minority enrollment (themselves intertwined) appear more closely related to patterns of crime, the relationships are not generalizable across crime types. The lack of strong relationships is not particularly surprising, as modest correlations between characteristics of the student body and school crime also were documented in the earliest incarnation of SSOCS data in 1999–2000 (e.g., see Miller, 2003). Moreover, research using

---

5. Minority status is defined in reference to the U.S. population, not a school's population.

a wide variety of data sources beyond SSOCS provides little compelling evidence that school size and location are significantly related to school crime incidents and only mixed evidence regarding the significance of economic disadvantage and/or racial composition (e.g., Cook, Gottfredson, and Na, 2010; Turanovic, Pratt, Kulig, and Cullen, 2019). Thus, criminologists assert that other school-level factors may be more important in affecting crime rates across schools. Three key factors that have emerged in the literature are school organization, school culture, and situational opportunity. We discuss them next.

Social (Dis)Organization and School Rates of Crime

As mentioned in Chapter 2, the related concepts of social organization and collective efficacy have been key to understanding neighborhood variability in crime for the past century (Bursik and Grasmick, 1993; Kornhauser, 1978; Sampson, 2012; Shaw and McKay, 1942). Here, we discuss research using these concepts to understand variation in school crime. For this purpose, we will predominantly use the term *school organization*, but we view the term as interchangeable with similar concepts, including *communal school organization* and *school efficacy*. Each of these terms refers to: (1) shared goals and norms among members of a school community, and (2) the ability of members of a school community to work collaboratively toward their shared goals and norms (Payne et al., 2003).[6] More specifically, these concepts encompass mutually respectful, trusting social relations among students, teachers, and school administrators and collective engagement among those parties in efforts to achieve common goals, including enforcement of school rules, management of school problems, and school improvements (Kirk, 2009). *Schools with strong school organization are thought to display higher levels of informal social control—the ability to regulate the (mis)behavior of students.*

Finding historical data on variation in levels of school organization is difficult, in part because of the complexity of the concept. However, Figure 7.3 illustrates trends in U.S. schools on a key aspect of school organization—the enforcement of school rules by teachers and principals. Changes in rule enforcement over time are modest and not perfectly linear, but a moderate increase in rule enforcement is evident, especially between the 1993 and 2008—during which time overall rates of school crime declined substan-

---

6. Some scholars use the term *school connectedness* in similar fashion (Vogel, Rees, Mc-Cuddy, and Carson, 2015).

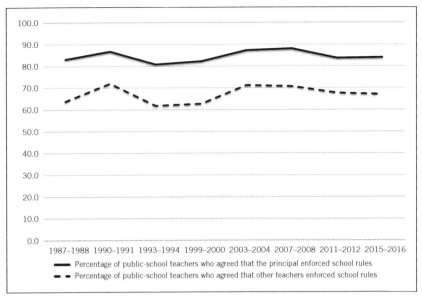

Figure 7.3 Percentage of teachers who reported that principals and other teachers at their school enforced school rules, select years 1987–88 through 2015–16

(U.S. Department of Education, National Center for Education Statistics, Schools and Staffing Survey [SASS], "Public School Teacher Data File," 1987–88, 1990–91, 1993–94, 1999–2000, 2003–04, 2007–08, and 2011–12; "Charter School Teacher Data File," 1999–2000; and National Teacher and Principal Survey [NTPS], "Public School Teacher Data File," 2015–16.)

tially. Does school organization vary across schools in a way that correlates with variations in rates of school crime? We delve into this question directly in the next section, examining research on the potential correlation between school organization and school crime. Two major mechanisms linking school organization to student offending and victimization are the focus. The first offers that school organization directly affects offending and victimization, independent of individual student differences. The second asserts that school organization moderates the risk for offending and victimization associated with student or community characteristics. We summarize findings from studies examining these two mechanisms in the subsections that follow.

Does School Organization Reduce Student Offending and Victimization, Independent of Student Differences?

Individual-level studies. Several studies explore whether school organization reduces student offending and/or victimization by estimating the effects of measures of *individual-level student perceptions of school organization* on student offending and/or victimization. Below, we summarize their key details:

- Welsh (2001) studied over 4,000 students in 11 Philadelphia middle schools and found that individual perceptions of rule clarity, perceived dignity/respect, and perceived student influence in school affairs were all related to lower levels of offending across student respondents (e.g., hitting others, threatening others, stealing, weapon carrying).
- Welsh (2001) also found that individual perceptions of rule clarity, dignity/respect, student influence in school affairs, and prioritization of school improvement were associated with lower levels of victimization across student respondents (e.g., having been hit or pushed, threatened, robbed, having property stolen).
- Schreck et al. (2003) analyzed data from over 6,000 6th–12th graders participating in the 1993 National Household Education Surveys Program-School Safety and Discipline Component (NHES-SSD). Their research showed that students who perceived greater levels of rule *un*fairness experienced higher odds of overall victimization, violent victimization, and theft victimization than students who perceived less rule unfairness.
- Several analyses of NCVS–SCS data reveal, collectively, that students who perceived clarity and fairness in school rules and in their enforcement experienced lower odds of several victimization experiences, including assault, theft, and destruction of property (Burrow and Apel, 2008; Kupchik and Farina, 2016).

School-level studies. Although informative, studies linking individual perceptions of school organization to offending and victimization are not ideal for assessing whether and how school context affects crime. After all, school organization is a characteristic of a collective occupying a place. Therefore, individual perceptions of organization might not be realistic or accurate. Furthermore, it is plausible that individual experiences with offending or victimization alter their perceptions of school organization, thus obfuscating causal effects of social organization on student offending or victimization. For these reasons, research that examines schools as key units of analysis, and that measures organization as a school-level construct, is preferable.

Researchers sometimes create school-level measures of organization by averaging individual survey respondents' perceptions of organization for each school. Then they observe the extent to which the resulting "school organization" measures correlate with school rates of offending and victimization. Gary and Denise Gottfredson's (1985) groundbreaking analysis of school crime in more than 600 secondary schools in the Safe School Study largely followed this approach.[7] A key finding from their research is that lower levels of cooperation between teachers and administrators (based on averaging teacher perceptions of cooperation within sampled schools) were associated with higher school-level rates of teacher victimization. A handful of more recent school-level studies focused on the effects of measures of "communal school organization" in analyses of data from the 1998 National Study of Delinquency Prevention in Schools (NSDPS). Results from these analyses include the following:

- Communal school organization—measured by aggregating within schools teachers' survey responses to questionnaire items assessing the supportive and collaborative nature of relationships among administrators, teachers, and students as well as the presence of common goals and norms—was related to lower rates of teacher victimization and student offending, but it was not significantly related to student rates of victimization (Payne et al., 2003).
- Communal school organization (measured similarly to Payne et al., 2003) reduced school crime (measured as an index combining teacher victimization, student victimization, and student offending), particularly in racially-ethnically heterogeneous schools (Payne, 2012).
- Schools in which students collectively perceived greater rule fairness and clarity experienced lower levels of student offending and victimization (Gottfredson et al., 2005).

Multilevel studies. The school-level studies just mentioned appropriately measure organization as a school-level concept, thus advancing our knowledge about the school organization–school crime linkage. Still, they are somewhat limited by not utilizing multilevel modeling techniques that distinguish school organization contextual effects from student difference effects (i.e., compositional effects). A better analytic approach is to use multilevel models that explicitly include two units of analysis: schools and students. In the latter models, organization is a school-level factor whose influence can be measured net of individual student differences.

Payne (2008) used a multilevel modeling framework in reanalysis of data from nearly 14,000 students in 253 of the schools that participated in

---

7. While technically not a multilevel analysis, Gottfredson and Gottfredson (1985) controlled for student and community compositional characteristics.

the NSDPS. In statistical models predicting levels of student offending, Payne included several measures of communal school organization—scales created by averaging within schools teacher responses to multiple survey items asking about supportive/collaborative relations as well as common norms and goals. Controlling for student-level differences within schools, these measures of communal school organization were associated with lower levels of student offending, suggesting a true contextual effect of communal school organization. A follow-up study by Payne (2009) reported that these measures of communal school organization exerted significant contextual effects on offending for both male and female students. Overlapping with Payne's findings, evidence from the program evaluation literature indicates that schools implementing programs with a focus on clarifying and consistently enforcing behavioral norms experience less school crime—a topic that will be discussed more fully in Chapter 8 (e.g., see Gottfredson, Cook, and Na, 2012).

Kirk (2009) conducted multilevel analysis of data from teachers and 6th- and 8th-grade students in 68 Chicago public schools. While controlling for individual and neighborhood differences, he estimated the extent to which being suspended from school (a proxy for school-based offending) was related to "school efficacy"—measured as the within-school aggregation of teachers' responses to survey items assessing the level of cohesion and trust among teachers as well as shared expectations for social control of student misbehavior. Findings indicated that school efficacy was significantly, inversely related to the likelihood of a student being suspended; as school efficacy increased, the odds of suspension declined.

Overall, evidence is mounting that school organization (or communal school organization, or school efficacy) is related to student offending and victimization (and teacher victimization), with the strongest evidence emerging from multilevel studies (Payne, 2008, 2009; Kirk, 2009).[8] The preceding evidence notwithstanding, several multilevel studies report null relationships between school-level measures of school organization (or similar concepts) and measures of secondary-school student offending or victimization (Fissel, Wilcox, and Tillyer, 2019; Tillyer et al., 2010, 2011; Welsh, 2003; Welsh, Greene, and Jenkins, 1999; Wilcox and Clayton, 2001). However,

---

8. It is worth noting that a recent meta-analysis supported the review provided here in showing that social disorganization (termed "negative school climate" in the meta-analysis) had the fifth- and thirteenth-highest effect sizes among 31 different predictors of K–12 student victimization and aggressive/delinquent behavior, respectively (Turanovic et al., 2019). However, caution must be used when comparing their findings with the conclusions drawn here, given the vastly different criteria for inclusion in the meta-analysis versus the studies under focus here.

methodological concerns limit the conclusiveness of evidence in several of these studies. Some studies reporting nonsignificant relationships between measures of school organization and school crime are based on analysis of data from a small number of schools in a single city—for example, Welsh's (2003) study of students in just 11 Philadelphia middle schools or Wilcox and Clayton's (2001) study of 21 schools in a single city. Such a small number of school contexts (and all from one city school district) restricts the degree of cross-school heterogeneity, thus limiting the likelihood of observing significant school-level effects.[9] Additionally, some studies reporting null effects of school-level social organization use outcome measures of "misconduct" that are particularly broad, picking up any behavior in which students "got in trouble for not following school rules" (Welsh et al., 1999). Such behavior conceivably includes tardiness, roaming the hallway without a pass, dress-code violations, and other noncriminal behavior. We contend that studies using these outcome measures are probably insufficient for assessing the relationship between school organization and school *crime*.

Finally, a handful of multilevel analyses of the Kentucky-based RSVP sample have reported null relationships between a measure of school organization (which they refer to as "school efficacy") and various measures of student offending and victimization, independent of individual-level correlates (e.g., Fissel et al., 2019; Tillyer et al., 2010, 2011, 2018). One interpretation of the null effects is that Kentucky schools do not demonstrate the variability in school efficacy seen at the national level. That potential limitation aside, RSVP-based studies arguably control for important underlying individual differences (i.e., low self-control, social bonds, peer associations, and lifestyle) more comprehensively than other studies of school organization to date due to the rich array of measures available in the dataset. Therefore, another interpretation of the null effects of school efficacy in RSVP is that school efficacy is not important, net of key individual-level differences (i.e., it may be a compositional effect in other studies showing it to be significant). However, an important caveat to either of these interpretations is that several RSVP-based studies find evidence of an alternative mechanism—through interaction with individual-level correlates, school efficacy helps to mitigate

---

9. Another issue is that Wilcox and Clayton's measure of "school capital" was based on aggregating within schools student responses to survey questions about attachment to school, church attendance, and religious commitment. Such a measure may tap some aspect of relational capital across the student body, but it does not explicitly get at the level of relational trust among school actors in order to achieve common goals, and is thus not comparable to most measures of school organization.

risk of offending and victimization. We next review the research testing this alternative mechanism.

Does School Organization Affect Student Offending and Victimization by Interacting with Individual Risk Factors?

The idea that school organization affects student behavior through an interaction with individual-level risk factors is corollary to research on neighborhoods showing that delinquency is affected by an interaction between individual-level risk factors and neighborhood social organization. For example, a study by Lynam et al. (2000) reported that neighborhood-level informal social control mitigated the effect of youths' low self-control on delinquent offending. They argued that delinquency risk factors exist across multiple domains (i.e., individual risk factors, school risk factors, neighborhood risk factors), and high levels of control in one domain could compensate for risk factors in other domains (e.g., Jones and Lynam, 2009; Vogel, Rees, McCuddy, and Carson, 2015). Thus, in Lynam and colleagues' study, strong control within the neighborhood domain partially compensated for the detrimental effect of weak control within the individual domain (low self-control).

While extending that multi-domain logic to settings beyond neighborhoods seems reasonable, only a limited body of work addresses interaction effects of this kind *in the school setting*. Studies that do are multilevel, with individuals *and* schools as units of analysis. That is, they examine *cross-level interactions* exploring the potential mitigating role that school organization has on the relationships between individual-level risk factors and measures of student offending or victimization. For example, in her multilevel analysis of the NSDPS data (described earlier in this chapter), Payne (2008) examined whether the effects of students' social bonds on delinquent offending varied with differences in the extent that schools were characterized by communal organization. She found that the deleterious effect of weak social bonds on student offending was mitigated in schools with higher levels of communal organization. In other words, while weak bonds put students at higher risk for offending, schools with greater communal organization helped offset the risk.

As alluded to earlier, several analyses of the Kentucky-based RSVP data similarly focus on whether their measure of school efficacy mitigates individual risk factors for student offending and victimization. These analyses measure school efficacy with a scale aggregating within-school teacher responses to multiple survey items about the perception of common goals and the degree of collaboration among students, teachers, and administrators. Johnson et al.'s (2019) analysis of student weapon carrying in the first two

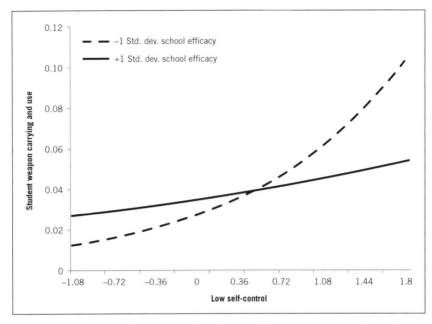

Figure 7.4 The effect of low self-control on student weapon carrying and use at low and high levels of school efficacy

(Original figure created by Samuel Peterson, based on quantitative results reported in Cheryl L. Johnson, P. Wilcox, and S. Peterson [2019]. Stressed out and strapped: Examining the link between psychological difficulties and student weapon carrying and use. *Criminal Justice and Behavior*, *46*, 980–998.)

waves of RSVP data (7th and 8th graders) revealed that strong school efficacy mitigated the positive effects of low self-control on student weapon carrying and use.[10] Figure 7.4 depicts this interaction effect. The dashed line represents the effect of low self-control in contexts of low school efficacy (at least one standard deviation below the sample mean level of school efficacy), whereas the solid line represents the effect of low self-control in contexts of strong school efficacy (at least one standard deviation above the sample mean level of school efficacy). Schools with strong school efficacy moderated the risk posed by low self-control for student involvement in offending in the form of weapon carrying and use.

In another analysis of the RSVP data, Tillyer et al. (2018) examined whether low self-control affected patterns of repeat assault victimization (experi-

---

10. The items tapping weapon carrying in the Johnson et al. (2019) index were in reference to in-school carrying specifically. The items tapping weapon use, however, picked up both in-school and out-of-school behavior.

encing multiple assaults within any one school year) and, if so, whether school efficacy mitigated its effects. They found that low self-control was significantly, positively related to repeat assault victimization (see Chapter 5), but the strength of that relationship was lessened by school efficacy. Thus, similar to Figure 7.4, Tillyer and colleagues observed that the relationship between low self-control and repeated victimization was stronger in schools with lower levels of school efficacy. Conversely, it was weaker in schools with higher efficacy.

Finally, Kirk (2009) examined whether his measure of school efficacy might compensate for weak control within the neighborhood, rather than individual, domain. He found that school efficacy's inverse association with odds of suspension was stronger when neighborhood collective efficacy was weak. Kirk (2009, p. 507) concluded that "a compensatory relation exists between the extent of collective efficacy in schools and in the surrounding neighborhood, such that the controlling influence of school collective efficacy on suspension is relatively greater in neighborhoods that lack collective efficacy." Conversely, his findings suggest that strong school efficacy lowers the risk associated with weak neighborhood-level collective efficacy.

Summary

To date, the empirical evidence from research on the effects of measures of school organization on school crime yields several key takeaways:

- Although evidence that school organization is associated with lower levels of school crime is common, much of it comes from studies of individual perceptions of school organization or studies including school-level variables only.
- The current gold standard for research examining effects of school organization is multilevel analysis including both school-level and student-level variables. Several large-scale multilevel studies find significant effects of school organization net of individual student characteristics, thus suggesting contextual rather than compositional effects (Kirk, 2009; Payne, 2008, 2009).
- Several multilevel studies report null effects of school organization based on samples of relatively small numbers of schools in a single city (Welsh, 2003; Wilcox and Clayton, 2001).
- Multilevel studies using RSVP data typically control for the largest array of individual student differences. These studies often have reported nonsignificant direct effects of a measure of school efficacy on school crime. However, they have also indicated that school efficacy influences school crime indirectly by, for example, miti-

gating the effects of low self-control on student assault victimization and student weapon carrying (Tillyer et al., 2018; Johnson et
al., 2019).

- Research using data from studies other than the RSVP, and examining other dimensions of school crime (e.g., general student offending, school suspension), also indicates that school organization (or efficacy) helps to reduce student offending and victimization
by attenuating risk in other domains (Payne, 2008; Kirk, 2009).

Culture and School Rates of Crime

Delinquent School Culture

As we discussed in Chapter 2, much of the criminological work addressing
the role of group culture identifies the neighborhood as the place wherein
youths receive messages about which behaviors are expected, condoned, or
tolerated. However, other work suggests a variety of group settings, including schools, are sites for the creation and transmission of culture. In his
seminal work describing the development and adoption of a culture conducive to violence—the code of the street—Elijah Anderson (1999) emphasized
the importance of what he called "staging areas." They are locations within
communities where people interact and collectively establish and display
cultural values. Common staging areas according to Anderson (1999) included places such as street corners, liquor stores or bars, neighborhood
basketball courts or recreation centers, and *schools*. Other research suggests
schools are characterized by meaningful cultural orientations representing
collective sentiments their students have about things such as the appropriateness of delinquent behavior (Brunson and Miller, 2009; Miller, 2008;
Vogel et al., 2015; Moule and Fox, 2021). Schools with a delinquent cultural
orientation—or *delinquent school culture*—are those where relatively large
percentages of students condone delinquent behavior, at least in certain
situations. Schools with such a cultural orientation arguably will have higher rates of crime. We discuss research that tests this argument next.

Criminologists studying the school culture–school crime relationship
articulate two distinct mechanisms by which a school's delinquent cultural
orientation might shape students' behavior. We refer to these mechanisms
as (1) culture as individual values and (2) culture in action (see Chapter 2;
see also Swartz et al., 2017). The *culture as individual values* perspective asserts
that a delinquent school culture acts as an agent of socialization, causing
individual students to embrace and adhere to delinquent values, resulting
in higher crime within the student body. In short, individuals internalize
the group norms, and their behavior reflects those values. Individuals adopt

the group culture as their own, so that their personal delinquent values drive their criminal behavior. The *culture as individual values* mechanism was previously discussed in the section on social learning and subcultural effects in Chapter 4, where the focus was on individual-level correlates of offending. Recall that Chapter 4 indicated there was strong support in the research literature suggesting that students' adherence to delinquent values was a direct correlate of their level of involvement in school delinquency. Because the *culture as individual values* mechanism implies that individuals adopt their personal values from the group, little divergence exists between measures of group values and individual values. Therefore, we would not expect to observe an effect of delinquent school culture on student behavior net of the influence of individual-level values (Swartz et al., 2017). In the absence of controls for individual values, delinquent school culture might affect delinquency, but the effect is *compositional*—due to the effects of un-measured individual differences in delinquent values.

As an alternative, the *culture in action* perspective contends that a group-level delinquent school culture exerts contextual effects that operate on student behavior net of individual student values. Individual students draw on and act in accordance with school-level cultural expectations prescribing delinquency even if their own value orientations are largely prosocial. For example, individuals who have not internalized delinquent values may still behave according to their school's delinquent culture—in order to gain respect or save face (i.e., impression-management purposes), to avoid future conflict (i.e., self-protection), or to imitate or model the behavior of one's peers (Anderson, 1999; Felson et al., 1994; Ousey and Wilcox, 2005). The *culture in action* perspective allows that a school's culture may act as a socialization agent, but differently than in the *culture as values* model. Rather than provoking wholesale repudiation of prosocial norms in favor of delinquent values, *school culture in action* provides an interactional framework that supports situational displays of student delinquency (Swartz et al., 2017). The *culture in action* mechanism is most relevant to this chapter's focus on place since it posits that delinquent school culture, as a school-level characteristic, can exert contextual effects on student behavior net of students' individual delinquent values.

As with the concept of "social organization," it is difficult to find comprehensive indicators of "delinquent school culture" over time for schools across the United States. However, Figure 7.5 illustrates trends in two proxy indicators that likely correlate with delinquent school culture—presence of gangs in school and availability of drugs in school—measured as the percentages of students who report that gangs and drugs are present in their schools. Keep in mind that students' aggregated perceptions of gangs/drugs are distinct from their individual gang membership or use of drugs, which

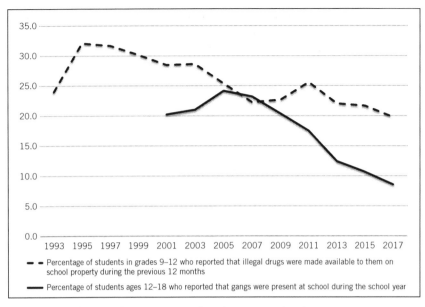

Figure 7.5 Percentage of students reporting that gangs
and drugs were present in school

(U.S. Department of Justice, Bureau of Justice Statistics, School Crime Supplement [SCS] to the
National Crime Victimization Survey, 2001 through 2017; Centers for Disease Control and Prevention,
Division of Adolescent and School Health, Youth Risk Behavior Surveillance System [YRBSS],
1993 through 2017.)

were individual-level correlates of offending in Chapter 4. Aggregated perceptions of gangs and drug problems in a school do not measure individual-
level behavior but rather the nature of the school context—in particular,
they serve as approximations of the extent to which students collectively
embrace delinquent norms. Per Figure 7.5, the percentages of students who
report presence of gangs and drugs in their schools have generally declined
over the past several decades—during which time overall rates of school
crime have declined as well. While these data provide useful images of
trends in proxy measures of school culture, we turn our attention next to
research that uses rigorous multivariate statistical analysis or in-depth qualitative analysis to examine the relationship between measures of delinquent
school culture and rates of school crime.

Does Delinquent School Culture Exhibit Contextual Effects
(Culture in Action)?

Initial quantitative studies. A handful of quantitative analyses of the NCVS-
SCS report that individual students perceiving greater drug availability and

gang presence in their schools are at increased risk for victimization, controlling for a whole host of potentially confounding factors (Burrow and Apel, 2008; Kupchik and Farina, 2016; Schreck et al., 2003; Wynne and Joo, 2011).[11] Such evidence points to a possible relationship between delinquent school culture and rates of school crime incidents, though the individual-level nature of the analyses precludes strong conclusions. Fortunately, school-level analyses of school rates of crime using the SSOCS data corroborate the individual-level analyses. They report that various indicators of a delinquent school cultural context—including number of gang disturbances, reports of bullying, reports of racial hostility, and other reports of student harassment and disrespect—are positively correlated with violent incidents, controlling for myriad school characteristics (Jennings, Khey, Maskaly, and Donner, 2011; Crawford and Burns, 2015, 2016; Swartz, Osborne, Dawson-Edwards, and Higgins, 2016). While these findings are notable, individual differences were uncontrolled, impeding the determination of whether effects of school culture measures are compositional or contextual.

Studies best suited to test the contextual *school culture in action* mechanism are multilevel in design, with measures tapping in to both individual-level and school-level delinquent values. Richard Felson and colleagues (1994) provided one of the first studies meeting this standard, though the data analyzed were collected 50 years ago. Their secondary analysis focused on data from nearly 2,000 boys across 87 public high schools who were part of the first two waves of the Youth in Transition (YIT) study—a longitudinal study of a panel of high-school boys in the late 1960 and early 1970s. They studied the effects of school culture and individual values on several dependent variables, including: (1) "interpersonal violence," an index composed of violent behaviors, some of which were specific to the school location (e.g., "got into a serious fight with a student in school"), and (2) "school delinquency," an index tapping school-specific but noncriminal forms of misbehavior (e.g., tardiness, cheating on tests). Key independent variables in their analysis were (1) individual-level violent values, based on student reports of their own acceptance of situational use of aggression, and (2) violent school culture, which captured the average level of acceptance of use of aggression across all students in the school. Results supported contextual effects of school culture on delinquency. Specifically, measures of violent school culture were associated with higher levels of interpersonal violence and school delinquency, independent of students' own beliefs about the appropriateness of violence. Nevertheless, it is difficult to draw firm conclusions about the ef-

---

11. Recent meta-analysis of a broad range of studies (well beyond the focus here on secondary schools in the U.S.) also report that "violent school context" is a top correlate of both individual student victimization and offending (Turanovic et al., 2019).

fect of delinquent school culture on school crime from this study. This is because "interpersonal violence" tapped behaviors that were not always specific to the school location, and "school delinquency" measured behaviors rarely considered criminal.[12]

Several other studies using more contemporary data explicitly examine school culture's effects on in-school criminal behavior. For example, Ousey and Wilcox's (2005) analysis of the first wave of the RSVP data investigated "school-based violent offending"—measured as the frequency with which students reported having physically attacked someone at school, having forced someone at school to give up their money or property, and having nonconsensually touched someone in a sexual manner at school. Their key independent variables were individual-level and school-level measures of attitudes regarding the appropriateness of violence—so, individual violent values and violent school culture, respectively. Multilevel regression analysis revealed that violent school culture was *not* significantly associated with school-based offending net of individual-level violent values. On the surface, this finding suggests a null contextual effect of violent school culture on student offending and contradicts Felson and colleagues' earlier conclusion. What might explain the difference? Differences in the historical time periods of the data, or the nature of the samples are possibilities. Other possible clues appear in ethnographic research, discussed next.

Key ethnographic detail. Brunson and Miller (2009) conducted qualitative research on the nature of conflicts among male students in inner-city St. Louis schools. Their work provides important nuance on the role of school culture in the genesis of student behavior. It also may help explain the contradictory findings reported in earlier quantitative research (e.g., Felson et al., 1994; Ousey and Wilcox, 2005). Brunson and Miller's (2009) in-depth student interviews revealed that school norms encouraged conflict resolution through violent means. For example, interviewees conveyed that their schools were settings in which, when boys started fighting, "people will start crowding around . . . [egg] stuff on . . . everybody crowd around cheerin' it on" (Brunson and Miller, 2009, p. 197). The interviews also revealed that school culture provided a message that, in the face of aggression, violent payback was expected. For example, one boy indicated that a common refrain heard at school in the midst of fights was "man, you let him whoop you like that? Get up and hit him back!" (p. 197).

---

12. A subsequent analysis of the YIT data by Brezina, Piquero, and Mazerolle (2001) also found that a school-level measure of students' approval of aggression was significantly, positively related to a measure of noncriminal student misconduct that tapped propensity for arguing with others students and teachers.

Though school culture promoted violent encounters, Brunson and Miller also observed that conflicts that started in school often intentionally ended outside of school, after the school day ended. For example, some boys they interviewed described situations where aggressive conflicts started in school, but school security stopped them. These conflicts typically resumed after school. Related to this point, other interviewees expressed concern over getting suspended if they fought at school, intentionally telling any in-school aggressors "I ain't gonna fight you at school . . . meet me outside" (Brunson and Miller, 2009, p. 202). Still others were willing to fight at school but only in secluded, weakly controlled locations, such as those known to be away from teachers and security guards (see also Astor et al., 1999).

Overall, Brunson and Miller's work paints a complex picture in terms of the effects of delinquent school culture on student (violent) offending. While delinquent school culture appears related to the occurrence of conflicts among youths, resolutions of those conflicts are likely to spill over into after-school hours. Hence, they often culminate in fights occurring outside of school. If so, observing the influence of school culture on in-school crime via typical quantitative analyses may be difficult. Indeed, studies like Felson and colleagues (1994), which estimated the impact of delinquent school culture on *both within- and outside-of-school* violence, may more readily capture contextual effects of school culture than studies like Ousey and Wilcox (2005), which focused only on the effect of delinquent school culture on *school-based* violent offending. Additionally, Brunson and Miller's (2009) research implies that the effects of delinquent school culture on in-school crime may take place only in selected in-school situations, where students perceive weak social control.

More evidence of the school culture-school control interplay. Building on the possibilities raised above, a subsequent study by Swartz et al. (2017) aimed to provide a more explicit quantitative test of the ways in which social control determines how and where delinquent school culture impacts student offending. Their analysis of all four waves of the RSVP data (over 3,000 7th through 10th graders in 103 schools) estimated effects of delinquent school culture, independent of individual-level delinquent values, on six offense-specific offending measures: (1) in-school assault, (2) in-school robbery, (3) in-school nonconsensual sexual touching, (4) out-of-school assault, (5) out-of-school robbery, and (6) out-of-school nonconsensual sexual touching. They found that school culture had a significant contextual effect on three of these six offending outcomes. Specifically, delinquent school culture was significantly related to higher frequency of in-school and out-of-school nonconsensual sexual touching as well as out-of-school assault. In a second part of their analysis, Swartz and colleagues (2017) examined whether delinquent school culture was more strongly related to in-school offending in situations where control is relatively weak (as measured by school efficacy). Results showed that the effect of delinquent school culture on robbery was contingent on the level of school efficacy; delinquent school culture increased robbery offending specifically among students in schools with weak school efficacy. In light of previous work, Swartz et al. (2017) reached two key conclusions about the school culture–school crime relationship: (1) there are more immediate opportunities to express delinquent school culture outside of the controlled confines of the school, and (2) the expression of violence in schools is likely confined to specific situations wherein students perceive weak control.

Summary

The concept of a delinquent *culture in action* is a promising contributor to efforts to understand cross-school variability in crime incidents. Although the body of work testing this idea remains relatively small, it provides some key takeaway points:

- Studies focused on a single-level unit of analysis (i.e., either individuals *or* schools) show that individual perceptions of delinquent school culture and school-level indicators of delinquent school culture are associated with school crime incidents. However, these studies cannot disentangle individual and contextual effects of culture.
- Multilevel studies with individuals nested within schools offer the best opportunities for investigating the contextual effect of delinquent school culture on school crime, net of individual delinquent values. Few meet those criteria, especially with data collected in the twenty-first century (Ousey and Wilcox, 2005; Swartz et al., 2017).
- Notwithstanding some limits on generalizability, studies employing the Kentucky-based RSVP data offer the most contemporary and comprehensive measurement of the effects of school-level culture. Evidence from those studies suggest that the effect of delinquent school culture on student offending and victimization is conditional. In particular, it is most apparent in situations where control is limited and/or opportunity is prevalent.

Situational Opportunity and School Rates of Crime

As we introduced in Chapter 2, *situational opportunity* refers to the extent to which motivated offenders can carry out offenses within a specific setting. When situational opportunity is great, the rate of crime incidents within the setting should be high. As is discussed below, situational opportunity overlaps somewhat with the concepts of social (dis)organization and delinquent school culture. At the same time, it has unique theoretical elements. Specifically, situational opportunity theory identifies five sub-concepts that are key to understanding opportunity for crime: effort, risk, reward, provocation, and excuses (e.g., Cornish and Clarke, 2003; Smith and Clarke, 2012). Utilizing these five concepts, the situational opportunity perspective offers that situational opportunity for crime is great in schools when:

1. Offending requires little *effort*—in other words, offenders face few challenges in carrying out the mechanics involved in crime within the school.
2. Offending is a *low-risk* endeavor, with offenders facing minimal odds of being detected and punished.
3. Offending offers clear and/or plentiful *rewards*.
4. There are stimuli that *provoke* criminal action.
5. There are *excuses* for offending (i.e., there is ambiguity in terms of whether offenders are responsible for their criminal actions).

Situational School Crime Prevention

Situational crime prevention (SCP) counteracts situational opportunity for crime. It refers to a set of techniques for blocking the opportunistic elements of settings, increasing the effort and risk associated with offending while also reducing the rewards, provocations, and excuses for offending. Scholarship on this issue has identified 25 general techniques to reduce situational opportunity and prevent crime. Table 7.4 provides a definitional overview of them, with examples of their application in school settings (Smith and Clarke, 2012; see also Tompson and Bowers, 2020).

The first column of Table 7.4 indicates that schools increase offender effort by engaging in various target hardening practices: controlling access to school grounds, school buildings, or specific locations within the school; screening school exits; deflecting offenders from problematic locations; and controlling the tools or weapons used in school crime. In fact, many schools implement these techniques through metal detectors, door locks, buzz-in/out systems, and book bag policies. The second column in Table 7.4 illustrates that schools can increase risks of detection associated with offending by extending guardianship practices among existing school personnel, reducing anonymity of students, and enhancing natural and formal surveillance as well as place management practices. Many schools engage in these techniques by hiring security/police personnel, installing security cameras, and providing ways for students and parents to report suspicious activity.

TABLE 7.4 THE 25 TECHNIQUES OF SITUATIONAL CRIME PREVENTION, APPLIED TO THE SCHOOL SETTING

INCREASE THE EFFORT Block or limit offender actions	INCREASE THE RISK Increase likelihood of detection	REDUCE THE REWARDS Limit visibility or value of specific targets/victims	REDUCE PROVOCATIONS Limit situational stimuli that may lead to criminal action	REMOVE EXCUSES Present situational controls that clarify offender responsibility
1. Target harden: Make it more difficult for students to target other students and their property *Example: Mandatory victimization prevention programming*	**6. Extend guardianship:** Incentivize action on the part of unofficial guardians *Example: Bystander training, anonymous tip line*	**11. Conceal targets:** Limit students' ability to see targets *Example: Individual student lockers/ locks*	**16. Reduce frustrations and stress:** Maintain calm settings and efficient procedures *Example: Reduce overcrowding, offer leisure/ enrichment activities*	**21. Set rules:** Clearly provide information about unacceptable behaviors in the school setting *Example: Unambiguous code of conduct*
2. Control access: Block access to school or places within school where criminal action can be carried out *Example: Locked doors, blocked off areas*	**7. Assist natural surveillance:** Increase the likelihood that potential guardians will see criminal action *Example: Glass walls in entry area; well-maintained landscaping*	**12. Remove targets:** Prohibit valuable targets in school *Example: School uniform policy that bans valued clothing/shoes*	**17. Avoid disputes:** Limit situations that promote or escalate conflicts between students *Example: Gang resistance training, staggered change-of-class periods, prohibition of hallway loitering*	**22. Post instructions:** Make it clear how students can meet the behavioral requirements *Example: Signs indicating requirements in specific school spaces*
3. Screen exits: Limit the ability of a student offender to leave the setting after criminal action *Example: Buzz-in/out doorway systems*	**8. Reduce anonymity:** Increase the likelihood that potential guardians will identify features of offenders *Example: ID badges*	**13. Identify property:** Make student property traceable *Example: ID tags/codes on all property*	**18. Reduce emotional arousal:** Limit emotionally insulting stimuli *Example: Collaboration among students, teachers, and administrators (communal school organization)*	**23. Alert conscience:** Provide reminders about unacceptable behavior *Example: Consistent, fair discipline for criminal action*

4. Deflect offenders: Change movement patterns of potential student offenders *Example: Dispersal of loitering students*	9. Utilize place managers: Use existing employees as guardians *Example: Teachers as monitors of other-than-classroom space*	14. Disrupt markets: Make it difficult for students to transfer stolen goods *Example: Partner with local pawn shops, SRO monitoring of online resale sites*	19. Neutralize peer pressure: Lessen students' desire to gain acceptance through criminal action *Example: Peer mentoring, nondelinquent school culture*	24. Assist compliance: Make it easy to behave according to expectations *Example: Student programming on conflict resolution; good-behavior-reinforcement programming*
5. Control tools/weapons: Limit offender access to or use of instrumentalities associated with particular modus operandi *Example: Metal detectors, book bag policy (clear bags, or ban all bags)*	10. Strengthen formal surveillance: Provide official guardians and/or increase their abilities to detect *Example: School police (SROs), security guards, security cameras*	15. Deny benefits: Make it difficult for students to use targets for intended purposes *Example: Facilitate security of phones and tablets (i.e., PIN protection)*	20. Discourage imitation: Limit knowledge of criminal action that might prompt other students to copy *Example: Promptly address disorderly conditions in the school; consistent, fair discipline for criminal action*	25. Control drugs and alcohol: Make it difficult to ingest illegal substances that distort judgment and lower inhibition *Example: Random drug searches*

TABLE 7.4 THE 25 TECHNIQUES OF SITUATIONAL CRIME PREVENTION, APPLIED TO THE SCHOOL SETTING (*continued*)

Source: Adapted from Smith, M. J., and Clarke, R. V. (2012). Situational crime prevention: Classifying techniques using "good enough" theory. In B. C. Welsh and D. P. Farrington (Eds.), *The Oxford handbook of crime prevention* (pp. 291–315). New York: Oxford University Press.

Columns three, four, and five of Table 7.4 similarly convey the techniques schools use to reduce rewards, provocations, and excuses, respectively.

Like the concepts "school organization" and "delinquent school culture" discussed earlier, "school-based situational opportunity" is a broad-ranging concept that is difficult to measure comprehensively. Thus, there is no standard, readily available measure for assessing variations in situational opportunity in U.S. schools over time. Important exceptions include national trends in school crime prevention, such as schools' implementation of access control, weapons control, electronic surveillance, and other guardianship measures, as reported in Figure 7.6. The trends indicate that use of these specific SCP techniques increased in U.S. schools over the course of the past several decades when overall rates of school crime declined. Such historical trends offer preliminary, descriptive evidence that school crime may, in fact, coincide with situational opportunity, though more rigorous evidence is

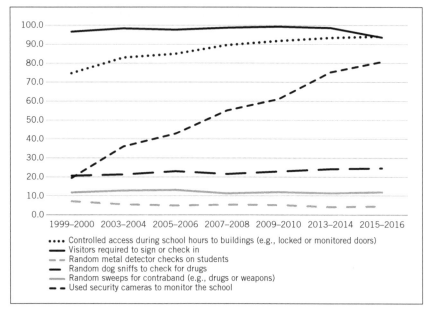

Figure 7.6 Percentage of public schools using safety and security features, 1999–2000 through 2015–2016

(U.S. Department of Education, National Center for Education Statistics, 1999–2000, 2003–04, 2005–06, 2007–08, 2009–10, and 2015–16 School Survey on Crime and Safety [SSOCS], 2000, 2004, 2006, 2008, 2010, and 2016; and Fast Response Survey System [FRSS], "School Safety and Discipline: 2013–14," FRSS 106, 2014.)

clearly in order. In the subsections to follow, we review the research aimed at examining more fully the potential correlation between situational opportunity and rates of school crime incidents. The relevant research includes multivariate quantitative analyses as well as detailed qualitative research addressing whether conditions indicative of situational opportunity are related to higher rates of school crime, or, conversely, whether use of SCP reduces school crime. The research reviewed focuses specifically on the effects of schools' characteristics related to four of the five theoretical concepts underlying situational opportunity: effort, risk, provocations, and excuses. Though schools also likely differ in the extent to which rewards of crime are obvious and available (see column 3, Table 7.4), we are aware of little research on that issue.

Does Situational Opportunity within School Environments Increase Student Offending and Victimization?

School context and "effort." Research since the 1980s underscores the idea that because of their structure and function, schools are places in which motivated offenders and accessible targets/victims readily converge. In their seminal work nearly three decades ago, Garofalo et al. (1987, pp. 329–330) noted, "The school domain is probably the most predominant location for the routine daily activities of adolescents, at least for 9 months of the year . . . bringing them into frequent contact with fellow students of similar ages . . . [who] have a relatively high rate of offending." In short, potential offenders and potential victims are within arm's reach of one another each school day. That said, research indicates there is variability in the ease with which crimes can occur across specific "sub-contexts" or "micro-settings" within any one school (Astor and Meyer, 2001; Astor et al., 1999; Brunson and Miller, 2009; Crowe, 1990). For example, research on micro-settings for school crime indicates that cafeterias are common sites for violence, likely because they are conducive to fights—they are places where large numbers of students congregate and where "ready-made props" for mischief are available in the form of food, beverages, serving trays, and the like (Brunson and Miller, 2009). Research also indicates that hallways are specific school sub-contexts where violent incidents cluster because they allow offenders to just "hang out" and access potential victims. Students interviewed as part of Brunson and Miller's research of inner-city St. Louis youths provided details to this effect: "Most of the fights really kick off in the hallways . . . you might find a group of guys standing somewhere and they just feel like they want to cause you trouble. And that's usually when that happens" (Brunson and Miller, 2009, p. 198; see also Astor et al., 1999). Additional indirect support for this idea comes from quantitative research indicating that rates of crime increase as the number of class changes increase (O'Neill and McGloin, 2007).

Other quantitative research examines the effectiveness of SCP tactics aimed at making crime more difficult throughout the school generally, as well as within specific micro-contexts. These measures include installation of metal detectors and door locks, book bag bans, and locker searches (see Table 7.4). Several types of research address the efficacy of such techniques:

- Individual-level analyses of NCVS-SCS data examine correlations between individual student perceptions of their school's use of SCP and individual student victimization experiences (Burrow and Apel, 2008; Kupchik and Farina, 2016; Schreck et al., 2003; Wynne and Joo, 2011). They generally report that students in schools that use metal detectors, door locks, locker searches, and book bag policies have similar victimization risk as those not exposed to those security measures.
- School-level analyses of SSOCS data focus on the correlation between schools' use of strategies to increase offender effort, as reported by principals, and rates of school crime incidents known

to principals (Crawford and Burns, 2015, 2016; Jennings et al., 2011; Na and Gottfredson, 2013; O'Neill and McGloin, 2007; Sevigny and Zhang, 2018). As a whole, these studies provide little evidence that schools' use of techniques such as metal detectors, door locks, locker searches, and book bag policies are related to their rates of crime. In fact, the few significant effects shown in these analyses suggest that measures designed to increase offender effort are associated with higher, not lower, levels of crime (Crawford and Burns, 2015; Schreck et al., 2003; but see Jennings et al., 2011).

- Tillyer and colleagues' (2011) multilevel analysis of wave 1 of the RSVP data reports that metal detectors, locker checks, or book bag bans, as reported by principals, are unrelated to student self-reported victimization.

There are several possible interpretations of the lack of research evidence supporting the effectiveness of situational prevention practices aimed at increasing offender effort. One is that schools are simply reactive in their implementation of such practices, with prevention efforts occurring only after there is a clear crime problem. If so, it would be difficult for researchers to observe preventive effects of these practices in the typical cross-sectional analysis. Another interpretation is that situational prevention practices, while theoretically reasonable, do not always work as intended. Interviews with students in qualitative studies point to practical limitations along these lines. For example, students interviewed by Brunson and Miller (2009) noted, "I've been to schools where they have metal detectors and kids still get guns in school. . . . In a way, it just make you think like, what is the system doing? I mean, they spend all this money on metal detectors, and here kids still walk up through the metal detectors with guns but they don't find 'em" (p. 200). In other qualitative research, students similarly remarked, "If somebody want to bring a gun in they can get slick. And that metal detector ain't going to stop them" (Astor et al., 1999, p. 29).

Yet another interpretation is that effects of effort-focused SCP on school crime might be more indirect, whereby SCP efforts attenuate individual risk factors for offending or victimization. Most research to date on the effectiveness of access control and weapons/contraband control considers only direct effects. One exception is Johnson and colleagues' (2019) study of weapon carrying and weapon use among students in the first two waves of RSVP. They found that a school-level index tapping access control, contraband control, weapons control, and surveillance techniques interacted with students' low self-control. Specifically, the greater risk of weapon carrying associated with low self-control was limited by higher levels of school security. Such a finding is a promising counterweight to earlier findings of null effects for many security practices. In short, SCP might reduce school crime via multiple mechanisms that to date have not been sufficiently evaluated in extant research. Indeed, the tendency of research to focus only on the direct effects of SCP may be masking important benefits of these popular techniques.

School context and "risk." As with "effort," there is mixed research evidence regarding situational opportunity's sub-concept of "risk"—or, the likelihood of detecting student offenders. On the one hand, some studies indicate students' perceptions of risk affect whether and where school crime occurs. For example, Astor and colleagues (1999) mapped violent incidents occurring in five Michigan schools and then interviewed students and teachers about these incidents and their locations. They found that "no severe violent events were reported in classrooms while a teacher was present" (p. 19). In contrast, violent events tended to cluster in places where students perceived that teacher responsibility for the space was ambiguous. These "unowned" places, like cafeterias and hallways, are spaces where teachers acted uncertain about their obligations for controlling student behavior. Brunson and Miller's (2009, p. 199) interviews of St. Louis students also indicated that perceived improbability of teacher intervention was key in determining good locations for fighting: "The school is real big . . . it's a whole lot of vacant parts of the school where you can just go. Ain't no teachers."

Many schools try to compensate for the fact that teachers cannot be everywhere, managing risk through other means. In particular, schools often try to increase risk of detection of student offending through use of formal surveillance measures, including professional police (school resource officers, or SROs), security guards, and security cameras. However, research indicates these measures are not associated with school crime as predicted by situational opportunity theory (Bouchard, Wang, and Beauregard, 2012; Burrow and Apel, 2008; Crawford and Burns, 2015, 2016; Fisher, Higgins, and Homer, 2021; Kupchik and Farina, 2016; Na and Gottfredson, 2013; O'Neil and McGloin, 2007; Schreck et al., 2003; Sevigny and Zhang, 2018; Tillyer et al., 2011; Wynne and Joo, 2011). In fact, some analyses of SSOCS data report that use of security guards, SROs, and/or some combination of formal surveillance techniques is associated with more, not less, school crime (e.g., Crawford and Burns, 2015, 2016; Gottfredson, Crosse, Tang, Bauer, Harmon, Hagen, and Greene, 2020; Jennings et al., 2011; Nickerson and Martens, 2008). Qualitative work reinforces the minimal effects of security guards on school crime, explicitly highlighting the poor quality of some school police personnel. For example, students interviewed by Astor and colleagues (1999, p. 30) indicated, "We've got the cheapest security guards you can get! They don't know what they are doing. . . . They aren't even trained. . . . And plus, they're not energetic. They out of shape."

It is important to note that many studies (including those cited above) evaluating effects of risk-enhancement strategies on school rates use cross-sectional data. Thus, they do not firmly establish the cause-and-effect temporality needed to determine if surveillance measures affect the likelihood of crime incidents. Previously mentioned studies of the effectiveness of access control and target hardening share this limitation. Consequently, it is arguable that use of police/security personnel or other security/risk enhancements positively correlates with school crime incidents because the prevention practices come after the fact; that is, in response to crime problems. If implementation of security is need-based, then schools engaging in such security practices will likely show more crime than schools that do not (Crawford and Burns, 2015; Jennings et al., 2011). Recent studies have attempted to better discern effects of surveillance techniques, particularly use of SROs and cameras. Their research designs explicitly establish temporal order (i.e., longitudinal studies), use matching to more rigorously control for differences between schools with and without SROs, or apply meta-analysis and systematic review techniques to combine research evidence (Fisher and Hennessy, 2016; Fisher et al., 2021; Gottfredson et al., 2012, 2020; Na and Gottfredson, 2013; Reingle Gonzalez et al., 2016; Swartz et al., 2016; Turanovic et al., 2019). Collectively, these studies reiterate the findings that additional police and electronic surveillance do little to reduce school crime. In fact, these strategies may increase punishment and decrease feelings of safety among students (a "criminalization effect" of school policing linked to concerns about a "school-to-prison pipeline" are discussed more fully in Chapter 8).

Although most of the research assessing school-based situational opportunity in the form of risk focuses on informal (teacher) and formal (police) surveillance, a few studies address other risk-enhancement techniques. For example, isolated studies indicate that extending guardianship by leveraging students' (or parents') anonymous tips/reports is unrelated to school crime rates (Nickerson and Martens, 2008; see Sevigny and Zhang, 2018, for review). Other research reports minimal effects on school crime of physical designs that enhance natural surveillance (i.e., clear sight lines) (Wilcox, Augustine, and Clayton, 2006).[13]

---

13. Wilcox, Augustine, and Clayton (2006) examined the effects of four distinct measures of school-level natural surveillance: clear sight lines from the main office, clear sight lines in hallways, clear sight lines from outside the school to the school grounds and buildings, and presence of entrapment areas (hiding spots) on the school's exterior grounds. The researchers examined the effects of these measures of natural surveillance on both student-reported victimization and teacher-witnessed incidents of student offending. None of the four surveillance measures were related to student-reported victimization. However, schools with stronger natural surveillance in the form of clear sight lines from outside the school onto school grounds had significantly lower incidents of teacher-witnessed crime.

School context and "provocations." From a situational opportunity perspective, school settings can provoke crime when they generate frustration and other forms of emotional arousal, foster disputes, or allow peer pressure and copycat (criminal) behavior to take root. As implied in Table 7.4, situational opportunity in the form of "provocation" goes hand in hand with the concepts of school (dis)organization and delinquent school culture discussed earlier in this chapter. Schools that are disorganized (rather than communally organized) are non-collaborative and fail to uphold school rules through fair, effective social control. This condition can provoke crime by breeding tension and encouraging imitation of delinquent behavior (i.e., "If they can get away with it, so can I"). Additionally, a delinquent school culture can provoke offending by creating an environment in which disputes are "egged on" and peer pressure is pervasive.

As discussed earlier in this chapter, several multivariate quantitative studies report that indicators of school organization and delinquent school culture are, in fact, related to student victimization and offending (e.g., Bouchard et al., 2012; Crawford and Burns, 2015, 2016; Jennings et al., 2011; Kirk, 2009; Kupchik and Farina, 2016; Payne, 2008; Schreck et al., 2003). Qualitative research supports the idea that one probable mechanism behind the effect of delinquent school culture, as indicated by *gang presence* specifically, is situational provocation. Students interviewed in the Brunson and Miller (2009, p. 196) study, for example, documented the emotional arousal associated with being in proximity to rival gang members for an entire school day: "You can sit in the classroom with somebody you don't like for like, two hours . . . if it's hot and you already got an attitude and you gotta look at this guy for two hours—a lot of times a fight'll break out" (see also Carson and Esbensen, 2019).

The situational opportunity perspective suggests that, beyond school disorganization and delinquent school culture, school disorder (e.g., litter, graffiti, noise, disrepair) also can be a source of provocation (see Table 7.4). The school disorder–school crime link is theoretically rooted in "broken windows theory" (Wilson and Kelling, 1982)—the idea that unchecked incivility invites more (and more serious forms of) disorder. If disorder continues to go "unrepaired," rule violations become entrenched. In short, school disorder provokes criminal action by encouraging imitation and reinforcing norms expecting misbehavior. In fact, there is some research suggesting that unchecked disorder in schools is associated with higher rates of student offending and victimization. For example, multilevel studies using the RSVP data show that general levels of physical disorder and misconduct among students in schools is related to increased risk of criminal victimization (Tillyer et al., 2010, 2011).

School context and excuses. Within situational opportunity theory, the sub-concept of "excuses" refers to a lack of clarity regarding offender responsibility. Excuses exist when settings fail to clarify that offenders are unambiguously responsible for their misbehavior. Per Table 7.4, one of the main ways that schools can limit excuses for offending is by setting clear rules and alerting students' consciences about those rules through consistent, fair enforcement of behavioral expectations. In this regard, the "excuses" aspect of situational opportunity overlaps substantially with the concept of school (dis)organization. Again, numerous studies reviewed earlier in this chapter report that students who perceive clear and fair rules in their school report fewer victimization experiences, and several other studies show that communal school organization or school efficacy lowers student offending and victimization (e.g., Burrow and Apel, 2008; Payne, 2008; Payne et al., 2003; Kirk, 2009; Schreck et al., 2003).

Beyond providing clear rules and consistent discipline, schools can limit excuses for offending by assisting compliance through, for example, positive behavioral reinforcement and providing students with the skills needed to resolve conflicts peacefully (see Table 7.4). In fact, programs aimed at reinforcement of good behavior, social skills training, and conflict resolution are plentiful in today's schools, and evaluations suggest that they are effective at reducing school crime (Gottfredson, 2001; Gottfredson et al., 2012). Finally, also indicated in Table 7.4, controlling students' use of drugs and alcohol is yet another strategy for removing potential excuses for student offending. Conversely, availability of drugs and alcohol within the school setting offers situational opportunity. Here again, situational opportunity overlaps with the concept of delinquent school culture (to the extent that drug availability is also a valid indicator of delinquent school culture). Numerous studies reviewed earlier report that drug availability at school is positively associated with student victimization experiences as well as overall rates of student offending. On the other hand, research also suggests that random searches used by many schools to control drugs are unrelated to rates of crime (Sevigny and Zhang, 2018).

Summary

Overall, the research to date suggests that situational opportunity is important for understanding school crime, with important caveats. The key points emerging from the research literature indicate that:

- Students consider effort and risk when deciding if, where, and when to engage in delinquent activity at school, with certain schools, and certain sub-contexts within schools, appearing to provide settings for nearly effortless and risk-free offending (Astor et al., 1999; Brunson and Miller, 2009).

- Schools vary in the extent to which they offer conditions that provoke disputes (i.e., disorganization, presence of rival gang members, deviant cultural norms) or provide excuses (i.e., unclear rules,
inconsistent discipline, available drugs), and such conditions are
related to rates of school crime (Bouchard et al., 2012; Crawford
and Burns, 2015, 2016; Jennings et al., 2011; Kirk, 2009; Kupchik
and Farina, 2016; Schreck et al., 2003).
- Some SCP techniques show strong effectiveness for reducing
school-based situational opportunity. These include teacher-based
place management, communal school organization, prosocial norms
(including the control of gangs and drugs), and clear avenues for
assisting compliance (e.g., conflict resolution training, good behavior reinforcement) (Astor et al., 1999; Burrow and Apel, 2008;
Gottfredson, 2001; Gottfredson et al., 2012; Payne 2008, 2009).[14]
- Evidence supporting other SCP techniques is less promising. The
weight of the evidence suggests that strategies aimed at controlling access, weapons, or contraband, as well as formal surveillance
strategies do not reduce school crime. However, most of the de-
signs/analyses do not account very well for the reactive nature of
situational prevention measures (i.e., there are selection effects),
thus obscuring their potential for crime prevention benefits. A
handful of recent studies of formal surveillance strategies (especially use of SROs/police) have incorporated research designs and
analytic strategies that handle this issue, but they also report few
(if any) crime-reduction effects (Fisher and Hennessy, 2016; Fisher
et al., 2021; Gottfredson et al., 2020; Na and Gottfredson, 2013; Reingle Gonzalez, Jetelina, and Jennings, 2016; Swartz et al., 2015).
- Most research on the effectiveness of access control, weapons control, and formal surveillance strategies considers only their direct
effects. Indirect effects operating through the mitigation of individual risk factors are not assessed in most studies. An important
exception is Johnson et al. (2019). Results from it suggest that these
SCP strategies attenuated the risk of low self-control on student
offending, thus providing a counterweight to the largely null effects of many such security practices.

---

14. We presented research relevant to each of the five key concepts underlying situational opportunity and prevention. It should be noted that a few previous studies combined measures that cut across those five SCP concepts into an overall security index, making it hard to
discern specific effects for effort, risk, and so on (e.g., Burrow and Apel, 2008; Johnson et al.,
2019; Nickerson and Martens, 2008). As such, reference to these studies was minimal.

Conclusion

In contrast to the focus on individual characteristics that are related to student offending and victimization (as in Chapters 4, 5, and 6), this chapter focused on aspects of the school environment that foster or impede school crime incidents. This chapter thus addressed the third side of the problem analysis triangle introduced in Chapter 1—the *place* where offenders and victims converge. This focus on places has roots in a century of criminological work which indicates that crime incidents are nonrandomly patterned across cities or regions within countries, neighborhoods within cities, and streets within neighborhoods. It is also rooted in criminological work suggesting that most crime is concentrated within a small subset of "risky facilities." Applying these ideas to school settings, we derive the implication that schools across the United States face differential exposure to crime and its related consequences. Many schools will experience very little crime, while others will endure a highly disproportionate amount. This fact is evident in data from national surveys (e.g., SSOCS) and more localized surveys (e.g., RSVP). Thus, while crime has declined on a national scale when viewed through a historical lens, it remains at unacceptable levels in a subset of high-risk schools.

What characteristics make some schools particularly risky? To answer this question, public discourse often focuses on school size, location, and the socioeconomic and racial-ethnic makeup of the student body. However, as reviewed in this chapter, the research evidence regarding the correlations between these school structural characteristics and school rates of crime is modest. Thus, it appears likely that variability in school crime rates results from other school-level factors. In Chapter 2, we highlighted the role that social (dis)organization, culture, and situational opportunity play in understanding crime across places, generally, and we pointed to the possible relevance of those concepts for understanding cross-school variability in rates of crime, specifically. Much of this chapter focused on whether the empirical research on school crime supports the importance of social (dis)organization, culture, and situational opportunity.

There is moderate research evidence supporting the explanatory importance of these three factors, with the caveat that relatively few studies to date provide rigorous estimates of their effects. Experimental designs with random assignment are rare in school crime research, and some multilevel, multivariate, quasi-experimental studies lack adequate controls for both individual student differences and potentially confounding school characteristics. The quasi-experimental studies that most fully control for these confounds indicate, overall, that the manner in which school organization, delinquent school culture, and school-based situational opportunity relate to school crime is not always direct. For example, several studies reported effects of school organization that were in interaction with risk factors from other domains (e.g., individual risk factors or community risk factors). Only a handful of studies have examined such interactions, but there is consistent evidence across these studies that measures of school organization reduce school crime by offsetting risk in other domains. Similarly, research evidence to date supports the idea that schools with a pervasive delinquent culture report more offending and victimization incidents, though delinquent school culture gets enacted by students only in settings where social control is weak. Finally, there is evidence that some indicators of (greater) situational opportunity are associated with higher overall levels of school crime and/or concentrated levels of crime in certain school sub-contexts. At the same time, there is evidence that some measures schools use to counter situational opportunity work only indirectly, by mitigating individual-level risk factors for offending. Implications of the research evidence reviewed here are discussed further in the next chapter, where we address prevailing recommendations for creating safer schools.

8

School Zone

Strategies in Search of Safety

G uided by the problem analysis triangle as a conceptual framework, the preceding chapters sought to understand motivations for student offending, factors making students suitable targets for victimization, and school characteristics facilitating or constraining crime. In this last chapter, our attention turns to school *responses* to crime or the threat of crime.

Just as offending and victimization vary over time and across school contexts, so do school responses to crime. Chapter 1 offered the first glimpse of the variation in school crime experiences and responses through the eyes of the authors of this book as well as our children. In the midwestern suburban high school that Pamela Wilcox attended in the mid-1980s, target hardening techniques that are currently commonplace were absent. There were no locked doors, no buzzers to push to gain entry, no metal detectors, and no security cameras. Police, school resource officers, private security, and drug-sniffing dogs were absent from the premises. However, inner-city schools just a few miles away from Wilcox's school were different. They installed metal detectors, employed unarmed security officers to patrol middle- and high-school grounds, and contracted with city police to patrol a downtown bus stop. Graham Ousey's mid-1980s high-school experience in a small Virginia city was similar to Wilcox's, though perhaps with a bit more police presence via occasional random searches for drugs in school lockers. "Shelter in place" or "active shooter" drills or general concerns about armed intruders were nowhere near the radar. In contrast, the school experiences of Ousey's children and those of Marie Tillyer's children suggest that the threat of crime occupies a place of general prominence, requiring regular occurrences of lockdowns and other preparatory drills (in anticipation of school shooters), despite all attending high-performing, economically advantaged schools in safe communities during the 2000s and 2010s.

With noted variations in school crime responses as a backdrop, several important questions arise: How do schools go about crime prevention? What are the prevailing strategies? How well are they grounded in theory and evidence from science? Addressing these questions comprehensively is beyond the scope of a single chapter. It likely requires a book-length treatment (see, e.g., Gottfredson, 2001; Kupchik, 2010, 2016). However, we can close by offering some central thoughts and analysis about currently popular approaches to school crime prevention, their emergence, their alignment with the problem analysis triangle, and their consistency with theory and evidence from social-scientific studies of school crime reported in earlier chapters.

We focus attention on four broad strategies used to varying degrees and often in combination by many of today's schools to address and prevent crime. In the next four sections, we present a more detailed discussion and assessment of each strategy. However, as an introduction, we begin by briefly outlining the basic tenets of each strategy and identifying its points of intersection with the problem analysis triangle framework applied throughout the book (see also Figure 8.1).

1. *Enhanced security and harsh discipline*
   - A strategy that aims to increase the certainty and severity of disciplinary responses to school crime by putting police in schools, securing the school building and grounds through mechanical surveillance (i.e., metal detectors, cameras), and using exclusionary punishments for rule violations
   - Addresses the "offender" and "place" sides of the problem analysis triangle

2. *Active assailant preparedness*
   - A strategy focused on reducing harm in cases of active school shooters by making the school space, and the students within, less vulnerable
   - Addresses the "victim" and "place" sides of the problem analysis triangle

3. *Therapeutic practices*
   - Strategies attempting to make students resistant to factors that put them at higher risk for delinquency and/or victimization

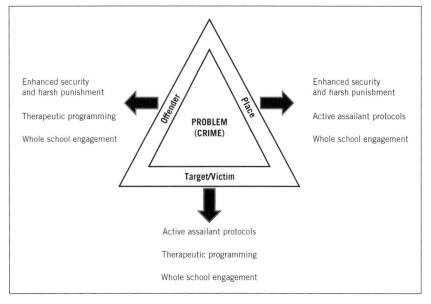

Figure 8.1 Four common approaches to addressing and reducing school crime and how they intersect with the problem analysis triangle

through school-based curricula teaching self-control, conflict resolution, and social competency, among other things
- Addresses the "offender" and "victim" sides of the problem analysis triangle
3. *Whole school engagement*
    - Strategies aimed at reducing crime by creating a supportive, integrative school environment that reinforces prosocial norms, provides effective informal social control, and prioritizes strong school relational networks
    - Focuses on the "place" side of the triangle; might also address "offenders" and "victims"

"Get Tough": Enhanced Security and Harsh Discipline

Rockmon Montrell "Rock" Allen, an 18-year-old from Jackson Mississippi, has never gone to jail. But school, he says, was close enough. . . . In the 10th and 11th grades . . . he was sent to in-school [suspension] whenever he spoke out of turn, questioned a teacher, was tardy, or refused to take off his hat. . . . Instead of being in class, Rock would sit in an empty room, doing nothing, for up to three days at a time. . . . A few weeks into the 12th grade, Rock . . . pulled out his cellphone during class. When his principal told him to put it away . . . Rock responded with a verbal threat: "I'm going to bust [the teacher] for taking everybody's phones," he said. For that outburst, he was sent to Madison County Academic Option Center, an "alternative school" 15 miles away. . . . At Rock's alternative school, there were no windows in the classrooms and hallways. Teams of seven police officers regularly walked in and out, searching students' jackets . . . ninth- and 12th-graders were all held together in the same crowded rooms and received no academic instruction for weeks at a time. By December, Rock . . . returned to his regular high school, where any infraction would mean getting sent back to the alternative school. Only a few days later, Rock was caught in the parking lot during lunch—a common practice that isn't against school rules—and charged with being "outside of his assigned area" in violation of his probation. He was sent back to the alternative school for the remainder of his senior year. (Hager, 2015, pp. 1–3)

Stories like Rock's, documented in 2015, illustrate a movement that began several decades prior. In the wake of rising rates of juvenile violence in the 1980s, and spurred further by several high-profile school shootings in the 1990s, school administrators and policymakers increasingly embraced a "get tough" approach to school crime (Addington, 2009; Hirschfield, 2018; Kupchik, 2010, 2016; Rocque and Snellings, 2018). It combined enhanced security and harsh discipline to increase the certainty and severity of disciplinary responses to violations of school rules.

To provide greater context, the "get tough" approach in schools coincided with punitive responses to adult crime, which were increasingly popular in the latter part of the twentieth century. Individuals ensnared in the criminal justice system during this era faced punitive policies and practices such as "three-strikes" laws that mandated a life sentence for a third felony conviction, legislative guidelines that mandated particular sentences for certain categories of crime (i.e., mandatory minimum sentences), and "super-max" facilities, where prisoners served entire sentences in solitary-confinement-like conditions. These policies contributed to sharp increases in imprisonment rates, a phenomenon now commonly called "mass incarceration." Federal legislation in the 1990s facilitated the analogous, punitive turn in the handling of crime in schools. For examples, congressional funding supported putting law-enforcement officers, commonly called school resource officers (or SROs) in schools. Additionally, Congress made educational funding contingent on a school's adoption of zero-tolerance policies mandating a one-year expulsion of any student found to have brought a weapon to school (Kupchik, 2010; Wolf and Kupchik, 2017). Backed by such legislative incentives, schools increasingly tackled rule breaking or its potential in a manner analogous to the criminal justice system rather than through more traditional school discipline practices. Crime scholars refer to this shift as the "prisonization of schools and the criminalization of students" (Payne and Welch, 2010, p. 1020; see also Hirschfield, 2018; Kupchik, 2010, 2016; Ramey, 2015).

Various manifestations of the "prisonization of schools and criminalization of students" appear in schools today. For instance, sworn law enforcement officers, once a rarity inside of schools, are now commonplace. Students witness daily the presence of police patrolling their schools. They are uniformed, armed, capable of making formal arrests, and sometimes accompanied by dogs that search students and their possessions for drugs or other contraband. In fact, fully two-thirds of public middle schools and nearly three-fourths of public high schools report using sworn law enforcement officers who routinely carry firearms (Wang et al., 2020). Additionally, many students are required to walk through metal detectors or electronically controlled egress doors—similar to those seen in many jails—before gaining entry to school hallways and classrooms. Students also are routinely subject to video surveillance within school buildings and on school grounds. Nearly 85% of public schools reported the use of security cameras for monitoring purposes in 2017–2018; less than 20% of schools did so two decades ago (Wang et al., 2020). School security is now a multibillion-dollar industry, and the public supports security-related expenditures. A recent nationwide survey of American adults revealed that over 70% of respondents expressed willingness to pay more taxes in order to fund security cameras, metal detectors, and stronger access control in schools (Burton, Pickett, Jonson, Cullen, and Burton, 2021).

Beyond prisonlike security, students routinely face mandatory punishment for violating rules, regardless of the severity of infractions. These mandatory punishments replace individualized and indeterminate punishments that schools embraced in the past. They often are "exclusionary," involving removal of the offending student from the classroom for days or months via arrest, suspension, expulsion, or placement in an alternative school. In fact, in any given academic year during the 2000s, serious disciplinary actions taken by U.S. public schools number in the hundreds of thousands (Wang et al., 2020).[1] Harsh disciplinary actions appear to have peaked in the 2005–2008 period, averaging approximately 800,000 serious punishments annually.

---

1. "Serious disciplinary action" defined in the SSOCS as suspension of five or more days, expulsion, or placement in an alternative school.

How does the "get tough" approach align with the problem analysis framework and school crime science?

The "get tough" approach simultaneously focuses on the "offender" and "place" sides of the problem analysis triangle while drawing on social control (deterrence) and situational opportunity theories of crime. First, strong security and use of harsh punishments serve as formal controls designed to suppress offender motivation and deter (further) student delinquency. At the same time, strong security and zero-tolerance disciplinary practices limit situational opportunities for motivated offenders and suitable targets to converge within the school environment. Hypothetically, enhanced guardianship of school spaces reduces opportunities while harsh punishments remove students who commit crime. Overall, it is clear that the "get tough" approach has roots in criminological theory—particularly, control-based deterrence theory and situational opportunity theory.

Research reviewed in Chapter 7 provided moderate support for situational opportunity theory as a tool for understanding school crime. Additionally, it provided evidence that some strategies to reduce opportunity through situational crime prevention were promising. However, Chapter 7 also indicated several of the most popular strategies for enhancing security—cameras and SROs—appear largely ineffective at reducing crime in schools. For example, recent longitudinal analysis of SSOCS data by Fisher et al. (2021) revealed no differences in the frequency of social disturbances or the volume of crime recorded between schools that implemented security cameras and those that did not. Another recent longitudinal study by Gottfredson and colleagues (2020) found that schools with increases in SRO staffing experienced *increased* numbers of drug- and weapon-related offenses and exclusionary disciplinary actions relative to a matched sample of comparison schools (see also Fisher and Hennessy, 2016; Jonson, 2017; Swartz et al., 2016). In short, use of SROs appears to widen the net of punishment without reducing instances of misbehavior. In turn, there is little evidence to date that harsh discipline deters students as intended, with several studies indicating it is unrelated to levels of school crime (Fissel et al., 2019; Way, 2011; see also Bordsky, 2016). This evidence aligns with the broader literature in criminology on deterrence that shows a negligible relationship between the severity of punishment and criminal offending (Paternoster and Bachman, 2013; Pratt, Cullen, Blevins, Daigle, and Madensen, 2006).

In contrast, there is considerable evidence that harsh discipline produces collateral damage among punished students. In particular, exclusionary punishment pushes students toward the juvenile and criminal justice systems—a process referred to as the "school-to-prison pipeline." For example, research evidence indicates that exclusionary discipline is associated with known risk factors for delinquency, including strained family and peer relations as well as school disengagement among those punished (Jacobsen, 2020; Kupchik, 2016; Pyne, 2019). Moreover, longitudinal studies indicate that school suspensions increase individuals' offending over time, heightening their risks of experiencing adverse outcomes in adulthood, including victimization, offending, and incarceration (Mowen, Brent, and Boman, 2020; Wolf and Kupchik, 2017). Making matters worse, there is racial patterning to harsh disciplinary practices. Research indicates this is experienced more commonly by racial-minority students and in schools with higher percentages of minority students (Hughes et al., 2022; Kupchik, 2016; 2020; Morris and Perry, 2017; Payne and Welch, 2010; Ramey, 2015; Rocque and Paternoster, 2011; Skiba, Michael, Nardo, and Peterson, 2002; Welch and Payne, 2010). Often these students already face socioeconomic inequities, and the collateral consequences of exclusionary punishment create additional disadvantages. Illustrative of this fact, one study reported that racial disparities in rates of suspension account for one-fifth of the disparity in school performance between African American and White students (Morris and Perry, 2016).

Due to the discriminatory patterns and adverse effects highlighted, a number of school districts across the country have, in recent years, instituted reforms aimed at reducing exclusionary discipline (Hirschfield, 2018). Fueled by scientific evidence of its ineffectiveness and "backfire effects," exclusionary punishment is a "get tough" practice that is trending downward. It is not extinct, however, with still nearly 300,000 harsh disciplinary actions taken by public schools in 2017–2018.

Summary

The "get tough" approach attempts to alter the school environment through enhanced security features and zero-tolerance, exclusionary discipline policies. However, a serious limitation of the approach is that it presumes a relationship between enhanced security/harsh discipline and school crime that scientific evidence does not support. Collectively, the research to date suggests that expensive security strategies offer little preventive value and may produce unintended effects, including increasing levels of fear, student referrals and arrests, and the use of exclusionary discipline. In turn, exclusionary discipline does not produce safe schools but is associated with numerous collateral consequences, including halting academic progress and enhancing risk of continued involvement in crime.

"Get Down!" Active Assailant Protocols

As Ajani Dartiguenave rode to school in Charlotte with his mom one morning in October, he heard on the radio that a student at Butler

High, about 20 miles away, had been gunned down in the hallway. Ajani, 12, didn't say anything about it at the time, recalled his mother, Claudia Charles, and she didn't discuss it with him.

They live in an upscale neighborhood where crime is rare. . . . Not once did she imagine that the violence they'd heard about on the radio would make him feel unsafe. Eleven days later Ajani was studying English literature at Governors' Village STEM Academy when someone on the intercom announced that the campus was being locked down. The seventh-grader didn't know that an anonymous threat—never in danger of being carried out—had elicited the response. He only knew that a boy in the community had been shot to death inside another school a week before, and that made Ajani think he would get shot too. So, as he and his friends sat on the floor, Ajani reached into his bookbag . . . he pulled out a pencil, writing first on an index card and then on a sheet of paper. At the top, he scribbled his home address and his mom's name.

"I am sorry for anything I have done," he wrote.

"I'm scared to death."

"I will miss you."

"I hope that you are going to be ok with me gone." (Rich and Cox, 2018, pp. 13–14)

Active assailant protocols, often generically referred to as "lockdowns," overlap in some ways with strategies defining the "get tough" approach to school security and discipline. Like "get tough" strategies, active assailant protocols became increasingly commonplace in the late 1990s amid public concerns about crime, and they are typically one aspect of schools' overall safety and security plans. However, these protocols emphasize *preparedness* over punitiveness. Moreover, U.S. schools adopted active assailant protocols in specific response to school shootings, not because of general concerns about a rising tide of urban youth violence, which motivated the "get tough" approach. In particular, the tragic mass shooting at affluent, suburban Columbine High School in 1999 sparked a moral panic about school shootings, centered around the notion that the unthinkable could happen anywhere (Addington, 2009; Jonson, 2017). In response, schools developed protocols to reduce harm to students when threats of gun violence surfaced. Training associated with those protocols are now a regular part of the school year for most students. In fact, in the 2017–2018 school year, 95% of public middle and high schools reported having a written protocol for active shooter situations and drilling students on lockdown emergency procedures (Wang et al., 2020). According to an analysis by the *Washington Post*, more than 4.1 million students (pre K–12), like Ajani Dartiguenave, endured an actual lockdown or a lockdown drill in 2017–18 (Rich and Cox, 2018).

Although discussions of active assailant procedures often imply "one size fits all," numerous strategies exist. Scholars classify the various strategies into three broad paradigms: (1) single-option, "traditional lockdown" approaches, (2) dual-option approaches, and (3) multi-option approaches (Jonson, Moon, and Gialopsos, 2020; Jonson, Moon, and Hendry, 2020). The single-option "traditional lockdown" approach emphasizes limiting exposure to an assailant by locking entry points, turning off lights, staying quiet, and taking cover. Dual-option approaches use the traditional lockdown as the foundation but add self-evacuation as a possible contingency should students be in the same room as an assailant or in a large, open area of the school during an intrusion (in both situations hiding behind a locked door is moot). Multi-option approaches build on traditional lockdowns in three important ways: (1) they advocate building of barricades out of objects in the students' environment (i.e., desks, chairs, shoes), (2) they support evacuation in a number of circumstances, and (3) they teach active resistance (i.e., throwing objects) as a response option should students find themselves face-to-face with an assailant (Jonson, Moon, and Hendry, 2020, p. 3).[2]

How do active assailant protocols align with the problem analysis framework and school crime science?

Active assailant protocols ignore factors motivating student offending but address ways students can protect themselves from serious harm while also providing strategies for securing places within schools (i.e., classrooms). Thus, they reduce opportunities for assailants to converge with victims. As such, active assailant protocols address the "target/victim" and "place" sides of the problem analysis triangle. In particular, these protocols encourage actions aligned with routine activity, target congruence, and situational opportunity theories (see Chapter 2). They provide strategies for removing potential victims from unsafe areas or "hardening" potential targets/victims (i.e., making them less vulnerable) while also denying assailants access to places within schools.

While built on sound theory, scientific evidence of the effectiveness of active assailant protocols to date is minimal. Furthermore, that evidence gives

---

2. Multi-response options are represented by various agencies with slogans such as "Run. Hide. Fight.", "Evacuate. Hide Out. Take Action.", and "Alert, Lockdown, Inform, Counter, and Evacuate." (www.alicetraining.com; https://www.dhs.gov/xlibrary/assets/active_shooter _booklet.pdf?0.7552442226207703; https://www.fema.gov/media-library-data/152356195 8719-f1eff6bc841d56b7873e018f73a4e024/ActiveShooter_508.pdf)

reason to see both promise and pitfalls in such programs. On one hand, the high numbers of fatalities and injuries at places like Columbine and Sandy Hook, which used traditional lockdown practices, are anecdotal evidence of ineffectiveness. On the other hand, post-hoc analysis of anecdotal data on students' actions during the shooting rampage at Virginia Tech in 2007 suggests that multi-option protocols might save lives. Jonson, Moon, and Hendry (2020) provided an overview of the student responses relative to numbers of injuries and fatalities across five classrooms targeted in the Virginia Tech incident. Their analysis indicated that active responses were associated with lower rates of fatalities and injuries. For example, in a classroom in which there was no apparent active resistance, 10 of the 14 students (71.4%) were killed, and 2 others were injured. In contrast, in another classroom, students barricaded the door with their feet, and a lightweight table prevented the offender from entering. None of the 12 students in that classroom died, and only one was injured (Jonson, Moon, and Hendry, 2020, p. 2).

Jonson, Moon, and Hendry (2020) also used simulations of school shootings—using Airsoft guns that shoot plastic pellets—to study "likely injury." Simulations occurred during a voluntary active assailant training. The researchers asked participants to respond, alternatively, to the simulated shooting using a single-option protocol (traditional lockdown) and then a multi-option protocol. Fifty percent fewer participants were shot in the simulation using the multi-option approach versus the simulation using the traditional lockdown approach.

Thus, multi-option active assailant protocols show promise, but we need additional scientific evidence on their effectiveness. Moreover, that evidence must be weighed against two other facts: (1) the exceptionally low overall risk of school shooting victimization and (2) the possibility of serious unintended consequences (e.g., Christakis, 2019; Fox and Friedel, 2019; Jonson, 2017). For example, opponents of assailant protocols argue that, while emergency preparations are understandable and done in good faith, current practices for drilling students on shooting events is likely causing psychological harm and should be abandoned ("Everytown for Gun Safety," 2020). Journalistic accounts of the trauma of active assailant drills and actual lockdowns provide gut-wrenching details of students sobbing, vomiting, and writing anguished farewell notes to parents while hunkered down on schoolroom floors (Christakis, 2019; Hamblin, 2018; Rich and Cox, 2018). In a recent piece for the *Atlantic*, Erika Christakis (2019, p. 4) summarizes other concerns:

> Preparing our children for profoundly unlikely events would be one thing if that preparation had no downsides. But, in this case, our ef-

forts may exact a high price. Time and resources spent on drills and structural upgrades to school facilities could otherwise be devoted to, say, a better science program or hiring more experienced teachers. Much more worrying: School-preparedness culture itself may be instilling in millions of children a distorted and foreboding view of their future. It's also encouraging adults to view children as associates in a shared mission to reduce gun violence, a problem whose real solutions, in fact, lie at some remove from the schoolyard.

Journalistic investigation of the psychological impact of active assault protocols is valuable, as is the policy work of advocacy groups. However, scientific analyses are necessary to grasp the extent and nature of beneficial as well as deleterious effects. Few such analyses exist to date. In an exception, Jonson, Moon, and Gialopsos (2020) used a post-training survey of 4th- through 12th-grade participants in a midwestern school district to examine the psychological effects of training in a multi-option protocol (ALICE). Their results indicated that 10% of students experienced a negative psychological outcome after ALICE training, whereas over 85% indicated ALICE either had no effect on their perceived safety or made them feel more confident or safe. Overall, students tended to be no less fearful of the ALICE training than other forms of emergency preparedness (such as tornado drills or training on "stranger danger"). The authors stress that their results were in relation to a *discussion-based* training as opposed to a training involving an *active drill or simulation*. Therefore, results are not generalizable to potentially more traumatizing active practice drills. Nonetheless, their results provide preliminary evidence that age-appropriate discussion-based active assailant training might provide some important agency to students while scaring relatively few in the process.

Summary

The emergency preparedness approach to school safety, centered on active assailant protocols, is immensely popular in education systems today. It addresses rare and specific school crimes—shootings. The goal of active assailant protocols is making spaces within schools less permeable and students less vulnerable. However, the effectiveness of this approach is still largely in question. The research to date suggests that multi-option active assailant protocols may reduce injury and fatalities in school shootings, but their implementation in schools has potential pitfalls. In particular, they can produce unintended trauma, especially if active shooter drills are part of the preparedness protocol or if schools employ lockdowns in response to unsubstantiated threats.

"Get Well": Therapeutic Practice

Nikkia Rowe, the principal of Renaissance Academy High School in West Baltimore, teaches a dating-abuse-prevention curriculum to ninth graders. Violence is a learned behavior, she explained, so she puts the burden on educators in her school—located in an impoverished black neighborhood—to focus on helping students, both victims and perpetrators, navigate trauma and learning their individual stories to shift behaviors and attitudes. "Schools are the training ground to address the abuse and to create that change of mind [to] change those habits," Rowe said. "Ultimately, those patterns that we see in schoolhouses continue into adulthood . . . if they're not receiving those lessons and those supports at home, we're obligated to do it." (Anderson, 2017, https://www.theatlantic.com/education/archive/2017/12/the-preventable-problem-that-schools-ignore/547604/)

Another common approach to the problem of school crime involves "therapeutic programming." We use this term in reference to a broad range of interventions whose primary goal is fostering positive human development and, more specifically, helping students become more resistant to risks for offending and victimization. As such, it emphasizes social support as opposed to punitiveness ("get tough") or emergency preparedness ("get down").

The therapeutic approach (also referred to as "prevention curricula") dates back to the late 1970s and early 1980s—an important period of rapid growth in research on school crime, due in large part to federal funds being poured into the collection of school-based survey data. Those data provided an unprecedented glimpse into the extent, nature, and correlates of adolescent involvement in school crime. They also prompted development of interventions addressing myriad individual problems or deficiencies exhibited by students involved in school crime (Gottfredson et al., 2012; Chouhy, Madero-Hernandez, and Turanovic, 2017; Kulig et al., 2019). There are generally two kinds of therapeutic programs: those focused most directly on addressing offending behavior and those explicitly dealing with victimization risk. That said, due to the victim-offender overlap, the line between these two general types can be murky, and numerous programs simultaneously address both offending and victimization (e.g., the dating-violence prevention program described by Baltimore principal Nikkia Rowe).

Offending-Focused Therapeutic Programming

Offending-focused therapeutic programs aim primarily at reducing delinquent behavior. Program curricula commonly used in schools today include those intended to foster the development of impulse control, cognitive skills, academic achievement, positive peer relations, and prosocial norms—often generally referred to as "socioemotional learning." The assumption is that these characteristics "reverse" known risk factors for offending. Therefore, they may reduce delinquency and other problematic outcomes among students. Examples of programs administered in middle and high schools include the following (Institute of Behavioral Science, University of Colorado, 2020; Institute of Education Sciences, 2020):

- LifeSkills Training (LST): A classroom-based curriculum that teaches middle- and high-school students self-regulation, social skills, and resistance skills in order to reduce substance use and disruptive/problem behavior.
- Too Good for Drugs & Violence: A program that intends to reduce drug use and violence among high-school students by teaching prosocial skills, positive character, and anti-drug/violence norms.

Though these programs intend to reduce delinquency, they can also indirectly serve to reduce victimization risk because many risk factors for offending overlap with the risk factors for victimization. Indeed, as we discussed in Chapters 4, 5, and 6, impulsivity, weak school bonds, and negative peer relations are associated with both offending and victimization.

Victimization-Focused Therapeutic Programming

Other therapeutic programs focus more specifically on reducing student victimization, especially in the form of bullying, broadly defined (i.e., bullying that encompasses delinquent behavior, such as assault). Victimization-focused programs commonly used in school today teach conflict resolution and social-competency skills, with an emphasis on helping students de-escalate tense situations and, in the process, reduce antagonistic tendencies. Victimization-focused programs also commonly teach awareness and help-seeking behaviors that can increase guardianship of victims or potential victims. A few of these programs include (Fox and Shjarback, 2016):

- WITS ("Walk away, Ignore it, Talk it out, and Seek help"): A program that aims to reduce student victimization by promoting healthy conflict resolution, social competency, and help-seeking.
- Steps to Respect: A program aimed at raising bullying awareness among school staff, parents, and students and promoting healthy conflict resolution.

How does a therapeutic approach align with the problem analysis framework and school crime science?

Therapeutic programming addresses the offender and victim sides of the problem analysis triangle, and both offender-focused and victim-focused therapeutic programs are rooted in criminological theory and research. For example, skills commonly taught in model therapeutic interventions—impulse control, emotional skills, cognitive skills, positive peer relations, prosocial norms, conflict resolution, and help-seeking—are inversely related to offending and victimization according to well-tested theories of delinquency, including control theories (self-control and social bond theories), strain theories, social learning theories, psychological trait theories, lifestyle-routine activities theories, and target congruence theories (see Chapter 2). In fact, the school crime literature provides ample evidence that these factors are associated with lower levels of student delinquency and victimization (see Chapters 4, 5, and 6).

Are school-based programs rooted in the correlates of individual offending and victimization effective at reducing crime and victimization? It depends. Some programs appear to work, while others do not. An exhaustive review of the expansive evaluation literature on individual school-based therapeutic programs is far more than we can accomplish in this chapter, but systematic scientific reviews provide useful syntheses. These reviews indicate that a number of school-based curricula are effective at reducing conduct problems, including substance use and violence, among students. Specifically, the more successful programs teach social and emotional competency using cognitive-behavioral techniques (Cook et al., 2010; Gottfredson, 2001; Gottfredson et al., 2012; Wilson and Lipsey, 2007). Examples of middle- and high-school-administered programs with strong records of reducing offending behavior include LifeSkills Training (LST) and Too Good for Drugs & Violence. Moreover, a systematic review of victimization programs concluded that antibullying programs, including the WITS and Steps to Respect programs mentioned above (Fox and Shjarback, 2016), show promise of effectiveness.

While effective programming exists, it is important to note that the majority of offender-focused therapeutic programs in use by schools are *not* supported by scientific evidence. They are unevaluated or found ineffective in studies (Gottfredson and Gottfredson, 2002). The D.A.R.E. program is an illustration. It was one of the early therapeutic programs, started in the early 1980s as a local partnership between the Los Angeles Unified School District and the LAPD. Its initial partnership team developed and delivered a 17-lesson school curriculum aimed at preventing student substance abuse and violence (D.A.R.E. America, n.d.). Over the course of three subsequent decades, D.A.R.E. expanded virally beyond Los Angeles. It became nearly universally administered in schools throughout the United States, supported by hundreds of millions of dollars annually, despite evidence of ineffectiveness (e.g., Clayton, Cattarello, and Johnstone, 1996; Rosenbaum, 2007; Telep and Weisburd, 2012).[3]

Sometimes the ineffectiveness of a program is due to a failure to clearly identify and address known risk factors, but in other cases, it is because aspects of program implementation are lacking. For example, the duration and intensity/dosage of a program can be problematic (i.e., too little or too much), or its protocol standardization weak (e.g., no instructor's manuals; unclear protocols). Furthermore, model programs that are effective according to some evaluations might fail in particular schools due to poor implementation qualities. Those administering a curriculum may not adhere to program protocols, or those delivering the program might lack enthusiasm, clarity, or positivity (Pettigrew, Graham, Miller-Day, Hecht, Krieger, and Shin, 2015). In fact, Gottfredson and Gottfredson's (2002, p. 3) process-evaluation research indicated "the quality of school-based prevention practices as they are implemented in the typical school is low." Factors increasing the quality of therapeutic program implementation were inclusive decision making about what programs to use, strong training and supervision of program providers, and strong support from the school principal.

Summary

Therapeutic programming attempts to address school crime by making students less motivated to offend or by making students less vulnerable to victimization. Research to date suggests there are theoretically based interventions that yield positive outcomes under rigorous evaluation. Nonetheless, schools often do not select proven programs and instead rely on those with little scientific backing. Moreover, using a science-supported model program is not a guarantee of success. This is because success often depends as much on quality implementation as it does on quality programming.

---

3. Initially resistant to change, D.A.R.E. America has revised its programming several times since 2000 due to noted ineffectiveness. In the early 2000s, D.A.R.E. officers began teaching a new curriculum, Take Charge of Your Life (TCYL). Rigorous evaluation indicated that TCYL failed to produce lasting positive outcomes (Sloboda et al., 2009). In 2009, D.A.R.E. America then adopted yet another curriculum, keepin' it REAL (kiR). Evidence of the effectiveness of D.A.R.E. officer-administered kiR is still unclear (e.g., Caputi and McLellan, 2017; Day, Miller-Day, Hecht, and Fehmie, 2017).

"Get Together": Whole School Engagement

We, as individuals, must somehow negotiate/dialogue with one another to create community. . . . I have been used to operating on my own, being responsible to me. . . . [Now] I'm always thinking of my responsibilities to the community. . . . I need to be a part of a community founded on respect, love and understanding. I need to be able to dialogue, to speak my truth and be willing to accord the same to others. . . . It's what we all need as human beings. (Owen, junior high teacher, as quoted in Vaandering, 2014, p. 522)

A final approach to achieving school safety is what we call "whole school engagement." This is a broad-ranging set of practices that, like the therapeutic practices discussed above, initially coincided with a flurry of federal-funded research on school crime in the late 1970s and early 1980s. Whole school engagement also overlaps with therapeutic programming in its focus on ways to bring about conformity through helping and healing. However, whole school practices are distinct because they target environmental risk factors as opposed to individual risk factors. Specifically, whole school engagement targets the social context of the school community. Three overlapping subcategories of practices align with this general whole school approach: (1) school-wide positive behavior supports, (2) communal school organization, and (3) restorative justice.

School-Wide Positive Behavioral Supports (SWPBS)

SWPBS are whole school practices aimed at creating a prosocial, nondelinquent school culture. They build from the idea a school's strong articulation of prosocial norms and values serves as a basis for (1) social organization, and thus external control, as well as (2) students' internalization of the norms, and thus internal control. In contrast, when a school's culture poorly articulates or reinforces prosocial norms and values, its "common opinion" no longer serves as effective external control or as a basis for prosocial student socialization and the development of internal control. To instill a prosocial school culture, SWPBS includes interventions that train school staff to remove rewards in response to unwanted behavior and provide rewards for desired behavior.

While SWPBS represents a fundamental approach rather than a single program or policy, many specific programs fall under its umbrella. Positive Action, for example, aims at individual students' social and emotional learning but also has a school-climate component that teaches principals and teachers how to reinforce student-focused classroom curricula through coordinated school efforts (e.g., Institute of Behavioral Science, University of Colorado, 2020). The Olweus Bullying Prevention Program (OBPP) is another well-known whole school program. It focuses on curbing bullying, delinquency, and violent victimization by changing schools' cultural norms. OBPP involves a classroom curriculum that defines and enforces rules regarding bullying and a school-wide component that consists of a committee-driven, systematic effort to ensure adult supervision and reinforcement of antibullying norms outside of the classroom (Institute of Behavioral Science, University of Colorado, 2020).

Communal School Organization (CSO)

CSO refers to school contexts in which "members know, care about and support one another, have common goals and sense of shared purpose, and to which they actively contribute and feel personally committed" (Solomon et al., 1997, p. 236). CSO and SWPBS both embrace the importance of a prosocial normative climate that is reinforced school-wide. However, CSO more distinctly stresses social cohesion and collective efficacy among all those in the school—administrators, teachers, and students (and students' parents). It more explicitly suggests that these various groups share a "sense of community" and work together to define and uphold school norms and solve school problems. CSO serves as a basis of social control, like school norms in SWPBS. However, CSO is based less in pure behaviorism; it also relies heavily on the principles of collectivism and legitimacy. Thus, CSO suggests that rewarding/reinforcing normative behavior is important, but so, too, are the processes by which school norms and their enforcement unfold. CSO favors a collaborative approach to process development and operation. The reasoning is that collective participation in the creation of school norms and policy engenders student-school connectedness, which students will want to avoid jeopardizing via rule-violating behaviors. Additionally, collaborative participation goes hand in hand with the development of perceptions that school policies are fair and legitimate. The more that students participate in the creation and enforcement of school rules, the more likely it is that students will perceive the system of control established by those rules as legitimate. In turn, higher perceived legitimacy should amplify conformity with rules.

Restorative Justice (RJ)

RJ is rooted in peacemaking and reconciliation practices of indigenous populations in the Americas, the South Pacific, New Zealand, and Australia as well as Canadian Mennonite communities (Morrison and Vaandering,

2012; Ortega, Lyubansky, Nettles, and Espelage, 2016; Payne and Welch, 2018). It has been an alternative to traditional criminal and juvenile justice for nearly a half century and used as a response to school misconduct in Australia since the 1990s (for recent examples, see Cardwell, Bennett, and Mazerolle, 2021; Mazerolle, Bennett, Antrobus, Cardwell, Eggins, and Piquero, 2019). Over the past 20 years, RJ has picked up steam as an alternative to harsh discipline practices in U.S. schools. Recent analysis indicates that schools in more than half the states implement some form of RJ (González, 2016).

Much like SWPBS and CSO, RJ is fundamentally a whole school approach, not a specific program per se. However, RJ is unique in several respects. First, it explicitly structures the input of offenders, victims, and community members in response to harms during a continuum of practices that include affective statements, informal and formal "conferences," and "peacemaking circles" (González, 2012). Second, RJ promotes alternative, restorative sanctions that serve to reintegrate offenders—including apologies, restitution, community service, and behavior modification agreements (Stinchcomb, Bazemore, and Riestenberg, 2006, p. 132). Through these mechanisms, RJ pursues justice with the core value of "repairing harm" created by school crime. Harm includes damages suffered by direct victim(s) of crime as well as deleterious consequences for others in the school community such as classmates, staff, and parents (Morrison and Vaandering, 2012; Stinchcomb et al., 2006). Throughout the process of repairing harm, RJ embraces another core value, stakeholder involvement. This means victims, offenders, and others in the school community are full participants in the justice process (Stinchcomb et al., 2006, p. 131). In particular, RJ seeks inclusion of victim, offender, and the broader school community. Together they define what harms are, outline ways of healing, and administer restorative sanctions or healing-related obligations (Stinchcomb et al., 2006, p. 132).

How do whole school practices align with the problem analysis framework and school crime science?

As indicated in the previous section, SWPBS aims to improve school normative cultures, CSO aims to enhance school efficacy and legitimacy, and RJ aims to repair school relational networks. While somewhat different, each of these whole school practices addresses the "place" side of the problem-analysis triangle (the school environment). Notably, RJ also addresses the individual needs of offenders and victims in the course of repairing the school-wide relational network. Thus, more than the other whole school approaches, RJ addresses all sides of the problem analysis triangle.

In terms of theoretical basis, SWPBS and CSO map well onto theories touting the influence of community culture and social organization (or collective efficacy). As discussed in Chapter 2, there are long-standing research traditions in criminology that apply these theoretical perspectives to explain between-community differences in crime. Furthermore, as detailed in Chapter 7, there is mounting evidence that they are applicable to understanding between-school differences in crime. For example, a number of studies reviewed in Chapter 7 find that rule clarity, school organization, and perceived school legitimacy/fairness are related to student offending and victimization (e.g., Burrow and Apel, 2008; Fissel et al., 2019; Gottfredson et al., 2005; Kirk, 2009; Payne, 2008, 2012; Payne et al., 2003; Way, 2011; Welsh, 2001).

While RJ is rooted in ideas about communitarianism that overlap theoretical concepts like social organization and collective efficacy, it most closely relates to reintegrative shaming theory and peacemaking criminology. Briefly, reintegrative shaming theory claims that the type of shaming used to hold individuals accountable for their actions affects their persistence in or desistance from crime. Shaming that stigmatizes (i.e., harsh, exclusionary discipline) is predicted to produce additional offending, whereas shaming that is reintegrative (i.e., RJ) promotes desistance (Braithwaite, 1989). Similarly, peacemaking criminology argues that offending and victimization will be lower in social contexts that address underlying social harms—when peace prevails (Pepinsky and Quinney, 1991; Wozniak, 2002).

Do interventions based on these theory-inspired whole school approaches actually reduce school crime? Evaluation studies reveal mixed evidence for some whole school approaches; evaluations are scant for others. On one hand, extensive evaluation literature on SWPBS indicates that model programs teaching prosocial norms enjoy success (Cook et al., 2010). Examples of such programs include the Positive Action and OBPP programs mentioned in the earlier description of SWPBS. Evaluations of Positive Action show that schools using this program exhibited lower subsequent levels of student violence and suspensions and greater acceptance of prosocial norms (e.g., Flay and Allred, 2003; Washburn et al., 2011). Findings across evaluations of OBPP are also positive, with participating schools often experiencing declines in students' self-reported bullying offending, bullying victimization, and other forms of delinquency (e.g., Farrington and Ttofi, 2009; Institute of Behavioral Science, University of Colorado, 2020). On the other hand, not all SWPBS programs consistently reduce school crime, and even successful programs fail to produce positive results in some schools.

CSO is measurable within schools, and research indicates that schools with greater CSO have lower rates of school crime (see Chapter 7; Cook et al., 2010; Payne et al., 2003; Payne, 2008). Yet there are fewer CSO-based interventions than SWPBS-based interventions. An exception is reorganizing school space to create smaller learning environments fostering stronger teacher-student connections and a greater overall "sense of community." This approach, referred to as "schools within schools," involves segmenting a large school into multiple, smaller units. This approach gained a great deal of popularity in the early 2000s, but rigorous evaluations of its effects are sorely lacking.

Comprehensive documentation of the effectiveness of RJ in U.S. schools is also lacking. Some empirical evidence of its effectiveness is found in descriptive data or case studies (e.g., Armour, 2015; González, 2012; Karp and Breslin, 2001; Ortega et al., 2016; Stinchcomb et al., 2006). In particular, several case studies have reported fewer student referrals, suspensions, and expulsions after implementing RJ, suggesting that it might be helpful in curbing misconduct and disrupting the school-to-prison pipeline associated with harsh disciplinary practices. But the evidence reported in more methodologically rigorous study designs offers mixed support. For example, a multilevel regression analysis of the effects of a disciplinary policy change within the Denver Public Schools—from exclusionary punishment to restorative interventions—indicated students who received restorative interventions in the first semester after the policy change were referred less often for misconduct in the second semester compared to peers not experiencing RJ (Anyon et al., 2016). In contrast, a randomized controlled trial across 13 Maine middle schools (7 treatment schools, 6 control schools) reported no differences in student connectedness, peer relationships, or victimization (Acosta et al., 2019).

As was also true for therapeutic programming, implementation quality is an important consideration in assessing the effectiveness of whole school interventions. A lack of positive outcomes does not mean a program will fail to reduce crime in all settings; negative results could be due to poor program implementation. Effects of implementation quality appear in Acosta and colleagues' (2019) research on RJ. They observed that individual students receiving a higher dosage of RJ practices reported better outcomes, including less victimization. Other research raises concerns about inequitable application, with RJ significantly less likely to be used in schools with higher percentages of Black or Hispanic students, and in schools with higher percentages of students eligible for free or reduced-price lunch (Payne and Welch, 2015, 2018). As such, if RJ is proven effective at crime reduction, its benefits may not disseminate to students in schools that are most in need of it.

Summary

Whole school engagement includes school-wide efforts to, among other things, reinforce positive behavior (i.e., SWPBS), create a collaborative community (i.e., CSO), and heal the harms occurring because of school crime (i.e., RJ). Individual studies as well as systematic reviews over the last several decades have consistently pointed out that "schools in which rules are clearly stated, are fair, and are consistently enforced, and in which students have participated in establishing mechanisms for reducing behavior, experience less disorder" (Cook et al., 2010, p. 317). Thus, support for SWPBS and CSO is apparent. The concept of RJ has a less lengthy history in U.S. secondary schools, so research addressing its merits for reducing school crime is still rather scant, though promising. Despite the good that can come from whole school engagement, it is important to note the vast discrepancies across schools in terms of their use of this approach and the quality of its implementation.

Conclusion

School crime has been declining at the national level, and the overall proportion of students in the U.S. who experience it is rather small. Still, as detailed in the preceding chapters, it remains a substantial problem felt by select youths and particular schools. The purpose of this volume was, throughout, to comprehensively examine school crime by highlighting the three distinct sides to the problem: student offenders, student victims, and school settings. We first reviewed theoretical constructs useful for understanding factors that make a small group of students at higher risk for offending, the characteristics that make some students disproportionately susceptible to victimization, and the factors that make some schools highly criminogenic places. Next, we provided a deep dive into research testing the applicability of those theoretical concepts for explaining students' self-reported involvement in school-based offending, their experiences of school-based victimization, and variation in rates of crime across schools. Finally, in this last chapter, we briefly described and reviewed evaluative research on four popular approaches that schools use to reduce school crime through actions targeting offenders, victims, and/or the school setting.

Our objective for this final chapter was not arbitration among the four approaches, declaration of a "winner," and endorsement of a particular policy recommendation for addressing school crime. Rather, our goal was to be illustrative. We aimed to demonstrate that, just as causes of school crime can be productively understood with a problem analysis framework, so too can school crime prevention efforts. In fact, the problem analysis framework is particularly useful in thinking about prevention because it implies three distinct avenues for crime reduction: (1) efforts that counter or control offender motivation, (2) efforts that protect students as potential victims, and (3) efforts that tackle the aspects of the school environment that facilitate or encourage crime. Prevention approaches that address any of these three avenues have garnered some empirical support, but missing are systematic efforts that combine the best of each into an integrated whole addressing all sides of the triangle framework. Moving forward, it would seem wise for schools to use a combination of practices such that all three sides of the crime triangle are targeted. However, as our discussion here shows, simply using approaches that purportedly address offenders, victims, and places is likely not enough. Schools should use approaches backed by sound science rather than rousing rhetoric, while also balancing possible collateral consequences and the likelihood of imperfect implementation.

References

Acosta, J., Chinman, M., Ebener, P., Malone, P. S., Phillips, A., and Wilks, A. (2019). Evaluation of a whole-school change intervention: Findings from a two-year cluster-randomized trial of the restorative practices intervention. *Journal of Youth and Adolescence*, *48*, 876–890.

Addington, L. A. (2003). Students' fear after Columbine: Findings from a randomized experiment. *Journal of Quantitative Criminology*, *19*, 367–387.

Addington, L. A. (2009). Cops and cameras: Public school security as a policy response to Columbine. *American Behavioral Scientist*, *52*, 1426–1446.

Agnew, R. (1985). A revised strain theory of delinquency. *Social Forces*, *64*, 151–167.

Agnew, R. (1989). A longitudinal test of the revised strain theory. *Journal of Quantitative Criminology*, *5*, 373–387.

Agnew, R. (1992). Foundation for a general strain theory of crime and delinquency. *Criminology*, *30*, 47–87.

Agnew, R. (2006). *Pressured into crime*. Los Angeles: Roxbury.

Agnew, R., Brezina, T., Wright, J. P., and Cullen, F. T. (2002). Strain, personality traits and delinquency: Extending general strain theory. *Criminology*, *40*, 43–72.

Agnew, R., and White, H. R. (1992). An empirical test of general strain theory. *Criminology*, *30*, 475–500.

Akers, R. L. (1973). *Deviant behavior: A social learning approach*. Belmont, CA: Wadsworth.

Alvarez, A., and Bachman, R. (1997). Predicting the fear of assault at school and while going to and from school in an adolescent population. *Violence and Victims*, *12*, 69–86.

Ancona, P. (1985). School task forces to hold meeting on problem areas. *Dayton Daily News*, April 23.

Anderson, E. (1999). *Code of the street: Decency, violence, and the moral life of the inner city*. New York: W. W. Norton.

Anderson, M. D. (2017). The preventable problem that schools ignore. *The Atlantic*, December 6. https://www.theatlantic.com/education/archive/2017/12/the-preventable -problem-that-schools-ignore/547604/. Accessed October 23, 2020.

Anyon, Y., Gregory, A., Stone, S., Farrar, J., Jenson, J. M., McQueen, J., Downing, B., Greer, E., and Simmons, J. (2016). Restorative interventions and school discipline sanctions in a large urban school district. *American Educational Research Journal, 53*, 1663–1697.

Armour, M. (2015). Restorative practices: Righting the wrongs of exclusionary school discipline. *University of Richmond Law Review, 50*, 999–1037.

Astor, R. A., and Meyer, H. A. (2001). The conceptualization of violence-prone school sub-contexts: Is the sum of the parts greater than the whole? *Urban Education, 36*, 374–399.

Astor, R. A., Meyer, H. A., and Behre, W. J. (1999). Unowned places and times: Maps and interviews about violence in high schools. *American Educational Research Journal, 36*, 3–42.

Bachman, R., Randolph, A., and Brown, B. L. (2011). Predicting perceptions of fear at school and going to and from school for African American and White students: The effects of school security measures. *Youth & Society, 43*, 705–726.

Barnes, J. C., and Beaver, K. M. (2012). Extending research on the victim–offender overlap: Evidence from a genetically informative analysis. *Journal of Interpersonal Violence, 27*, 3299–3321.

Barrett, K. L., Jennings, W. G., and Lynch, M. J. (2012). The relation between youth fear and avoidance of crime in school and academic experiences. *Journal of School Violence, 11*, 1–20.

Berg, M. T., and Felson, R. B. (2020). A social interactionist approach to the victim-offender overlap. *Journal of Quantitative Criminology, 36*, 153–181.

Berg, M. T., and Loeber, R. (2011). Examining the neighborhood context of the violent offending-victimization relationship: A prospective investigation. *Journal of Quantitative Criminology, 27*, 427–451.

Berg, M. T., and Loeber, R. (2015). Violent conduct and victimization risk in the urban illicit drug economy: A prospective investigation. *Justice Quarterly, 32*, 32–55.

Berg, M. T., and Mulford, C. F. (2020). Reappraising and redirecting research on the victim-offender overlap. *Trauma, Violence, & Abuse, 21*, 16–30.

Berg, M. T., Stewart, E. A., Schreck, C. J., and Simons, R. L. (2012). The victim-offender overlap in context. Examining the role of neighborhood street culture. *Criminology, 50*, 359–390.

Billy, J. O. G., Wenzlow, A. T., and Grady, W. R. (1998). National longitudinal study of adolescent health: Public use contextual database. Carolina Population Center, University of North Carolina at Chapel Hill.

Blake, J. J., Lunch, E. M., Zhou, Z., Kowk, O., and Benz, M. (2012). National prevalence rates of bully victimization among students with disabilities in the United States. *School Psychology Quarterly, 27*, 210–222.

Bordsky, S. (2016). Is discipline reform really helping decrease school violence? *The Atlantic*, June 28. https://www.theatlantic.com/education/archive/2016/06/school-vio lence-restorative-justice/488945/. Accessed October 23, 2020.

Bouchard, M., Wang, W., and Beauregard, E. (2012). Social capital, opportunity, and school-based victimization. *Violence and Victims, 27*, 656–673.

Bradshaw, C. P., Rodgers, C. R. R., Ghandour, L. A., and Garbarino, J. (2009). Social-cognitive mediators of the association between community violence exposure and aggressive behavior. *Social Psychology Quarterly, 24*, 199–210.

Braga, A. A., Hureau, D. M., and Papachristos, A. V. (2011). The relevance of micro places to citywide robbery trends: A longitudinal analysis of robbery incidents at street corners and block faces in Boston. *Journal of Research in Crime and Delinquency, 48*, 7–32.

Braithwaite, J. (1989). *Crime, shame and reintegration.* Cambridge (England): Cambridge University Press.

Brantingham, P. J., and Brantingham, P. L. (Eds.). (1981). *Environmental criminology.* Beverly Hills, CA: Sage.

Brantingham, P. L., and Brantingham, P. J. (1993). Nodes, paths and edges: Considerations on the complexity of crime and the physical environment. *Journal of Environmental Psychology, 13*, 3–28.

Bray, D. (1991). Officers take turns watching over students. *Dayton Daily News*, March 9. https://www.daytondailynews.com/news/archive/. Accessed November 12, 2018.

Brener, N., Kann, L., Shanklin, S., Kinchen, S., Eaton, D. K., Hawkins, J., Flint, K. H. (2013). Centers for Disease Control and Prevention: Methodology of the Youth Risk Behavior Surveillance System—2013. MMWR Recomm Rep. 2013; 62 (RR–1): 1–20.

Brener, N., Simon, T. R., Anderson, M., Barrios, L. C., and Small, M. L. (2002). Effect of the incident at Columbine on students' violence- and suicide-related behaviors. *American Journal of Preventive Medicine, 22*, 146–150.

Brezina, T., Agnew, R., Cullen, F. T., and Wright, J. P. (2004). The code of the street: A quantitative assessment of Elijah Anderson's subculture of violence thesis and its contribution to youth violence research. *Youth Violence and Juvenile Justice, 2*, 303–328.

Brezina, T., Piquero, A. R., and Mazerolle, P. (2001). Student anger and aggressive behavior in school: An initial test of Agnew's macro-level strain theory. *Journal of Research in Crime and Delinquency, 38*, 362–386.

Brick, J. M., Collins, M., Nolin, M. J., Ha, P. C., Levinsohn, M., and Chandler, K. (1994). National Household Education Survey of 1993: School Safety and Discipline Data File User's Manual (NCES 94-218). U.S. Department of Education. Washington, DC: National Center for Education Statistics.

Brunson, R. K., and Miller, J. (2009). Schools, neighborhoods, and adolescent conflicts: A situational examination of reciprocal dynamics. *Justice Quarterly, 26*, 183–210.

Burrow, J. D., and Apel, R. (2008). Youth behavior, school structure, and student risk of victimization. *Justice Quarterly, 25*, 349–380.

Bursik, R. J., and Grasmick, H. G. (1993). *Neighborhoods and crime: The dimensions of effective community control.* New York: Lexington Books.

Burton, A. L., Pickett, J. T., Jonson, C. L., Cullen, F. T., and Burton, V. S., Jr. (2021). Public support for policies to reduce school shootings: A moral-altruistic model. *Journal of Research in Crime and Delinquency, 58*, 269–305.

Butler, L. C., Kulig, T. C., Fisher, B. S., and Wilcox, P. (2019). Victimization at schools and on college and university campuses: Historical developments and applications of opportunity framework. In M. D. Krohn, G. Penly Hall, A. J. Lizotte, and N. Hendrix (Eds.), *Handbook on crime and deviance* (2nd ed., pp. 53–84). New York: Springer.

Campbell Augustine, M., Wilcox, P., Ousey, G. C., and Clayton, R. R. (2002). Opportunity theory and adolescent school-based victimization. *Violence and Victims, 17*, 233–253.

Caputi, T. L., and McLellan, T. (2017). Truth and D.A.R.E.: Is D.A.R.E.'s new keepin' it REAL curriculum suitable for American nationwide implementation? *Drugs: Education, Prevention and Policy*, 24, 49–57.

Cardwell, S. M., Bennett, S., and Mazerolle, L. (2021). Bully victimization, truancy, and violent offending: Evidence from the ASEP Truancy Reduction Experiment. *Youth Violence and Juvenile Justice, 19*, 5–26.

Carson, D. C., and Esbensen, F. A. (2019). Gangs in school: Exploring the experiences of gang-involved youth. *Youth Violence and Juvenile Justice, 17*, 3–23.

Caspi, A., Moffitt T. E., Silva, P. A., Stouthamer-Loeber, M., Krueger, R. F., and Schmutte, P. S. (1994). Are some people crime-prone? Replications of the personality-crime relationship across countries, genders, races, and methods. *Criminology, 32*, 163–196.

Centers for Disease Control and Prevention. (2019). Youth Risk Behavior Survey Questionnaire. https://www.cdc.gov/yrbs. Accessed January 8, 2020.

Centers for Disease Control and Prevention. (n.d.). Trends in the Prevalence of Behaviors that Contribute to Violence on School Property, National YRBS: 1991–2017. https://www.cdc.gov/healthyyouth/data/yrbs/pdf/trends/2017_violence_school_property_trend_yrbs.pdf. Accessed January 9, 2020.

Cho, S., Hong, J. S., Espelage, D. L., and Choi, K. (2017). Applying the lifestyle routine activities theory to understand physical and nonphysical peer victimization. *Journal of Aggression, Maltreatment & Trauma, 26*, 297–315.

Chouhy, C., Madero-Hernandez, A., and Turanovic, J. J. (2017). The extent, nature, and consequences of school victimization: A review of surveys and recent research. *Victims & Offenders, 12*, 823–844.

Christakis, E. (2019). Active shooter drills are terribly misguided. *The Atlantic*, March 13. https://www.theatlantic.com/magazine/archive/2019/03/active-shooter-drills-erika-christakis/580426/. Accessed September 20, 2020.

Clarke, R. V. (2010). Crime science. In E. McLaughlin and T. Newburn (Eds.), *The SAGE handbook of criminological theory* (pp. 271–283). London: SAGE.

Clayton, R. R., Cattarello, A. M., and Johnstone, B. M. (1996). The effectiveness of Drug Abuse Resistance Education (Project DARE): 5-year follow-up results. *Preventive Medicine, 25*, 307–318.

Cloward, R. A., and Ohlin, L. E. (1960). *Delinquency and opportunity: A theory of delinquent gangs.* New York: Free Press.

Cohen, A. K. (1955). *Delinquent boys: The culture of the gang.* Glencoe, IL: Free Press.

Cohen, A. K., Lindesmith, A. R., and Schuessler, K. (Eds.). (1956). *The Sutherland papers.* Bloomington: Indiana University Press.

Cohen, L. E., and Felson, M. (1979). Social change and crime rate trends: A routine activity approach. *American Sociological Review, 46*, 588–608.

Cohen, L. E., Felson, M., and Land, K. C. (1980). Property crime rates in the United States: A macrodynamic analysis, 1947–1977; with ex ante forecasts for the mid-1980s. *American Journal of Sociology, 86*, 90–118.

Cohen, L. E., Kluegel, J. R., and Land, K. C. (1981). Social inequality and predatory criminal victimization: An exposition and test of a formal theory. *American Sociological Review, 46*, 505–524.

Connell, N. M. (2018). Fear of crime at school: Understanding student perceptions of safety as function of historical context. *Youth Violence and Juvenile Justice, 16*, 124–136.

Cook, P. J., Gottfredson, D. C., and Na, C. (2010). School crime control and prevention. *Crime and Justice, 39*, 313–440.

Cornish, D. B., and Clarke, R. V. (2003). Opportunities, precipitators and criminal decisions: A reply to Wortley's critique of situational crime prevention. *Crime Prevention Studies, 16*, 41–96.

Crawford, C., and Burns, R. (2015). Preventing school violence: assessing armed guardians, school policy, and context. *Policing: An International Journal of Police Strategies & Management, 38*, 631–647.

Crawford, C., and Burns, R. (2016). Reducing school violence. *Policing: An International Journal of Police Strategies & Management, 39*, 455–477.

Crowe, T. (1990). Designing safer schools. *School Safety*, Fall, 9–13.

Cullen, F. T. (2011). Beyond adolescence-limited criminology: Choosing our future—The American Society of Criminology 2010 Sutherland Address. *Criminology, 49*, 287–330.

Cullen, F. T., and Kulig, T. C. (2018). Evaluating theories of environmental criminology: Strengths and weaknesses. In G. J. N. Bruinsma and S. D. Johnson (Eds.), *The Oxford handbook of environmental criminology* (pp. 160–174). New York: Oxford University Press.

Curtin, T. R., Ingels, S. J., Wu, S., and Heuer, R. (2002). National Education Longitudinal Study of 1988: Base-Year to Fourth Follow-up Data File User's Manual. Washington, DC: National Center for Education Statistics, U.S. Department of Education.

D.A.R.E. America. (n.d.). D.A.R.E's story as a leader in drug prevention education. https://dare.org/history/. Accessed October 9, 2020.

Day, L. E., Miller-Day, M., Hecht, M. L., and Fehmie, D. (2017). Coming to the new DARE: A preliminary test of the officer-taught elementary keepin' it REAL curriculum. *Addictive Behaviors, 74*, 67–73.

DeCoster, S., and Kort-Butler, L. (2006). How general is general strain theory? Assessing determinancy and indeterminancy across life domains. *Journal of Research in Crime and Delinquency, 43*, 297–325.

DeLisi, M. (2013). Revisiting Lombroso. In F. T Cullen and P. Wilcox (Eds.), *The Oxford handbook of criminological theory* (pp. 5–21). New York: Oxford University Press.

DeRidder, D. T. D., Lensvelt-Mulders, G., Finkenauer, C., Stok, F. M., and Baumeister, R. F. (2012). Taking stock of self-control: A meta-analysis of how trait self-control relates to a wide range of behaviors. *Personality and Social Psychology Review, 16*, 76–99.

DeVoe, J. F. (2007). *The protective behaviors of student victims: Responses to direct and indirect bullying.* Unpublished Ph.D. dissertation. University of Maryland, College Park.

Dijkstra, J. K., Lindenberg, S., Veenstra, R., Steglich, C., Isaacs, J., Card, N. A., and Hodges E. V. E. (2010). Influence of selection processes in weapon carrying during adolescence: The roles of status, aggression, and vulnerability. *Criminology, 48*, 187–220.

Diliberti, M., Jackson, M., Correa, S., Padgett, Z., and Hansen, R. (2019). Crime, Violence, Discipline, and Safety in U.S. Public Schools: Findings from the School Survey on Crime and Safety: 2017–2018. Washington, DC: National Center for Education Statistics, U.S. Department of Education.

DiPietro, S. M., Slocum, L. A., and Esbensen, F. A. (2015). School climate and violence: Does immigrant status matter? *Youth Violence and Juvenile Justice, 13*, 299–322.

Eck, J. E. (2001). Policing and crime event concentration. In R. Meier, L. Kennedy, and V. Sacco (Eds.), *The process and structure of crime: Criminal events and crime analysis* (pp. 249–276). New Brunswick, NJ: Transaction.

Eck, J. E., Clarke, R. V., and Guerette, R. T. (2007). Risky facilities: Crime concentration in homogeneous sets of establishments and facilities. In G. Farrell, K. H. Bowers, S. D. Johnson, and M. Townsley (Eds.), *Imagination for crime prevention: Essays in honour of Ken Pease* (vol. 21, pp. 225–264). Monsey, NY: Criminal Justice Press.

Eck, J. E., and Guerette, R. T. (2012). Place-based crime prevention: Theory, evidence, and policy. In B. C. Welsh and D. P. Farrington (Eds.), *The Oxford handbook of crime prevention* (pp. 354–383). New York: Oxford University Press.

Elvey, K., and McNeeley, S. (2019). Target congruence as a means of understanding risk of intimate partner violence: A comparison of male and female college students in the United States. *Crime & Delinquency, 65*, 1823–1849.

Estrada, J. N., Jr., Gilreath, T. D., Astor, R. A., and Benbenishty, R. (2014). Gang membership, school violence, and the mediating effects of risk and protective behaviors in California high schools. *Journal of School Violence, 13*, 228–251.

Everytown for Gun Safety. (2020). The impact of school safety drills for active shootings. https://everytownresearch.org/report/the-impact-of-school-safety-drills-for-active-shootings/. Accessed September 23, 2020.

Farrell, G. (1992). Multiple victimisation: Its extent and significance. *International Review of Victimology, 2*, 85–102.

Farrell, G. (1995). Preventing repeat victimization. *Crime and Justice, 19*, 469–534.

Farrell, G., and Pease, K. (1993). Once bitten, twice bitten: Repeat victimization and its implications for crime prevention. Crime Prevention Unit Paper 46. London, England: Home Office.

Farrell, G., Phillips, C., and Pease, K. (1995). Like taking candy: Why does repeat victimization occur? *British Journal of Criminology, 35*, 385–399.

Farrell, G., Tseloni, A., and Pease, K. (2005). Repeat victimization in the ICVS and the NCVS. *Crime Prevention and Community Safety, 7*, 7–18.

Farrington, D. P., and Ttofi, M. M. (2009). School-based programs to reduce bullying and victimization. *Campbell Systematic Reviews, 5*, i–148.

Felson, M. (1986). Linking criminal choices, informal control, and criminal outcomes. In D. B. Cornish and R. V. Clarke (Eds.), *The reasoning criminal: Rational choice perspectives on offending* (pp. 119–28). New York: Springer-Verlag.

Felson, M. (1987). Routine activities and crime prevention in the developing metropolis. *Criminology, 25*, 911–931.

Felson M., Belanger, M. E., Bichler, G. M., Bruzinski, C. D., Campbell, G. S., Fried, C. L., Grofik, K. C., Mazur, I. S., O'Regan, A. B., Sweeney, P. J., and Ullman, A. L. (1996). Redesigning hell: preventing crime and disorder at the Port Authority bus terminal. In R.V. Clarke (Ed.), *Preventing mass transit crime* (pp. 5–92). Monsey, NY: Criminal Justice Press.

Felson, R. B. (1996). Big people hit little people: Sex differences in physical power and interpersonal violence. *Criminology, 34*, 433–452.

Felson, R. B., Berg, M. T., Rogers, E. M., and Krajewski, A. (2018). Disputatiousness and the victim-offender overlap. *Journal of Research in Crime and Delinquency, 55*, 351–389.

Felson, R. B., Liska, A. E., South, S. J., and McNulty, T. L. (1994). The subculture of violence and delinquency: Individual vs. school context effects. *Social Forces, 73*, 155–173.

Ferraro, K. F. (1995). *Fear of crime: Interpreting victimization risk.* Albany, NY: SUNY Press.

Ferraro, K. F., and LaGrange, R. (1987). The measurement of fear of crime. *Sociological Inquiry, 57*, 70–101.

Finigan-Carr, N. M., Cheng, T. L., Gielen, A., Haynie, D. L., and Simons-Morton, B. (2015). Using the theory of planned behavior to predict aggression and weapon carrying in urban African American early adolescent youth. *Health Education & Behavior, 42*, 220–230.

Finkelhor, D., and Asdigian, N. L. (1996). Risk factors for youth victimization: Beyond a lifestyles/routine activities theory approach. *Violence and Victims, 11*, 3–19.

Lauritsen, J. L., and Davis Quinet, K. F. (1995). Repeat victimization among adolescents and young adults. *Journal of Quantitative Criminology, 11*, 143–166.

Lauritsen, J. L., and Laub, J. H. (2007). Understanding the link between victimization and offending: New reflections on an old idea. *Crime Prevention Studies, 22*, 55–75.

Lauritsen, J. L., Sampson, R. J., and Laub, J. H. (1991). The link between offending and victimization among adolescents. *Criminology, 29*, 265–292.

Lee, D. R., and Cohen, J. W. (2008). Examining strain in a school context. *Youth Violence and Juvenile Justice, 6*, 115–135.

Lessne, D., and Harmalkar, S. (2013). Student Reports of Bullying and Cyber-Bullying: Results from the 2011 School Crime Supplement to the National Crime Victimization Survey (NCES 2013–329). Washington, DC: U.S. Department of Education, National Center for Education Statistics.

Lessne, D., and Yanez, C. (2016). Student Reports of Bullying: Results from the 2015 School Crime Supplement to the National Crime Victimization Survey. Washington, DC: National Center for Education Statistics, U.S. Department of Education.

Lessne, D., and Yanez, C. (2018). Changes in Bullying Victimization and Hate-Related Words at School Since 2007. Washington, DC: National Center for Education Statistics, U.S. Department of Education.

Lombroso, C., and Horton, H. P. (1911). *Crime, its causes and remedies.* Boston: Little, Brown and Company.

Lynam, D. R., Caspi, A., Moffit, T. E., Wikström, P. O., Loeber, R., and Novak, S. (2000). The interaction between impulsivity and neighborhood context on offending: The effects of impulsivity are stronger in poorer neighborhoods. *Journal of Abnormal Psychology, 109*, 563–574.

Macmillan, R. (2001). Violence and life course: The consequences of victimization for personal and social development. *Annual Review of Sociology, 27*, 1–22.

Madensen, T. D., and Eck, J. E. (2013). Crime places and place management. In F. T. Cullen and P. Wilcox (Eds.), *The Oxford handbook of criminological theory* (pp. 554–578). New York: Oxford University Press.

Madero-Hernandez, A., and Fisher, B. S. (2013). Routine activity theory. In F. T. Cullen and P. Wilcox (Eds.), *The Oxford handbook of criminological theory* (pp. 513–534). New York: Oxford University Press.

Madison, N. (1986). Fairview to keep discipline tough. *The Journal Herald*, February 17.

Madison, N. (1987). Students spruce up Colonel White's image. *Dayton Daily News*, February 23.

Malecki, C. K., and Demaray, M. K. (2003). Carrying a weapon to school and perceptions of social support in an urban middle school. *Journal of Emotional and Behavioral Disorders, 11*, 169–178.

Manson S., Schroeder, J., Van Riper, D., and Ruggles, S. (2018). *IPUMS national historical geographic information system: Version 13.0* [database]. Minneapolis: University of Minnesota. http://doi.org/10.18128/D050.V13.0. Accessed March 5, 2019.

Marsh, S. C., and Evans, W. P. (2007). Carrying a weapon to school: The influence of youth assets at home and school. *Journal of School Violence, 6*, 131–147.

May, D. C. (1999). Scared kids, unattached kids, or peer pressure: Why do students carry firearms to school? *Youth & Society, 31*, 100–127.

May, D. C., and Dunaway, R. G. (2000). Predictors of fear of criminal victimization at school among adolescents. *Sociological Spectrum, 20*, 149–168.

Mazerolle, L., Bennett, S., Antrobus, E., Cardwell, S. M., Eggins, E., and Piquero, A. R. (2019). Disrupting the pathway from truancy to delinquency: A randomized field trial test of the longitudinal impact of a school engagement program. *Journal of Quantitative Criminology, 35,* 663–689.

Mazerolle, P., Burton, V. S., Cullen, F. T., Evans, T. D., and Payne, G. L. (2000). Strain, anger, and delinquent adaptations: Specifying general strain theory. *Journal of Criminal Justice, 28,* 89–101.

McGloin, J. M., Schreck, C. J., Stewart, E. A., and Ousey, G. C. (2011). Predicting the violent offenders: The discriminant validity of the subculture of violence. *Criminology, 49,* 767–794.

McNeeley, S. (2015). Lifestyle-routine activities and crime events. *Journal of Contemporary Criminal Justice, 31,* 30–52.

McNeeley, S., and Wilcox, P. (2015a). The code of the street and violent versus property crime victimization. *Violence and Victims, 30,* 1049–1067.

McNeeley, S., and Wilcox, P. (2015b). Street codes, routine activities, neighbourhood context and victimization. *British Journal of Criminology, 55,* 921–943.

Melde, C. (2009). Lifestyle, rational choice, and adolescent fear: A test of a risk-assessment framework. *Criminology, 47,* 781–812.

Melde, C., and Esbensen, F. (2009). The victim-offender overlap and fear of in-school victimization: A longitudinal examination of risk assessment models. *Crime & Delinquency, 55,* 499–525.

Menard, S. (2002). Short- and long-term consequences of adolescent victimization. Washington, DC: U.S. Department of Justice, Office of Justice Programs, Office of Juvenile Justice and Delinquency Prevention.

Merton, Robert K. (1938). Social structure and anomie. *American Sociological Review, 3,* 672–682.

Messner, S. F., Lu, Z., Zhang, L., and Liu, J. (2007). Risks of criminal victimization in contemporary urban China: An application of lifestyle/routine activities theory. *Justice Quarterly, 24,* 496–522.

Meyer-Adams, N., and Connor, B. T. (2008). School violence: Bullying behaviors and the psychosocial school environment in middle schools. *Children & Schools, 30,* 211–221.

Miethe, T. D., and McDowall, D. (1993). Contextual effects in models of criminal victimization. *Social Forces, 71,* 741–759.

Milam, A. C., Spitzmueller, C., and Penney, L. M. (2009). Investigating individual differences among targets of workplace incivility. *Journal of Occupational Health Psychology, 14,* 58.

Miller, A. M. (2003). *Violence in U.S. public schools: 2000 School Survey on Crime and Safety,* NCES 2004-314 REVISED. U.S. Department of Education, National Center for Education Statistics. Washington, DC: U.S. Government Printing Office.

Miller, J. (2008). *Getting played: African American girls, urban inequality, and gendered violence.* New York: NYU Press.

Miller, W. B. (1958). Lower class culture as a generating milieu of gang delinquency. *Journal of Social Issues, 14,* 5–19.

Moffitt, T. E. (1993). Adolescence-limited and life-course persistent antisocial behavior: A developmental taxonomy. *Psychological Review, 100,* 674–701.

Moon, B., and Alarid, L. F. (2015). School bullying, low self-control and opportunity. *Journal of Interpersonal Violence, 30,* 839–856.

Morris, E. W., and Perry, B. L. (2016). The punishment gap: School suspension and racial disparities in achievement. *Social Problems, 63,* 68–86.

Morris, E. W., and Perry, B. L. (2017). Girls behaving badly? Race, gender, and subjective evaluation in the discipline of African American girls. *Sociology of Education, 90*, 127–148.

Morrison, B. E., and Vaandering, D. (2012). Restorative justice: Pedagogy, praxis, and discipline. *Journal of School Violence, 11*, 138–155.

Moule, R. K., Jr., and Fox, B. (2021). Belief in the code of the street and individual involvement in offending: A meta-analysis. *Youth Violence and Juvenile Justice, 19*, 227–247.

Mowen, T. J., Brent, J. J., and Boman, J. H. (2020). The effect of school discipline on offending across time. *Justice Quarterly, 37*, 739–760.

Mowen, T. J., and Freng, A. (2019). Is more necessarily better? School security and perceptions of safety among students and parents in the United States. *American Journal of Criminal Justice, 44*, 376–394.

Mustaine, E. E., and Tewksbury, R. (1998). Predicting risks of larceny theft victimization: A routine activity analysis using refined lifestyle measures. *Criminology, 36*, 829–858.

Musu, L., Zhang, A., Wang, K., Zhang, J., and Oudekerk, B. A. (2019). *Indicators of school crime and safety: 2018* (NCES 2019-047/NCJ 252571). National Center for Education Statistics, U.S. Department of Education, and Bureau of Justice Statistics, Office of Justice Programs, U.S. Department of Justice. Washington, DC.

Musu-Gillette, L., Zhang, A., Wang, K., Zhang, J., Diliberti, M., and Oudekerk, B. A. (2018). *Indicators of school crime and safety: 2017*. Washington, DC: National Center for Education Statistics, U.S. Department of Education.

Muula, A. S., Rudatsikira, E., and Siziya, S. (2008). Correlates of weapon carrying among high school students in the United States. *Annals of General Psychiatry, 7*, 1–8.

Myers, W., Turanovic, J. J., Lloyd, K. M., and Pratt, T. C. (2020). The victimization of LGBTQ students at school: A meta-analysis. *Journal of School Violence, 19*, 421–432.

Na, C., and Gottfredson, D. C. (2013). Police officers in schools: Effects on school crime and the processing of offending behaviors. *Justice Quarterly, 30*, 619–650.

Na, C., and Paternoster, R. (2012). Can self-control change substantially over time? Rethinking the relationship between self- and social control. *Criminology, 50*, 427–462.

Nansel, T. R., Overpeck, M. D., Haynie, D. L., Run, W. J., Scheidt, P. C. (2003). Relationships between bullying and violence among US youth. *Archives of Pediatric & Adolescent Medicine, 157*, 348–353.

National Center on Addiction and Substance Abuse at Columbia University. (2010). *National survey of American attitudes on substance abuse XV: Teens and parents, 2010*. New York: National Center on Addiction and Substance Abuse at Columbia University. http://www.casacolumbia.org/upload/2010/20100819teensurvey.pdf.

Nickerson, A. B., and Martens, M. P. (2008). School violence: Associations with control, security/enforcement, educational/therapeutic approaches, and demographic factors. *School Psychology Review, 37*, 228–243.

Nofziger, S. (2009). Deviant lifestyles and violent victimization at school. *Journal of Interpersonal Violence, 24*, 1494–1517.

O'Neill, L., and McGloin, J. M. (2007). Considering the efficacy of situational crime prevention in schools. *Journal of Criminal Justice, 35*, 511–523.

Ortega, L., Lyubansky, M., Nettles, S., and Espelage, D. L. (2016). Outcomes of a restorative circles program in a high school setting. *Psychology of Violence, 6*, 459–468.

Ousey, G. C., and Wilcox, P. (2005). Subcultural values and violent delinquency: A multilevel analysis in middle schools. *Youth Violence and Juvenile Justice*, 3, 3–22.

Ousey, G. C., and Wilcox, P. (2007). The intersection of antisocial propensity and life-course varying predictors of delinquency: Differences by method of estimation and implications for theory. *Criminology*, 45, 313–354.

Ousey, G. C., Wilcox, P., and Brummel, S. (2008). Déjà vu all over again: Investigating temporal continuity of adolescent victimization. *Journal of Quantitative Criminology*, 24, 307–335.

Ousey, G. C., Wilcox, P., and Fisher, B. S. (2011). Something old, something new: Revisiting competing hypotheses of the victimization-offending relationship among adolescents. *Journal of Quantitative Criminology*, 27, 53–84.

Ousey, G. C., Wilcox, P., and Schreck, C. J. (2015). Violent victimization, confluence of risks and the nature of criminal behavior: Testing main and interactive effects from Agnew's extension of general strain theory. *Journal of Criminal Justice*, 43, 164–173.

Patchin, J. W., and Hinduja, S. (2011). Traditional and nontraditional bullying among youth: A test of general strain theory. *Youth & Society*, 43, 727–751.

Paternoster, R., and Bachman, R. (2013). Perceptual deterrence theory. In F. T. Cullen and P. Wilcox (Eds.), *The Oxford handbook of criminological theory* (pp. 649–671). New York: Oxford University Press.

Paternoster, R., and Mazerolle, P. (1994). General strain theory and delinquency: A replication and extension. *Journal of Research in Crime and Delinquency*, 31, 235–263.

Payne, A. A. (2008). A multilevel analysis of the relationships among communal school organization, student bonding, and delinquency. *Journal of Research in Crime and Delinquency* 45, 429–455.

Payne, A. A. (2009). Girls, boys, and schools: Gender differences in the relationships between school-related factors and student deviance. *Criminology*, 47, 1167–1200.

Payne, A. A. (2012). Communal school organization effects on school disorder: Interactions with school structure. *Deviant Behavior*, 33, 507–524.

Payne, A. A., Gottfredson, D. C., and Gottfredson, G. D. (2003). Schools as communities: The relationships among communal school organization, student bonding, and school disorder. *Criminology*, 41, 749–777.

Payne, A. A., and Welch, K. (2010). Modeling the effects of racial threat on punitive and restorative school discipline practices. *Criminology*, 48, 1019–1062.

Payne, A. A., and Welch, K. (2015). Restorative justice in schools: The influence of race on restorative discipline. *Youth & Society*, 47, 539–564.

Payne, A. A., and Welch, K. (2018). The effect of school conditions on the use of restorative justice in schools. *Youth Violence and Juvenile Justice*, 16, 224–240.

Peguero, A. A. (2009). Victimizing the children of immigrants: Latino and Asian American student victimization. *Youth & Society*, 41, 186–208.

Peguero, A. A. (2011a). Violence, schools, and dropping out: Racial and ethnic disparities in the educational consequence of student victimization. *Journal of Interpersonal Violence*, 26, 3753–3772.

Peguero, A. A. (2011b). Immigration, schools and violence: Assimilation and student misbehavior. *Sociological Spectrum*, 31, 695–717.

Peguero, A. A. (2013). An adolescent victimization immigrant paradox? School-based routines, lifestyles, and victimization across immigration generations. *Journal of Youth and Adolescence*, 42, 1759–1773.

Peguero, A. A., and Jiang, X. (2014). Social control across immigrant generations: Adolescent violence at school and examining the immigrant paradox. *Journal of Criminal Justice* 42, 276–287.

Peguero, A. A., and Popp, A. M. (2012). Youth violence at school and the intersection of gender, race, and ethnicity. *Journal of Criminal Justice, 40*, 1–9.

Peguero, A. A., Popp, A. M., and Koo, D. J. (2015). Race, ethnicity, and school-based adolescent victimization. *Crime & Delinquency, 61*, 323–349.

Peguero, A. A., Popp, A. M., Latimore, T. L., Shekarkhar, Z., and Koo, D. J. (2011). Social control theory and school misbehavior: Examining the role of race and ethnicity. *Youth Violence and Juvenile Justice, 9*, 259–275.

Pepinsky, H. E., and Quinney, R. (Eds.). (1991). *Criminology as peacemaking.* Bloomington: Indiana University Press.

Perry, B. L., and Morris, E. W. (2014). Suspending progress: Collateral consequences of exclusionary punishment in public schools. *American Sociological Review, 79*, 1067–1087.

Perumean-Chaney, S. E., and Sutton, L. M. (2013). Students and perceived school safety: The impact of school security measures. *American Journal of Criminal Justice, 38*, 570–588.

Peskin, M., Gao, Y., Glenn, A. L., Rudo-Hutt, A., Yang, Y., and Raine, A. (2013). Biology and crime. In F. T. Cullen and P. Wilcox (Eds.), *The Oxford handbook of criminological theory* (pp. 22–39). New York: Oxford University Press.

Peterson, S., Lasky, N. V., Fisher, B. S., and Wilcox, P. (2018). Gendered opportunity and school-based victimization: An integrated approach. *Youth Violence and Juvenile Justice, 16*, 137–155.

Pettigrew, J., Graham, J. W., Miller-Day, M., Hecht, M. L., Krieger, J. L., and Shin, Y. J. (2015). Adherence and delivery: Implementation quality and program outcomes for the seventh-grade keepin' it REAL program. *Prevention Science, 16*, 90–99.

Pinchevsky, G. M., Fagan, A. A., and Wright, E. M. (2014). Victimization experiences and adolescent substance use: Does the type and degree of victimization matter? *Journal of Interpersonal Violence, 29*, 299–319.

Piquero, A. R., MacDonald, J. M., Dobrin, A., Daigle, L., and Cullen, F. T. (2005). Studying the relationship between violent death and violent arrest. *Journal of Quantitative Criminology, 21*, 55–71.

Planty, M., and Strom, K. J. (2007). Understanding the role of repeat victims in the production of annual US victimization rates. *Journal of Quantitative Criminology, 23*, 179–200.

Popp, A. M., and Peguero, A. A. (2011). Routine activities and victimization at school: The significance of gender. *Journal of Interpersonal Violence, 26*, 2413–2436.

Pratt, T. C., and Cullen, F. T. (2000). The empirical status of Gottfredson and Hirschi's general theory of crime: A meta-analysis. *Criminology, 38*, 931–964.

Pratt, T. C., Cullen, F. T., Blevins, K. R., Daigle, L. E., and Madensen, T. D. (2006). The empirical status of deterrence theory: A meta-analysis. In F. T. Cullen, J. P. Wright, and K. R. Blevins (Eds.), *Taking stock: The status of criminological theory—Advances in criminological theory* (Vol. 15, pp. 367–395). New Brunswick, NJ: Transaction Publishers.

Pratt, T. C., Turanovic, J. J., Fox, K. A., and Wright, K. A. (2014). Self-control and victimization: A meta-analysis. *Criminology, 52*, 87–116.

Pyne, J. (2019). Suspended attitudes: Exclusion and emotional disengagement from school. *Sociology of Education, 92*, 59–82.

Rader, N. E. (2004). The threat of victimization: A theoretical reconceptualization of fear of crime. *Sociological Spectrum, 24*, 689–704.

Raine, A. (2014). *The anatomy of violence: The biological roots of crime.* New York: Vintage Books.

Raine, A., Buchsbaum, M., and LaCasse, L. (1997). Brain abnormalities in murderers indicated by positron emission tomography. *Biological Psychiatry, 42*, 495–508.

Ramey, D. M. (2015). The social structure of criminalized and medicalized school discipline. *Sociology of Education, 88*, 181–201.

Randa, R. (2013). The influence of the cyber-social environment on fear of victimization: Cyberbullying and school. *Security Journal, 26*, 331–348.

Randa, R., and Reyns, B. W. (2014). Cyberbullying victimization and adaptive avoidance behaviors at school. *Victims & Offenders, 9*, 255–275.

Randa, R., and Wilcox, P. (2010). School disorder, victimization, and general v. place-specific student avoidance. *Journal of Criminal Justice, 38*, 854–861.

Reingle Gonzalez, J. M., Jetelina, K. K., and Jennings, W. G. (2016). Structural school safety measures, SROs, and school-related delinquent behavior and perceptions of safety: A state-of-the-art review. *Policing: An International Journal of Police Strategies & Management, 39*, 438–454.

Reisig, M. D., and Holtfreter, K. (2018). The victim-offender overlap in late adulthood. *Journal of Elder Abuse & Neglect, 30*, 144–166.

Reisig, M. D., Pratt, T. C., and Holtfreter, K. (2009). Perceived risk of internet theft victimization: Examining the effects of social vulnerability and financial impulsivity. *Criminal Justice and Behavior, 36*, 369–384.

Reiss, A. (1981). Towards a revitalization of theory and research on victimization by crime. *Journal of Criminal Law & Criminology, 72*, 704–713.

Rich, S., and Cox, J. W. (2018). School lockdowns: How school lockdowns traumatize children. *The Washington Post*, December 26. https://www.washingtonpost.com/classic-apps/numerous-school-lockdowns-are-traumatizing-kids/2018/12/26/db3fe398-ff1a-11e8-862a-b6a6f3ce8199_story.html. Accessed September 21, 2020.

Rocque, M. (2012). Exploring school rampage shootings: Research, theory, and policy. *The Social Science Journal, 49*, 304–313.

Rocque, M., and Paternoster, R. (2011). Understanding the antecedents of the "school-to-jail" link: The relationship between race and school discipline. *Journal of Criminal Law & Criminology*, 633–665.

Rocque, M., and Snellings, Q. (2018). The new disciplinology: Research, theory, and remaining puzzles on the school-to-prison pipeline. *Journal of Criminal Justice, 59*, 3–11.

Rosenbaum, D. P. (2007). Just say no to DARE. *Criminology & Public Policy, 6*, 815.

Sampson, R. J. (2012). *Great American city: Chicago and the enduring neighborhood effect*. Chicago: University of Chicago Press.

Sampson, R. J., and Bean, L. (2006). Cultural mechanisms and killing fields: A revised theory of community-level racial inequality. In R. Peterson, L. Krivo, and J. Hagan (Eds.), *The many colors of crime: Inequalities of race, ethnicity and crime in America* (pp. 8–36). New York: New York University Press.

Sampson, R. J., and Groves, W. B. (1989). Community structure and crime: Testing social-disorganization theory. *American Journal of Sociology, 94*, 774–802.

Sampson, R. J., Raudenbush, S. W., and Earls, F. (1997). Neighborhoods and violent crime: A multilevel study of collective efficacy. *Science, 277*, 918–924.

Schreck, C. J. (1999). Criminal victimization and low self-control: An extension and test of a general theory of crime. *Justice Quarterly, 16*, 633–654.

Schreck, C. J., Berg, M. T., Ousey, G. C., Stewart, E. A., and Miller, J. M. (2017). Does the nature of the victimization-offending association fluctuate over the life course? An examination of adolescence and early adulthood. *Crime & Delinquency, 63*, 786–813.

Schreck, C. J., and Fisher, B. S. (2004). Specifying the influence of family and peers on violent victimization: Extending routine activities and lifestyles theories. *Journal of Interpersonal Violence, 19,* 1021–1041.

Schreck, C. J., and Miller, J. M. (2003). Sources of fear of crime at school. *Journal of School Violence, 2,* 57–79.

Schreck, C. J., Miller, J. M., and Gibson, C. L. (2003). Trouble in the school yard: A study of the risk factors of victimization at school. *Crime & Delinquency, 49,* 460–484.

Schreck, C. J., Ousey, G. C., Fisher, B. S., and Wilcox, P. (2012). Examining what makes violent crime victims unique: Extending statistical methods for studying specialization to the analysis of crime victims. *Journal of Quantitative Criminology, 28,* 651–671.

Schreck, C. J., Stewart, E. A., and Fisher, B. S. (2006). Self-control, victimization, and their influence on risky lifestyles: A longitudinal analysis using panel data. *Journal of Quantitative Criminology, 22,* 319–340.

Schreck, C. J., Stewart, E. A., and Osgood, D. W. (2008). A reappraisal of the overlap of violent offenders and victims. *Criminology, 46,* 871–906.

Schreck, C. J., Wright, R. A., and Miller, J. M. (2002). A study of individual and situational antecedents of violent victimization. *Justice Quarterly, 19,* 159–180.

Scruggs. O. E. (1992). Williams seeks community help after Dunbar gun incident. *Dayton Daily News,* March 28. https://www.daytondailynews.com/news/archive/. Accessed November 12, 2018.

Seldin, M., and Yanez, C. (2019). Student Reports of Bullying: Results from the 2017 School Crime Supplement to the National Crime Victimization Survey. Washington, DC: National Center for Education Statistics, U.S. Department of Education.

Sellin, T. (1938). *Culture conflict and crime.* New York: Social Science Research Council.

Sevigny, E. L., and Zhang, G. (2018). Do barriers to crime prevention moderate the effects of situational crime prevention policies on violent crime in high schools? *Journal of School Violence, 17,* 164–179.

Shaw, C. R. (1929). *Delinquency areas.* Chicago: University of Chicago Press.

Shaw, C. R., and McKay, H. D. (1942). *Juvenile delinquency and urban areas.* Chicago: University of Chicago Press.

Sherman, L., Gartin, P., and Buerger, M. (1989). Hot spots of predatory crime: Routine activities and the criminology of place. *Criminology, 27,* 27–55.

Silver, E. (2002). Mental disorder and violent victimization: The mediating role of involvement in conflicted social relationships. *Criminology, 40,* 191–212.

Skiba, R. J., Michael, R. S., Nardo, A. C., and Peterson, R. L. (2002). The color of discipline: Sources of racial and gender disproportionality in school punishment. *The Urban Review, 34,* 317–342.

Sloboda, Z., Stephens, R. C., Stephens, P. C., Grey, S. F., Teasdale, B., Hawthorne, R. D., Williams, J., and Marquette, J. F. (2009). The Adolescent Substance Abuse Prevention Study: A randomized field trial of a universal substance abuse prevention program. *Drug and Alcohol Dependence, 102,* 1–10.

Smith, M. J., and Clarke, R. V. (2012). Situational crime prevention: Classifying techniques using "good enough" theory. In B. C. Welsh and D. P. Farrington (Eds.), *The Oxford handbook of crime prevention* (pp. 291–315). New York: Oxford University Press.

Smith, M. S. (1996). *Crime prevention through environmental design parking facilities: Research in brief.* NCJ 157310. Washington, DC: U.S. Department of Justice, Office of Justice Programs, National Institute of Justice.

Solomon, D., Battistich, V., Kim, D., and Watson, M. (1997). Teacher practices associated with students' sense of the classroom as a community. *Social Psychology of Education*, *1*, 235–267.

Spano, R., and Nagy, S. (2005). Social guardianship and social isolation: An application and extension of lifestyle/routine activities theory to rural adolescents. *Rural Sociology*, *70*, 414–437.

Stabbing occurs on school bus. (1987). *Dayton Daily News*, March 10.

Stewart, E. A., Elifson, K. W., and Sterk, C. E. (2004). Integrating the general theory of crime into an explanation of violent victimization among female offenders. *Justice Quarterly*, *21*, 159–181.

Stewart, E. A., Schreck, C. J., and Simons, R. L. (2006). "I ain't gonna let no one disrespect me": Does the code of the street reduce or increase violent victimization among African American adolescents? *Journal of Research in Crime and Delinquency*, *43*, 427–458.

Stewart, E. A., and Simons, R. L. (2010). Race, code of the street, and violent delinquency: A multilevel investigation of neighborhood street culture and individual norms of violence. *Criminology*, *48*, 569–605.

Stinchcomb, J. B., Bazemore, G., and Riestenberg, N. (2006). Beyond zero tolerance: Restoring justice in secondary schools. *Youth Violence and Juvenile Justice*, *4*, 123–147.

Stolen uniforms sought. (1984). *The Journal Herald*, February 8.

Sullivan, C. J., Ousey, G. C., and Wilcox, P. (2016). Similar mechanism? A comparative longitudinal study of adolescent violence and victimization. *Journal of Interpersonal Violence*, *31*, 1367–1392.

Sullivan, C. J., Wilcox, P., and Ousey, G. C. (2011). Trajectories of victimization from early to mid-adolescence. *Criminal Justice and Behavior*, *38*, 85–104.

Sullivan, K. (1985). 3 charged in retaliation action. *The Journal Herald*, May 1.

Sutherland, Edwin H. (1947). *Principles of criminology, 4th ed.* Philadelphia: Lippincott.

Swartz, K., Osborne, D. L., Dawson-Edwards, C., and Higgins, G. E. (2016). Policing schools: Examining the impact of place management activities on school violence. *American Journal of Criminal Justice*, *41*, 465–483.

Swartz, K., Wilcox, P., and Ousey, G. C. (2017). Culture as values or culture in action? Street codes and student violent offending. *Victims & Offenders*, *12*, 868–890.

Swidler, A. (1986). Culture in action: Symbols and strategies. *American Sociological Review*, *51*, 273–286.

Telep, C. W., and Weisburd, D. (2012). What is known about the effectiveness of police practices in reducing crime and disorder? *Police Quarterly*, *15*, 331–357.

Thomas, W. I., and Znaniecki, F. (1920). *The Polish peasant in Europe and America: Monograph of an immigrant group, Volume IV, Disorganization and reorganization in Poland.* Boston: Gorham Press.

Tillyer, M. S., Fisher, B. S., and Wilcox, P. (2011). The effects of school crime prevention on students' violent victimization, risk perception and fear of crime: A multilevel opportunity perspective. *Justice Quarterly*, *28*, 249–277.

Tillyer, M. S., Gialopsos, B. M., and Wilcox, P. (2016). The short-term repeat sexual victimization of adolescents in school. *Crime & Delinquency*, *62*, 81–106.

Tillyer, M. S., Wilcox, P., and Fissel, E. R. (2018). Violence in schools: Repeat victimization, low self-control, and the mitigating influence of school efficacy. *Journal of Quantitative Criminology*, *34*, 609–632.

Tillyer, M. S., Wilcox, P., and Gialopsos, B. M. (2010). Adolescent school-based sexual victimization: Exploring the role of opportunity in a gender-specific multilevel analysis. *Journal of Criminal Justice*, *38*, 1071–1081.

Tillyer, M. S., and Wright, E. M. (2014). Intimate partner violence and the victim-offender overlap. *Journal of Research in Crime and Delinquency, 51*, 29–55.

Tompson, L., and Bowers, K. (2020). Gang violence in Enfield, London. In M. S. Scott and R. V. Clarke (Eds.), *Problem-oriented policing: Successful case studies* (pp. 40–52). New York: Routledge.

Tseloni, A., Wittebrood, K., Farrell, G., and Pease, K. (2004). Burglary victimization in England and Wales, the United States and the Netherlands: A cross-national comparative test of routine activities and lifestyle theories. *British Journal of Criminology, 44*, 66–91.

Turanovic, J. J., and Pratt, T. C. (2014). "Can't stop, won't stop": Self-control, risky lifestyles, and repeat victimization. *Journal of Quantitative Criminology, 30*, 29–56.

Turanovic, J. J., Pratt, T. C., Kulig, T. C., and Cullen, F. T. (2019). *Individual, institutional, and community sources of school violence: A meta-analysis.* NCJRS 253934. Washington DC: U.S. Department of Justice, Office of Justice Programs.

Turanovic, J. J., Reisig, M. D., and Pratt, T. C. (2015). Risky lifestyles, low self-control, and violent victimization across gendered pathways to crime. *Journal of Quantitative Criminology, 31*, 183–206.

Turner, H. A., Finkelhor, D., and Ormrod, R. (2010). The effects of adolescent victimization on self-concept and depressive symptoms. *Child Maltreatment, 15*, 76–90.

Unnever, J. D., Pratt, T. C., and Cullen, F. T. (2003). Parental management, ADHD and delinquent involvement: Reassessing Gottfredson and Hirschi's general theory. *Justice Quarterly, 20*, 471–500.

U.S. Census Bureau. (1992). *1990 Census of population, general population characteristics, Ohio (1990-CP-1-37).* https://www2.census.gov/library/publications/decennial/1990/cp-1/cp-1-37.pdf. Accessed February 21, 2019.

U.S. Census Bureau. (2018). *American Factfinder. Community Facts. American Community Survey, 2017 (5-year estimates).* Generated by Graham Ousey using American FactFinder. https://factfinder.census.gov/faces/nav/jsf/pages/index.xhtml. Accessed March 5, 2019.

U.S. Department of Education. (2016). School Survey on Crime and Safety, Principal Questionnaire, 2015–2016 School Year. https://nces.ed.gov/surveys/ssocs/pdf/SSOCS_2016_Questionnaire.pdf. Accessed January 9, 2020.

U.S. Department of Justice, Federal Bureau of Investigation. (2020). *Crime in the United States, 2019.* Table 1: Crime in the United States, by Volume and Rate per 100,000 Inhabitants, 2000–2019. https://ucr.fbi.gov/crime-in-the-u.s/2019/crime-in-the-u.s.-2019/tables/table-1 Accessed November 18, 2020.

U.S. Department of Justice. Office of Justice Programs. Bureau of Justice Statistics. National Crime Victimization Survey: School Crime Supplement. (2015). Ann Arbor, MI: Inter-university Consortium for Political and Social Research [distributor], 2016–12–20. https://doi.org/10.3886/ICPSR36354.v1.

Vaandering, D. (2014). Relational restorative justice pedagogy in educator professional development. *Curriculum Inquiry, 44*, 508–530.

Virginia State Police. (2020). *Crime in Virginia 2019.* Richmond, VA: Virginia Uniform Crime Reporting Program, Department of State Police.

Vogel, M., and Barton, M. S. (2011). Impulsivity, school context and school misconduct. *Youth & Society, 45*, 455–479.

Vogel, M., Rees, C. E., McCuddy, T., and Carson, D. C. (2015). The highs that bind: School context, social status and marijuana use. *Journal of Youth and Adolescence, 44*, 1153–1164.

Waldner, L. K., and Berg, J. (2008). Explaining antigay violence using target congruence: An application of revised routine activities theory. *Violence and Victims, 23,* 267–287.

Wallace, L. H., and May, D. C. (2005). The impact of parental attachment and feelings of isolation on adolescent fear of crime at school. *Adolescence, 40,* 457–474.

Wallace, L. H., Moak, S. C., and Moore, N. T. (2005). Religion as an insulator of delinquency in schools. *American Journal of Criminal Justice, 29,* 217–233.

Wallace, L. H., Patchin, J. W., and May, J. D. (2005). Reactions of victimized youth: Strain as an explanation of school delinquency. *Western Criminology Review, 6,* 104–116.

Wang, J. W., Iannotti, R. J., and Nansel, T. R. (2009). School bullying among adolescents in the United States: Physical, verbal, relational, and cyber. *Journal of Adolescent Health, 45,* 368–375.

Wang, K., Chen, Y., Zhang, J., and Oudekerk, B. A. (2020). *Indicators of school crime and safety: 2019* (NCES 2020-063/NCJ 254485). National Center for Education Statistics, U.S. Department of Education, and Bureau of Justice Statistics, Office of Justice Programs, U.S. Department of Justice. Washington, DC.

Washburn, I. J., Acock, A., Vuchinich, S., Snyder, F., Li, K. K., Ji, P., Day, J., DuBois, D., and Flay, B. R.. (2011). Effects of a social-emotional and character development program on the trajectory of behaviors associated with social-emotional and character development: Findings from three randomized trials. *Prevention Science, 12,* 314–323.

Way, S. M. (2011). School discipline and disruptive classroom behavior: The moderating effects of student perceptions. *The Sociological Quarterly, 52,* 346–375.

Weisburd, D., Groff, E. R., and Yang, S. M. (2012). *The criminology of place: Street segments and our understanding of the crime problem.* New York: Oxford University Press.

Welch, K., and Payne, A. A. (2010). Racial threat and punitive school discipline. *Social Problems, 57,* 25–48.

Welsh, W. N. (2001). Effects of student and school factors on five measures of school disorder. *Justice Quarterly, 18,* 911–947.

Welsh, W. N. (2003). Individual and institutional predictors of school disorder. *Youth Violence and Juvenile Justice, 1,* 346–368.

Welsh, W. N., Greene, J. R., and Jenkins, P. H. (1999). School disorder: The influence of individual, institutional, and community factors. *Criminology, 37,* 73–116.

Welsh, W., Jenkins, P., and Greene, J. (1997). Building a culture and climate of safety in public schools in Philadelphia: School-based management and violence reduction. Philadelphia: Center for Public Policy.

Whitaker, C. J., and Bastian, L. D. (1991). Teenage Victims: A National Crime Survey Report. Washington, DC: Department of Justice, Office of Justice Programs, Bureau of Justice Statistics.

Wilcox, P., Campbell Augustine, M., Bryan, J. P., and Roberts, S. D. (2005). The "reality" of middle-school crime: Objective vs. subjective experiences among a sample of Kentucky youth. *Journal of School Violence, 4,* 3–28.

Wilcox, P., Campbell Augustine, M. C., and Clayton R. R. (2006). Physical environment and crime and misconduct in Kentucky schools. *Journal of Primary Prevention, 27,* 293–313.

Wilcox, P., and Clayton, R. R. (2001). A multilevel analysis of school-based weapon possession. *Justice Quarterly, 18,* 509–541.

Wilcox, P., and Cullen, F. T. (2018). Situational opportunity theories of crime. *Annual Review of Criminology, 1,* 123–148.

Wilcox, P., Cullen, F. T., and Feldmeyer, B. (2018). *Communities and crime: An enduring American challenge*. Philadelphia: Temple University Press.

Wilcox, P., Gialopsos, B. M., and Land, K. C. (2013). Multilevel criminal opportunity. In F. T. Cullen and P. Wilcox (Eds.), *The Oxford handbook of criminological theory* (pp. 579–601). New York: Oxford University Press.

Wilcox, P., Madensen, T. D., and Tillyer, M. S. (2007). Guardianship in context: Implications for burglary victimization risk and prevention. *Criminology, 45,* 771–803.

Wilcox, P., May, D. C., and Roberts, S. D. (2006). Student weapon possession and "fear and victimization hypothesis": Unraveling the temporal order. *Justice Quarterly, 23,* 502–529.

Wilcox, P., Sullivan, C. J., Jones, S., and van Gelder, J.-L. (2014). Personality and opportunity: An integrated approach to offending and victimization. *Criminal Justice and Behavior, 41,* 880–901.

Wilcox, P., Tillyer, M. S., and Fisher, B. S. (2009). Gendered opportunity? School-based adolescent victimization. *Journal of Research in Crime and Delinquency, 46,* 245–269.

Wilcox Rountree, P. (2000). Weapons at school: Are the predictors generalizable across context? *Sociological Spectrum, 20,* 291–324.

Wilson, J. Q., and Kelling, G. L. (1982). Broken windows. *Atlantic Monthly, 249* (3), 29–38.

Wilson, S. J., and Lipsey, M. W. (2007). School-based interventions for aggressive and disruptive behavior: Update of a meta-analysis. *American Journal of Preventive Medicine, 33,* S130–S143.

Wittebrood, K., and P. Nieuwbeerta. (2000). Criminal victimization during one's life course: The effects of previous victimization and patterns of routine activities. *Journal of Research in Crime and Delinquency, 37,* 91–122.

Wolf, K. C., and Kupchik, A. (2017). School suspensions and adverse experiences in adulthood. *Justice Quarterly, 34,* 407–430.

Wolfgang, M. E. (1958). *Patterns in Criminal Homicide*. Philadelphia: University of Pennsylvania Press.

Wolfgang, M. E., and Ferracuti, F. (1967). *The subculture of violence: Towards an integrated theory in criminology*. London: Tavistock.

Wolfgang, M. E., Figlio, R. M., and Sellin, T. (1972). *Delinquency in a birth cohort*. Chicago: University of Chicago Press.

Wozniak, J. F. (2002). Toward a theoretical model of peacemaking criminology: An essay in honor of Richard Quinney. *Crime & Delinquency, 48,* 204–231.

Wright, R., and Decker, S. H. (1997). *Armed robbers in action: Stickups and street culture*. Northeastern University Press.

Wu, J., and Pyrooz, D. C. (2016). Uncovering the pathways between gang membership and violent victimization. *Journal of Quantitative Criminology, 32,* 531–559.

Wynne, S. L., and Joo, H. J. (2011). Predictors of school victimization: individual, familial, and school factors. *Crime & Delinquency, 57,* 458–488.

Yanez, C., and Lessne, D. (2018). *Student victimization in U.S. schools: Results from the 2015 School Crime Supplement to the National Crime Victimization Survey*. (NCES 2018-106rev). Washington, DC: U.S. Department of Education, National Center for Education Statistics.

Yanez, C., and Seldin, M. (2019). *Student victimization in U.S. schools: Results from the 2017 School Crime Supplement to the National Crime Victimization Survey* (NCES 2019–064). Washington, DC: U.S. Department of Education, National Center for Education Statistics.

Yang, Y., Raine, A., Colletti, P., Toga, A. W., and Narr, K. L. (2010). Morphological alterations in the prefrontal cortex and the amygdala in unsuccessful psychopaths. *Journal of Abnormal Psychology, 119*, 546–554.

Yang, Y., Raine, A., Lencz, T., Bihrle, S., LaCasse, L., and Colletti, P. (2005). Volume reduction in prefrontal gray matter in unsuccessful criminal psychopaths. *Biological Psychiatry, 57*, 1103–1108.

Zavala, E., and Spohn, R. E. (2013). The role of vicarious and anticipated strain on the overlap of violent perpetration and victimization: A test of general strain theory. *American Journal of Criminal Justice, 38*, 119–140.

Zaykowski, H., and Gunter, W. (2012). Youth victimization: School climate or deviant lifestyles? *Journal of Interpersonal Violence, 27*, 431–452.

Zaykowski, H., and Gunter, W. D. (2013). Gender differences in victimization risk: Exploring the role of deviant lifestyles. *Violence and Victims, 28*, 241–356.

Index

Pamela Wilcox is a Professor in the Department of Sociology and Criminology at Pennsylvania State University. She is the coauthor of *Criminal Circumstance: A Dynamic, Multicontextual Criminal Opportunity Theory* and *Communities and Crime: An Enduring American Challenge* (Temple), and the coeditor of *Challenging Criminological Theory: The Legacy of Ruth Rosner Kornhauser.*

Graham C. Ousey is a Professor in the Department of Sociology at William & Mary.

Marie Skubak Tillyer is a Professor in the Department of Criminology and Criminal Justice at the University of Texas at San Antonio.

Made in United States
Orlando, FL
11 January 2024